Archbishop
LEFEBVRE
and the
VATICAN

Rev. Fr. François Laisney

1999 edition by Angelus Press contains slight revisions and updates
throughout the text introduced by Rev. Fr. Kenneth Novak.

ANGELUS PRESS
2915 FOREST AVENUE,
KANSAS CITY, MISSOURI 64109

On the front cover: (top left to bottom right) Archbishop Marcel Lefebvre, Pope John Paul II, Joseph Cardinal Ratzinger, Pope Paul VI.
On the back cover: (top left to bottom right) Edward Cardinal Gagnon, Paul Augustin Cardinal Mayer, Dom Gérard Calvet, O.S.B.

ANGELUS PRESS

2915 FOREST AVENUE
KANSAS CITY, MISSOURI 64109
PHONE (816) 753-3150
FAX (816) 753-3557
ORDER LINE 1-800-966-7337
WWW.ANGELUSPRESS.ORG

ISBN 0-935952-69-1

Printed in the United States of America

FIRST EDITION—February 1989
SECOND EDITION—April 1999
THIRD EDITION—August 2004

Library of Congress Cataloging-in-Publication Data

Archbishop Lefebvre and the Vatican, 1987-1988 / Fr. François Laisney, editor. – 2nd ed.
    p.   cm.
    Includes bibliographical references.
    ISBN 0-935952-69-1 (alk. paper)
    1. Lefebvre, Marcel, 1905-1991.   2. Catholic traditionalist movement.
    I. Lefebvre, Marcel, 1905-1991. II. Laisney, François, 1957-
BX4705.L474A73 1998
282'.092–dc21
                                     98–30197
                                         CIP

CONTENTS

PROLOGUE

(1974)

PART I

THE DOCUMENTS

(1987)

(1988)

PART II

ADDITIONAL DOCUMENTATION

(1988)

(1992)

PART III

EPILOGUE

FOREWORD TO FIRST EDITION

In this book you will find a complete set of the documents exchanged between Rome and Archbishop Lefebvre in the time leading up to and immediately following the episcopal consecrations of June 30, 1988.

Just as a court of law will insist upon the authentic documents to get at the truth, so in this historic clash between two radically opposed views of the Catholic Church and the Catholic Faith, there is no substitute for reading the original texts of what both sides had to say.

To these texts all that has been added is a narrative by Fr. François Laisney,[1] Editor of the Angelus Press, to connect them in their sequence and to set them in their context, with a few footnotes to uncover the issues at stake from the standpoint of the Society of Saint Pius X.

However, let the documents speak for themselves.

† Richard Williamson

Winona, Minnesota
August 25, 1988

---

[1] Rev. Fr. François Laisney is currently the General Bursar of the Society of Saint Pius X and is based in Menzingen, Switzerland.

PREFACE TO THE FIRST EDITION

Much has been written by many people on the subject of the consecrations of bishops performed by their Excellencies Archbishop Lefebvre and Bishop de Castro Mayer on June 30, 1988. Many documents were not available in English at that time, which made it difficult for some to understand the reasons for this "Operation Survival" of Tradition.

We have made a great effort to collect all the relevant documents. We present the most complete dossier now available. A few documents have already been published in our special issue of *The Angelus* in July 1988[2], but are reprinted here for the sake of continuity in the events. We refer the reader to this issue for other excellent documents such as the Declaration of Bishop de Castro Mayer [included in the second edition], the canonical study of Fr. Rudolf Kaschewsky.

In Part II of this volume we have added a few other documents surrounding the relations between Archbishop Lefebvre and the Vatican. Unfortunately too many conservative Catholics do not want to face reality, or they dream of a better world than the one we live in. They may be conscious of the errors taught by the bishops in America, but do not want to see their source in Vatican II and their support in Rome. These documents may help them to realize the gravity of the crisis of the Church, and how this crisis is just the application of the false principles of Religious Liberty, Ecumenism and Collegiality introduced at the Second Vatican Council. They will also realize that, unfortunately, in Rome there is the will to abide with these false principles, and to impose them on Dom Gérard and those who want to go with the May 5th Protocol, thus introducing the poison into the apple.

My comments, boldfaced and in a different typestyle, have been added either before or after the text of the documents.

The first impression one receives in reading these documents, other newspapers, commentaries, declarations and private letters, is that the Vatican and Archbishop Lefebvre are not on the same wavelength. Right from the beginning Archbishop Lefebvre takes his stand on *Faith*: he wants the continuation of the transmission of the Deposit of Faith, in all its entirety and purity; he wants the continuation of the most perfect expression of the Catholic Faith which is in the traditional liturgy, most apt to give the graces needed by the faithful for the salvation of their souls; he did not blind

---

[2]   Available from Angelus Press, 2918 Tracy Avenue, Kansas City, MO 64109.

himself, refusing to see the crisis of the Faith in so many souls poisoned by the conciliar reforms. He was convinced that the best service he could render to the Church and to the Pope himself was to fulfil his mission as a successor of the Apostles, transmitting the Faith to the next generation, without giving up under the pressures of the modernists who have infiltrated even the Roman Curia. This is why he asked to provide shepherds, successors of the Apostles, for the continuation of this mission; no request was more legitimate. The faithful could see this at the level of Faith; one wrote to me: "My Catholic sense tells me that Archbishop Lefebvre has done what had to be done in these strange and most serious times in the Church, and that he is not opposed to the Pope, but rather is more united to him than many others; his orthodoxy in doctrine and Liturgy is impeccable, his break is with Modernism..." This was a reaction of the *sensus fidei.*

On the other hand, many of those who have criticized him based themselves on *Church politics.* "Could he not have trusted God a little more and tested the agreement at least for a time? Then, if Rome did all the dire things that were predicted, it would have been time enough to risk excommunication."[3]

This was not a reaction of Faith, but of Church politics. If there had been a risk of valid excommunication, Archbishop Lefebvre would never have done it; it is only because he was convinced that such an action was necessary from a motive of Faith, for a real necessity for the good of the Church, and therefore legitimate, that he did it. Convinced it was good, he did it publicly, not hiding as others who conferred episcopal consecrations in a completely different context. Those in the Roman Curia who wanted to please both Archbishop Lefebvre and the local bishops were at that level too.

Others, even after more than 20 years of being deceived "in the name of obedience," still do not realize that "Satan's masterstroke is to have succeeded in sowing disobedience to all Tradition through obedience." They have not yet learned by experience what St. Peter, the first Pope, said: "We ought to obey God rather than men." St. Thomas teaches that obedience is a moral virtue, thus in between a default (disobedience) and an excess (servility); in two simple questions of his *Summa Theologica*, he masterfully exposes the solution to the dilemma of these souls: IIa IIæ Q.104, A.4: "Should we obey God in everything? Yes." A.5:

> Should the subjects obey their superiors in everything? *Sed contra* is what is said in the Acts of the Apostles, "we ought to obey God rather than man." But sometimes the precepts of the prelates (*sic*) are against God.

---

[3] *The Remnant,* Aug. 15, 1988, p.7.

> Therefore one must not obey the prelates in everything….Therefore, one can distinguish three kinds of obedience: one sufficient to salvation, by which one obeys in the things he is obliged to; a second one which is perfect, by which one obeys in all lawful things; a third one that is indiscreet (therefore sinful), by which one obeys even in the unlawful things.

He also teaches that there are many other virtues more important than obedience, such as faith, hope, charity, religion...Some have come to realize that obedience to the local bishop is not a theological virtue, but they still consider that obedience to the pope is a theological virtue (one against which there cannot be an excess). The history of the Church and the lives of the saints show that this is not true. Since the supreme authority has been given by Our Lord to Peter in order to transmit the deposit of Faith, the best obedience to the pope is to do what is necessary for the transmission of the Faith, especially when so many strive to distort this Faith.

I hope that this book will help the reader to strengthen his Faith and fight the good fight as St. Paul, who said at the end of his life:

> I have fought a good fight, I have finished my course, I have kept the Faith. As to the rest there is laid up for me a crown of justice which the Lord, the Just Judge, will render me in that day: and not only to me, but to them also that love His coming (II Tim. 4:7-8).

May the Blessed Virgin Mary, Guardian of the Faith, "terrible as an army in array," lead us in this good fight, knowing that "he who shall persevere until the end, this one shall be saved" (Mt. 24:13).

Fr. François Laisney
December 8, 1988
Feast of the Immaculate Conception

PREFACE TO THE SECOND EDITION

The fact that the first edition of this book was quickly exhausted manifests the demand for the full documentation regarding one of the most important moments of the 20th century for the Roman Catholic Church, the episcopal consecrations of four Bishops by Archbishop Lefebvre and Bishop de Castro Mayer on June 30, 1988.

This second edition adds in the first part some important documents not available at the time of the first edition, though none of these documents are essential. I mainly added the missing documents up to June 30, mostly letters between the Vatican and Archbishop Lefebvre. However I added some comments to the letter of May 6, and to the motu proprio *Ecclesia Dei*.

I restricted myself to add only two more documents after the Consecrations. First, the article of Fr. Paul Crane; being not in favor of the Consecrations, he cannot be accused of partiality, yet he points out very well one core element of the decision of Archbishop Lefebvre: Courage! Fortitude! Second, a letter from Fr. Bisig showing how the Society of St. Peter positively encourages people to go to the New Mass.

Many more documents could have been added concerning the implementation of the motu proprio *Ecclesia Dei*, but I think this should be the subject of a whole book. That would be beyond the scope of this one. Suffice to say here that those who had at first questioned the prudence of Archbishop Lefebvre's decision have now come to see the wisdom of his decision.

It is easier to destroy than to build. Archbishop Lefebvre had been a builder when so many others were either destroying or letting destroy. He could not let the future of the spiritual edifice of so many souls who had kept Tradition or returned to it, in the hands of those destroyers. He had been a good shepherd who took care of the abandoned and wounded souls when so many bad shepherds were either mercenaries or wolves in shepherds' clothes. He could not let the sheep in the care of these mercenaries or wolves. As a successor of the Apostles, his duty was to provide some good builders, some good shepherds for them; he asked for the Pope's approval which was given to him theoretically on May 5, 1988, but with no date and no definite candidate to consecrate. When he asked for a concrete date, conciliar Rome screamed that he was breaking the negotiations. Conscious of his duty towards God and towards these souls, he provided these good shepherds. By their fruits you shall know them.

May their work be fruitful through the intercession of the Blessed Virgin Mary for the glory of God and for the salvation of souls.

Fr. François Laisney
June 9, 1994
Feast of the Sacred Heart of Jesus

PROLOGUE

NOVEMBER 21, 1974

THE DECLARATION

Detractors say that Archbishop Lefebvre "upped the ante" in his later years prior to the consecration of bishops. We include the following document which is an evident proof to the contrary.

Let us recall the situation. Two Apostolic Visitors, sent from Rome to inspect the Society of Saint Pius X Seminary in Ecône on November 11-13, 1974, created considerable scandal as a result of the opinions they expressed in the presence of His Grace's seminarians and professors. These two Visitors from Rome considered it normal and inevitable that there should be married clergy; they did not believe there was an Immutable Truth and they also had doubts concerning the traditional concept of Our Lord's Resurrection. In reaction to the scandal occasioned by these opinions of the Apostolic Visitors, Archbishop Lefebvre considered it necessary to make clear where he stood in relation to the Rome represented by this attitude of mind. His Grace rejected the views expressed by the Visitors, even if they were currently acceptable in the Rome which they represented in an official capacity.[4]

In the words of Archbishop Lefebvre: "After telling me of the favorable impression the Seminary had made on the Apostolic Visitors no further reference was made to the Society or to the Seminary, either on February 13, or March 3. It was exclusively a question of my Declaration of November 21, 1974, which had been made as a result of the Apostolic Visitation."[5]

Thus, this document is at the very beginning of the clash between Rome and Archbishop Lefebvre and his work. The "stakes" have never changed!

The Declaration

We adhere with our whole heart, and with our whole soul to Catholic Rome, the Guardian of the Catholic Faith and of those traditions necessary for the maintenance of that Faith, to eternal Rome, Mistress of Wisdom and Truth.

Because of this adherence we refuse and have always refused to follow the Rome of neo-Modernist and neo-Protestant tendencies, such as were

---

[4] See *Apologia Pro Marcel Lefebvre*, Vol. I, p.37 (available from Angelus Press).
[5] *ibid.*, p.41.

clearly manifested during the Second Vatican Council, and after the Council in all the resulting reforms.

All these reforms have, indeed, contributed and still contribute to the demolition of the Church, to the ruin of the priesthood, to the destruction of the Holy Sacrifice and the Sacraments, to the disappearance of religious life, and to naturalistic and Teilhardian teaching in universities, seminaries, and catechetics, a teaching born of Liberalism and Protestantism many times condemned by the solemn magisterium of the Church. No authority, even the very highest in the hierarchy, can constrain us to abandon or to diminish our Catholic Faith, such as it has been clearly expressed and professed by the Church's magisterium for 19 centuries.

"But though we, or an angel from heaven, preach a gospel to you besides that which we have preached to you, let him be anathema" (Gal. 1:8).

Is this not what the Holy Father is repeating to us today? And if a certain contradiction is apparent in his words and actions, as well as in the acts of various Roman Congregations, then we choose what has always been taught, and we turn a deaf ear to the innovations which are destroying the Church.

The *lex orandi* (law of prayer) cannot be profoundly changed without changing the *lex credendi* (law of belief). The New Mass is in line with the new catechism, the new priesthood, new seminaries, new universities, and the charismatic or Pentecostal church, all of which are in opposition to orthodoxy and to the age-old magisterium.

This reform, since it has issued from Liberalism and from Modernism, is entirely corrupt. It comes from heresy and results in heresy, even if all its acts are not formally heretical. It is thus impossible for any faithful Catholic who is aware of these things to adopt this reform, or to submit to it in any way at all. To ensure our salvation, the only attitude of fidelity to the Church and to Catholic doctrine, is a categorical refusal to accept the reform.

It is for this reason that, without any rebellion, bitterness or resentment, we pursue our work of the formation of priests under the star of the age-old magisterium, in the conviction that we can thus do no greater service to the holy Catholic Church, to the Sovereign Pontiff, and to future generations.

For this reason we hold firmly to all that has been believed and practiced by the Church of all time, in her faith, morals, worship, catechetical instruction, priestly formation and her institutions, and codified in the books which appeared before the Modernist influence of the late Council. Meanwhile, we wait for the true Light of Tradition to dispel the darkness which obscures the sky of Eternal Rome.

By acting thus we are sure, with the grace of God, and the help of the
Blessed Virgin Mary, St. Joseph and St. Pius X, of remaining faithful to the
Catholic and Roman Church, to all the successors of St. Peter, and of be-
ing *fideles dispensatores mysteriorum Domini nostri Jesu Christi in Spiritu
Sancto.*

† Marcel Lefebvre
Rome on the Feast of the Presentation
of the Blessed Virgin Mary

Some conservative Catholics may object that it seems
illegitimate to distinguish between two Romes, or rather, two
tendencies in Rome. However, this distinction of an "eternal
Rome, Mistress of Wisdom and Truth" versus a "neo-Modernist
Rome and neo-Protestant tendencies," can be put in parallel with
a frightening passage of the discourse of Pope Paul VI to the
Council Fathers, on the very last day of the Council, December 7,
1965: "At the Council, the Church...dealt with man–with man as
he presents himself in reality to the modern world: the living man,
the man wholly occupied with self, with man not only making
himself the center of all his occupations, but also daring to
pretend to be the principle and the last end of all things. The
whole phenomenal man, *i.e.,* clad with his innumerable
appearances, raised himself in front of the gathering of the
Fathers of the Council....The lay and profane humanism at last
appeared in its terrible stature, and, in a certain way, has defied
the Council. The religion of God Who made Himself man
encountered the religion (it is, indeed, one) of man making
himself God. What happened? A shock, a fight, an anathema?
That could have happened; it did not take place. The old story of
the Samaritan was the model of the spirituality of the Council. A
boundless sympathy filled it....At least, acknowledge its merit,
you modern humanists, who renounce the transcendence of the
Supreme Things, and recognize our new humanism: we, more
than anyone, have the worship of man."[6]

The "religion of God Who made Himself man" is what Archbishop
Lefebvre calls the "eternal Rome, Mistress of Wisdom and Truth."
The Vatican's "new humanism" that "more than anyone has the
worship of man," is what Archbishop Lefebvre calls the
"neo-Modernist Rome and neo-Protestant tendencies."

May I say that the Society of Saint Pius X does not have "the
worship of man"! We adore the only One, True God, Father, Son
and Holy Ghost! We adore Jesus Christ, God made man, but we
do not adore man making himself God. With St. Paul, we reject
the compromise with modern humanism: "Bear not the yoke with
unbelievers. For what participation hath justice with injustice? Or
what fellowship hath light with darkness? And what concord hath
Christ with Belial? Or what part hath the faithful with the

---

6   *Documentation Catholique,* 1966, pp.63*ff.*

unbeliever? And what agreement hath the temple of God with idols?" (II Cor. 6:14-16). When the Pope returns to the spirit of St. Paul, there will be no need of a "Protocol" nor even the lifting of any penalty. He will see that all these were but a persecution waged by the worshippers of "man making himself God," against the adorers of "God Who made Himself man." A clash between these two different attitudes towards modern humanism was thus inevitable.

PART I

THE DOCUMENTS

JUNE 29, 1987

ORDINATION SERMON OF ARCHBISHOP MARCEL LEFEBVRE

Ecône, Switzerland[7]

My dear Brethren,

Let us give thanks to God, Who allows us to meet again here at Ecône to participate together in this magnificent ceremony of priestly ordination, which is the *raison d'être* [*i.e.*, the reason for its being] and the crowning event of our seminaries.

Seminaries without ordinations would no longer be Catholic seminaries, seminaries of the Church. And this is why, having the joy of imposing our hands onto these new priests, we thank God, who has permitted our seminaries to continue to live and even to expand, since Ecône has spread to Flavigny and thus a larger number of young people who want to become true Catholic priests can find both the formation and the graces necessary to grow into true and holy priests.

My dear friends, I am first going to direct to you some words of edification and of encouragement. You are going to be ordained in the Catholic Mass. You are not going to be ordained in the neo-Protestant Mass. And this Catholic Mass has been, is still, and always will be the great priestly program, the great program of the Christian life. To modify this Mass is also to change the priestly ideal and the Christian ideal, the Catholic ideal. Indeed, this Holy Mass is, before all else, the Cross of Jesus, the continuation of the Cross of Jesus. The veil of the temple is torn because Jesus died on the Cross. The Old Testament disappeared in order to give place to the New Testament. Was everything then changed? Yes and no. Without a doubt all the rites of the ancient law and a certain conception of the law of God were changed; but the main point of the law of the Old Testament was transformed into a living vision of the law of love. What are the Ten Commandments, if not to love God and to love our neighbor? It is Our Lord Jesus Christ Himself who told us this. And this law of love from now

---

[7]   Reprint from *The Angelus*, July 1987 (available from Angelus Press).

on is no longer inscribed only on stones but in the Sacrifice of Our Lord Jesus Christ. He is the law of love and He has shown it on the Cross. What more beautiful manifestation of this law of love and of this charity could Our Lord give than dying on the Cross for the glory of His Father and for the salvation of souls?

It is then this law of love that Jesus preached to us on the Cross and that He preaches to us every day at the Holy Sacrifice of the Mass. It is this law of love that has been put into your hearts and into your souls, my dear friends, by the grace of baptism, which, indeed, has transformed and deeply united you to Our Lord Jesus Christ in order to bring into effect His law of love and of charity.

The Holy Sacrifice of the Mass, which, as the Good Lord is going to give you the grace for it, you will celebrate—I hope—all the days of your life, will keep up this grace that you have received at your baptism, when your godfather and godmother said that they were devoting themselves to Our Lord Jesus Christ and renouncing all the temptations of this world. That is what you will repeat every day from now on: "My God, O Jesus, I devote myself to Thee forever. I want to be Thy priest, he who preaches the law of love by example and by word. Remove me from all of this world and from its temptations. Keep me from all the influences of this world, which is in the service of Satan, and from disobedience to God."

In this way your souls will be comforted before the Cross of Our Lord Jesus Christ, before His Blood, before His Body, which you will have in front of you on the altar and which you yourselves will make come down from Heaven by the words of consecration that you will pronounce. What a sublime mystery: God obedient to men to offer and continue His Sacrifice. That will be the design of your priestly life: to penetrate the souls who will come to you and who will take part in your Holy Sacrifice of the Mass, with these sentiments of love towards God, of love towards your neighbor, right up to the sacrifice of yourself. And God knows that Our Lord Jesus Christ gives us the example for this: up to the sacrifice of self, up to death if necessary, up to pouring out your blood to remain united to Our Lord Jesus Christ. May that be your resolution. That is why you must be attached to the life and death of Our Lord at the Holy Sacrifice of the Mass that you are going to celebrate with me.

Do not let yourselves be seduced by the attractions of the world and by its appeal in order to transform this Holy Sacrifice of the Mass into a purely human assembly!

I desire ardently that these sentiments remain in you for all of your priestly life. Be apostles, as the older priests are, every place where they have been sent, like these dear priests who are present here, who are gathered around you and who are happy to lay their hands upon you. Priests of

Our Lord Jesus Christ, priests of Love Crucified, of Jesus Crucified, and not priests *of* the world and *for* the world.

My very dear brethren, permit me to take advantage of these circumstances to point out to you the situation in which we find ourselves today, as we customarily do on the occasion of this ceremony of priestly ordinations.

It must be said. I cannot remain silent. I cannot hide it. This year has been a very serious year for the Catholic Church, for us Catholics, for us Catholic priests.

You know this, different writers have reported it, that I have had the occasion to say that I was waiting for signs from Providence to carry out the acts that seemed to me necessary for the continuation of the Catholic Church. I must acknowledge now that I am convinced that these signs have come.

What are they? There are two: Assisi, and the response that has been made to us from Rome to the objections that we had formulated with regard to religious liberty.

Assisi took place last October 27th, and the answer from Rome to our objections on the errors of Vatican II relating to religious liberty reached us at the beginning of March. In itself it is even more serious than Assisi. Assisi is an historical fact, an action. But the response to our objections on religious liberty is an affirmation of principles, and so that is very grave. It is one thing simply to perform a grave and scandalous act; it is something else to affirm false and erroneous principles, which as a consequence have disastrous conclusions in practice.

This is why Providence has willed that by a certain joining of circumstances we have drawn up a book that has just appeared, *Ils L'ont Découronné—They Have Uncrowned Him.*[8] They have uncrowned Him! Who has uncrowned, and who has been uncrowned?

Who has been uncrowned? Our Lord Jesus Christ.

Who has uncrowned Him? The Roman authorities of today.

And this uncrowning was manifested in an obvious way at the time of the ceremony of Assisi.

Jesus Christ is uncrowned. He is no longer the King, the universal King, the King whom we proclaim from the Feast of Christmas right up to His Ascension. All the religious feasts proclaim the royalty of Our Lord Jesus Christ. All during the liturgical year, we sing: *Rex regum, et Dominus dominantium*—King of kings and Lord of lords!

---

[8]   *They Have Uncrowned Him,* published by the Angelus Press, in English, and by *Editions Fideliter* in French.

And behold! Instead of magnifying the royalty of Our Lord Jesus Christ, a pantheon of all religions is instituted! Just as the pagan emperors of Rome had made that pantheon of all the religions, today it is the Roman authorities of the Church who are doing it!

This is a tremendous scandal for souls, for Catholics, to see thus cast into doubt the universal Kingship of Our Lord Jesus Christ. It is precisely that which is called Liberalism.

Liberalism is the institution of man's freedom *vis-à-vis* God. As a consequence, the man who in his conscience believes, hopes, professes any religion becomes as respectable as the one who says that he is professing the true religion.

The State, civil society, is no longer capable of knowing what is the true religion. This is what has been stated to us in the document that we have received from Rome. The State is incompetent in religious matters and thus cannot decide which is the true or the false religion. By this fact itself, the State must let all religious errors, whatever they are, spread out in this "autonomous social space"—as they call it—which is, in practice, all the life of the State, because man is free to have his own religion.

We say, "No, no, and no!"

And the Holy Mass shows us this. There is a law, a law of love, that Our Lord Jesus Christ on the Cross claims, proclaims, and preaches to us. He says to us, "You must obey the law of love. Whoever does not obey the law of love is not worthy of eternal life." It is then an obligatory law. We are not free to choose our religion. There is only one! The one that Our Lord Jesus Christ proclaimed from the height of His Cross.

Liberalism has become the idol of our modern times, an idol that is now adored in most of the countries of the world, even in the Catholic countries. It is this liberty of man in regard to God, which defies God, which wants to make its own religion, of the rights of man, its own commandments, with its lay associations, with secular States, with a secular education, without God—that is Liberalism. How is it possible that the Roman authorities profess and encourage this Liberalism in the declaration of Vatican II on Religious Liberty? It is that which, in my view, is very serious. Rome is in darkness, in the darkness of error. It is impossible for us to deny it.

How can we tolerate, from our point of view as Catholics and so much the more from our viewpoint as priests, that spectacle that could be seen at Assisi: St. Peter's Church, which was given to the Buddhists to celebrate their pagan worship there? Was it conceivable to see them perform their pagan ceremony in front of the tabernacle of Our Lord Jesus Christ—no doubt empty—but covered by their idol, by Buddha, and this in a Catholic church, a church of Our Lord Jesus Christ? There they are; the facts speak for themselves. It is impossible for us to conceive a more serious error.

How could that actually be done? Let us leave the answer to the Good Lord. It is He Who manages all things. It is Our Lord Jesus Christ Who is the master of events. It is He Who knows what will be the future of this hold of errors on Rome and the highest authorities, from the Pope and the Cardinals and passing through all the bishops of the world, for all the bishops of the world follow the false ideas of the Council on ecumenism and Liberalism.

God alone knows where that is going to lead; but, for us, if we want to remain Catholic and if we want to continue the Church, we have some indefeasible duties. We have serious obligations which oblige us, first of all, to multiply the priests who believe in Our Lord Jesus Christ, in His royalty, in His social Kingship according to the doctrine of the Church.

That is why I am happy that the book on Liberalism has appeared,[9] so that everyone can be nourished by it and understand well the struggle we are carrying on.

This is not a human battle. We are in close combat with Satan. It is a struggle that demands all the supernatural forces which we need in order to fight against him who wants to destroy the Church radically, who wishes the destruction of the work of Our Lord Jesus Christ. He has wanted this ever since Our Lord was born, and he wants to go on abolishing and destroying His Mystical Body, wiping out His reign and all His institutions, whatever they may be. We have to be conscious of this dramatic, apocalyptic struggle in which we live and not minimize it. To the extent that we minimize it, our eagerness in the battle grows less. We become weaker and dare no more to proclaim the Truth. We no longer dare to proclaim the social Kingship of Our Lord, because that sounds bad to the ears of the secular and atheistic world. To say that Our Lord Jesus Christ should reign in society seems to be a folly to the world. We are taken for laggards, old-fashioned, frozen in the Middle Ages. "All of that belongs to the past. It is finished. That time has ended. It is no longer possible that Our Lord Jesus Christ can reign in society." We could perhaps suffer a little of the tendency to be afraid of this public opinion that is against us, because we affirm the Kingship of Our Lord. Let us not be surprised then that the demonstrations that we can hold in favor of the social Kingship of Our Lord raise up in front of us an army directed by Satan in order to impede our influence from growing and even to destroy it.

This is why we are happy today to do these priestly ordinations, and we sincerely think that it is not possible to abandon this work which the

---

[9]   *They Have Uncrowned Him,* by Archbishop Lefebvre.

Good Lord has put into our hands. For, in truth, it was not I who founded it, but indeed Our Lord—and that in unbelievable circumstances. Now, after 15 years of existence, our Society has reached worldwide dimensions.

Thanks be to God, many other initiatives have also risen up with us, around us. All the men and women religious who are attending this ceremony have also risen up themselves to proclaim the royalty of Our Lord Jesus Christ, and they will not abandon Him.

Are we going to abandon Him, let Him be crucified a second time, and also leave the Church in the state of the Passion that she is living right now, and all that without our coming to her aid?

What will become of souls if no one any more proclaims the divinity of Our Lord Jesus Christ? What will become of them if we do not give them the real grace which they need for their salvation?

It is a question of obvious necessity. We must be convinced of this. This is why it is likely that I will give myself some successors in order to be able to continue this work, because Rome is in darkness. For now, Rome is no longer listening to the voice of Truth.

What echo have our appeals received?

There you have 20 years that I have been going to Rome—writing, speaking, sending documents to say: "Follow Tradition. Come back to Tradition, or else the Church is going to her ruin. You who have been placed into the succession of those who have built up the Church, you must continue to build Her up, and not demolish Her." They are deaf to our appeals!

The last document that we have received proves this fully; they are closing themselves up in their errors. They are locking themselves into darkness. And they are going to lead souls into apostasy, very simply, to the ruin of the divinity of Our Lord Jesus Christ, to the destruction of the Catholic and Christian Faith.

This is why, if God asks it of us, we will not hesitate to give ourselves auxiliaries in order to continue this work; for we cannot think that God wants it to be destroyed, that He wills that souls be abandoned, and that by this fact itself the Church will have no more pastors. We are living in an age that is completely exceptional. We must realize this. The situation is no longer normal, quite particularly in Rome.

Read the newspaper, *SiSiNoNo* [available bi-monthly since 1993 in *The Angelus* magazine from Angelus Press], published by the dear sisters who have come to see Ecône, and to find here an encouragement to pursue the work that they are accomplishing. This newspaper gives some very precise indications about the Roman situation. A situation that is hard to believe, such that history has never known one like it. Never has history seen the Pope turning himself into some kind of guardian of the pantheon of all religions, as I have brought it to mind, making himself the Pontiff of Liberalism.

Let anyone tell me whether such a situation has ever existed in the Church. What should we do in the face of such a reality? Weep, without a doubt. Oh, we mourn and our heart is broken and sorrowful. We would give our life, our blood, for the situation to change. But the situation is such, the work which the Good Lord has put into our hands is such, that in face of this darkness of Rome, this stubbornness of the Roman authorities in their error, this refusal to return to the Truth and to Tradition, it seems to me that the Good Lord is asking that the Church continue. This is why it is likely that I should, before rendering an account of my life to the Good Lord, perform some episcopal consecrations.

My dear friends, my dear brethren, let us pray with all our heart. Let us pray to the Most Holy Virgin Mary. We are going to go to Fatima on August 22 to ask Our Lady of Fatima to help us.

They have not wanted to reveal her secret. They have buried the message of the Virgin Mary. Without a doubt this message was supposed to prevent what is happening today. If her message had been known, it is very probable that we would not have gone so far and that the situation in Rome would not be what it is today. The popes have refused to publish the message of the Most Holy Virgin. The punishments pronounced by the Virgin Mary are coming. The apostasy foretold in the Scriptures is arriving. The coming of the Antichrist approaches. This is clearly evident.

Faced by this completely exceptional situation, we must also take exceptional measures.

My very dear brethren, my very dear friends, during this Mass we are going to pray particularly to the holy Apostles Peter and Paul, guardians of the Church, so that they will enlighten us, so that they will help us, so that they will grant us the gift of Fortitude and of Wisdom, in order to pursue their work and that of all their successors.

Let us ask this above all of the Most Holy Virgin Mary, and let us consecrate our persons, our families, our cities, to the Hearts of Jesus and of Mary.

In the Name of the Father and of the Son, and of the Holy Ghost. Amen.

JULY 8, 1987

LETTER OF ARCHBISHOP LEFEBVRE TO CARDINAL RATZINGER

Eminence,

After a serious examination of the answer from the Sacred Congregation for the Faith to the *Dubia*[10], as well as to the objections which we have submitted to it concerning the conciliar *Declaration on Religious Liberty*, would you please find enclosed our judgment on the matter, and our justification of this judgment. May I enclose documents which will manifest that this judgment is not a personal opinion, but rather that of authorized persons. Since it so happens that I have just published during these past few days a book on this subject called *They Have Uncrowned Him,* I consider it my duty to respectfully offer you a copy.

During the past few months, we have received several important studies which came from Roman universities and episcopal conferences. I send you a critique of the document of Fr. Cesboué, which was sent to us by the French episcopal conference.

I add a few other miscellaneous writings on the same subject in order to show that our refusal of the liberal principles of the conciliar Declaration is not founded on personal or sentimental opinions, but on the infallible magisterium of the Church. Therefore you will find:

1) thoughts of Cardinal Browne,
2) remarks of the *Cœtus Internationalis*, that is, the group of the Council Fathers opposed to Religious Liberty,
3) the critique of Msgr. Husseau of the Catholic University of Angers,
4) the critique of Fr. de Sainte-Marie Salleron, former professor at Teresianum,

---

[10] In 1985, Cardinal Ratzinger asked the Archbishop to write down his objections to the *Declaration on Religious Liberty*. In October 1985, a long study of 120 pages was sent to Rome, questioning many points of this Decree: this study is called the *Dubia*. An English translation will appear at some time in the future.

5)   the letter of Bishop de Castro Mayer, then Bishop of Campos, Brazil, addressed to Pope Paul VI, with its enclosure.

It appears that we can conclude that the Liberal doctrine of Religious Liberty and the traditional doctrine are radically opposed. A choice had to be made between the draft of the *schema* of Cardinal Ottaviani and that of Cardinal Béa, on the same subject.

At the last meeting of the Central Commission preparatory to the Council there was a heated opposition between these two Cardinals. Cardinal Béa then affirmed that his thesis was absolutely opposed to that of Cardinal Ottaviani. Nothing has changed since. The traditional magisterium is opposed to the Liberal thesis founded on a false conception of human dignity and on an erroneous definition of civil society. The problem is to know who is right—Cardinal Ottaviani or Cardinal Béa.

The practical consequences of the Liberal thesis adopted by the Holy See after the Council are disastrous and anti-Christian. It is the uncrowning of Our Lord Jesus Christ, with the reduction to an equal status before the law of all religions leading to an apostate ecumenism as that of Assisi.

In order to prevent the auto-demolition of the Church we beg the Holy Father, through your mediation, to allow the free exercise of Tradition by procuring for Tradition the means to live and develop itself for the salvation of the Catholic Church and the salvation of souls: that the traditional foundations may be recognized, especially the seminaries; that His Excellency de Castro Mayer and myself may consecrate some auxiliaries of our choice in order to give to the Church the graces of Tradition, the only source of the renewal of the Church.

Eminence, after almost 20 years of pressing requests so that the experience of Tradition be encouraged and blessed, requests always left unanswered, this is probably the final appeal in the sight of God and of the Church. The Holy Father and yourself will bear the responsibility of a definitive rupture with the past of the Church and its magisterium.

The magisterium of today is not sufficient by itself to be called Catholic unless it is the transmission of the Deposit of Faith, that is, of Tradition.[11] A new magisterium without roots in the past, and all the more if it is opposed to the magisterium of all times, can only be schismatic and heretical.

The permanent will to annihilate Tradition is a suicidal will, which justifies, by its very existence, true and faithful Catholics when they make the decisions necessary for the survival of the Church and the salvation of souls.

---

[11]   Emphasis added by Editor.

Our Lady of Fatima, I am sure, blesses this final appeal in this 70th anniversary of her apparitions and messages. May you not be for a second time deaf to her appeal.

I am, Your Eminence,

† Marcel Lefebvre
July 8, 1987

July 28, 1987

Letter of Cardinal Ratzinger to Archbishop Lefebvre

Excellency,

I thank you sincerely for your letter of July 8, and for your recent book with its dedication; I will not fail to read it with interest. The file that you have sent me concerning the answer of the Sacred Congregation to the *Dubia* on Religious Liberty shall be studied with all the required attention and the results shall be sent to you in good time.

Your great desire to safeguard Tradition by procuring for it "the means to live and develop" manifests your attachment to the Faith of all times, but can only be realized in communion with the Vicar of Christ to whom the Deposit of Faith and the government of the Church are entrusted.

The Holy Father understands your cares and shares them. Therefore, in his name, I offer you a new proposal, thereby wishing to give you a final possibility for agreement on the problems that you bear at heart: the canonical situation of the Society of Saint Pius X and the future of your seminaries. Here are its contents:

1)   The Holy See cannot give auxiliaries to the Society of Saint Pius X unless it possesses an adequate juridical structure and unless the relations with the Apostolic See are solved beforehand.

2)   The Holy See is disposed to nominate without delay and without previous conditions a Cardinal Visitor for the purpose of finding for the Society of Saint Pius X a juridical status in conformity with the rules of the present Canon Law.

3)   According to the divine institution of the Church, such a juridical status necessarily includes reverence and obedience on the part of the superiors and members of the Society to the Successor of Peter, Vicar of Christ (see the norms indicated in *Lumen Gentium*, §25). Within the limits of this obedience and the framework of the canonical rules, the Holy See is disposed to concede to the Society a rightful autonomy and to guarantee:

     a)   the continuity of the liturgy according to the liturgical books as they were in the Church in 1962;

b) the right to train seminarians in its own seminaries according to the particular charisma of the Society;

c) the priestly ordination of candidates to the priesthood, under the responsibility which the Cardinal Visitor would assume, until further decision.

4) Until the approbation of the final juridical status of the Society, the Cardinal Visitor shall guarantee the orthodoxy of the teachings in your seminaries, the ecclesial spirit and the unity with the Holy See. During this period the Cardinal Visitor shall make the decision concerning admission of seminarians to the priesthood, taking into account the recommendation of the competent superiors.

5) The juridical status that has to be found shall outline the modalities of positive and fitting relations between the Society and different dioceses, according to the rules set by the Law in similar cases.

I ask you, Excellency, to consider attentively this proposal so that a positive and equitable solution may be found, assuring the continuity of your work in submission to the authority of the Church.

If, in spite of the multiple efforts of the Holy See towards a reconciliation, you persist in your project of giving to yourself one or more auxiliaries without the agreement of the Pope and against him, it will clearly appear to everyone that the "final rupture," which you mention in your letter, in no way could be attributed to the Church, but would exclusively depend upon your personal initiative. Its consequences would be grievous for the Church—that you say you love so much—for yourself and for your work.

Divinely instituted, the Church has the promises of the assistance of Christ until the end of time. The breaking of its unity by an act of grievous disobedience on your part would cause incalculable damage and would destroy the future of your work itself, since outside of unity with Peter it would have no future except the ruin of all that you have desired and undertaken. History has oftentimes witnessed the uselessness of an apostolate accomplished outside of the submission to the Church and to its head.

By giving a personal interpretation of the texts of the magisterium, you would paradoxically give an example of this Liberalism which you fight so strongly, and would act contrarily to the goal you pursue. Indeed, it is to Peter that the Lord has entrusted the government of His Church; the Pope is therefore the principal artisan of her unity. Assured of the promises of Christ, he will never be able to oppose in the Church the authentic magisterium and holy Tradition.

Excellency, do you find my words severe? I would have liked to express myself in another way, but the gravity of the matter at stake does not give me any other choice. Anyhow, I am sure you acknowledge the generosity of the proposal which is made to you in the name of the Holy Father, and which constitutes a real means to safeguard your work in the unity and catholicity of the Church.

At the beginning of this Marian Year, to the Virgin "*Mater Ecclesiæ*" I entrust the solution of this long disagreement which opposes us, confident that her powerful intercession will obtain the graces and light necessary for this. With the assurance of my prayer, please receive, Excellency, the expression of my respectful devotion in the Lord.

Joseph Card. Ratzinger

The accusation of personal interpretation of the magisterium is a false accusation; Archbishop Lefebvre has received and kept faithfully the interpretations of the Popes which were taught to him by Fr. Le Floch at the French Seminary in Rome. The documents which the Archbishop had attached to his letter of July 8, 1987 manifested it.

Archbishop Lefebvre hesitated a long time before answering this letter. He feared the extensive power of the Visitor. It is useful to make the reader aware that there was a precedent. An order of nuns called the Dominican Sisters of the Holy Name of Jesus, founded last century, had an excellent adviser in the 1950's, Fr. Calmel, O.P., and an excellent Mother Superior, Mother Hélène Jamet. Under such guidance, the order revised their Rule before the Council, with the purpose to unify their religious life and their teaching life: they teach by the example of their religious life, and their teaching is offered to God as a part of their religious life. After the Second Vatican Council, every religious order was asked to update its Rule in order to conform it to the "spirit of the Council." Since they had changed their Rule ten years before, they refused to again change it. Much pressure was exercised on them to change it. In 1974, in order to avoid constant tension within the community, the superior, Mother Anne Marie Simoulin, decided to send the sisters who wanted to keep the old Rule to make a foundation at Brignoles with Fr. Calmel who was faithful to the traditional Dominican Mass; she stayed with the others.

The bishop imposed a Visitor on the sisters who remained. This Visitor had extensive powers too. His actions were the cause of great upheaval; he supported the few sisters who wanted to modernize the Rule. Though the Dominican Mass had never been banned and many Dominican priests were still able to say it, Mother Simoulin had much difficulty in having it said. For instance, the Visitor proposed that the sisters would have the

traditional Dominican Mass, while the students would have the *Novus Ordo*. Mother Simoulin explained that it was impossible for them to teach the students in such a situation. After a year of such controversy, Mother Simoulin decided to take with her the sisters who did not want such an impossible situation, and founded the second traditional Dominican school at Fanjeaux. There were 40 nuns in these two traditional foundations, while the rest of the Order, that is, about 160 nuns stayed with the Visitor.

Together now there are around 200 traditional Dominican nuns in 12 traditional Dominican schools in France. They already have 15 American-born sisters, and have founded a school in Post Falls, Idaho in 1991, their first foundation in the US. The rest of the original Order, because of lack of vocations and the death of the older sisters, has dwindled to around 60 nuns.

OCTOBER 1, 1987

LETTER OF ARCHBISHOP LEFEBVRE TO CARDINAL RATZINGER

Eminence,

Shall your letter of July 28 be the dawn of a solution? A few clues allow us to hope for it:

- The absence of a declaration makes us think that, at last, we are recognized as perfectly Catholic.[12]
- The extensive contacts with a Cardinal who would visit us answers our wishes oftentimes expressed.
- The continuity of the liturgy according to the liturgical books as they were in the Church in 1962, deeply satisfies us.
- The right to continue the formation of our seminarians as we are currently doing, according to the norms of the Sacred Congregation for the Seminaries, is also for us the assurance of perpetuity for our work.

In order to go further towards a solution it seems indispensable to meet with the Visitor, either by his coming to Ecône or Rickenbach, in Switzerland, or by our meeting him at Albano, in order to be able to study possible concrete means of this definitive solution.

It is out of the question to relinquish authority over our seminarians. It would be opposed to the very right that you intend to give us.

I will be in Albano between October 16 and 20. I dare hope that the wish expressed above shall be able to be realized at that date in order to open the way.

Fr. du Chalard shall carry this letter to you. He will be able to bring back your answer.

Thanking you in advance, I beg Your Eminence to accept my respectful and fraternal sentiments in *Christo et Maria*.

† Marcel Lefebvre

P.S. We strongly wish that the Cardinal Visitor be Cardinal Gagnon.

---

[12] Note that Cardinal Ratzinger went back on this point and required a doctrinal declaration in the Protocol of Accord of May 5, 1988.

OCTOBER 29, 1987

COMMUNIQUÉ FROM CARDINAL RATZINGER TO THE BISHOPS' SYNOD

After meeting with Archbishop Lefebvre on October 18, 1987, the Cardinal agreed to send a Visitor who would observe and report his findings.

Concerning the present dialogue between the Holy See and Archbishop Marcel Lefebvre, I am enabled to give to the Bishops' Synod the following information:

As it has already been announced by the Press Office of the Holy See, a meeting with the prelate took place on October 18, at the end of which the prelate accepted the proposal concerning the nomination of an Apostolic Visitor whose mission would be to gather all the elements of information which would enable us to solve the canonical situation of "the Priestly Society of Saint Pius X."

On this subject I can now add that the Holy Father has nominated the Apostolic Visitor in the person of His Eminence Edward Gagnon,[13] who will give him directly an account of the progress of his mission.

It goes without saying that the hoped-for final solution relies on the necessary condition of the obedience due to the Sovereign Pontiff and of fidelity to the magisterium of the Church.

---

[13] Born in Port-Daniel, in the diocese of Gaspé, Canada, on January 15, 1918, he began his theological studies in the Major Seminary of Montreal. He earned a B.A. degree in Theology in 1940, and a doctorate in 1941. Ordained on August 15, 1940, between 1941 and 1944 he attended courses in canon law at the University of Laval in Quebec. After 1945, he taught Moral Theology and Canon Law at the Major Seminary in the Laval Theology Department. From 1954 to 1960, he was head of the Major Seminary of Saint Boniface. He was a *peritus* during the Second Vatican Council. From 1966 to 1970 he was Father Provincial of the Sulpetians for Canada, Japan and Latin America. Named Bishop of St. Paul, Alberta on February 19, 1969, and Archbishop of Giustiniana on July 7, 1983, he was made a cardinal by Pope John Paul II during the Consistory of May 25, 1985. He has held several important posts in the Vatican Curia. Formerly president of the Pontifical Council for the Family, on January 3, 1991 he was named President of the Pontifical Committee for International Eucharistic Congresses. (*Inside the Vatican*, June-July 1996, p.16.)

NOVEMBER 21, 1987

LETTER OF ARCHBISHOP LEFEBVRE TO CARDINAL GAGNON

During the Visitation of the Society and of traditional institutions by Cardinal Gagnon, Archbishop Lefebvre wrote a letter to him to explain in what spirit he conceives of a normalization of the Society's relationship with Rome.

† Ecône
November 21, 1987
Feast of the Presentation of the Most Holy Virgin Mary

Your Eminence,

You have been able to see and listen to the members of the Society, examine their formation, be present with them in their ministry, and listen to the faithful who rely on them for their sanctification.

You have conversed likewise with religious and with nuns who find in the Society either their origin, or their spiritual assistance, or the graces of their ordination and religious expression.

No doubt you may have noticed here and there some exaggeration, a little bitterness. But I cannot doubt that you have found a climate of Faith, of devotion, of zeal for truth and sanctity, which you once knew. This climate of Catholic Tradition is producing extraordinary fruits whose value you must recognize.

Thus we are forming a great family, living in this Catholic ambience and atmosphere, attached to the Roman Church, attached to Peter and his successors, but absolutely and radically allergic to the conciliar spirit of religious liberty, ecumenism, collegiality, and the spirit of Assisi—the fruits of Modernism and Liberalism condemned so many times by the Holy See.

The consequences of this spirit are disastrous, and we flee from them as from a disease pestilential to our minds and hearts; we are doing everything we can to protect ourselves from it, and protect also the young people of our Catholic households.

Compare us to Israel in the midst of the perverse nations, to the Maccabees, and again to all these holy reformers of the clergy: St. Charles Borromeo, St. Vincent de Paul, St. John Eudes, Monsieur Olier.

Here is the reality: we are forming an army intent on remaining Catholic no matter what the price, as we witness the de-Christianisation taking place both outside and inside the Church.

We willingly agree to being recognized by the Pope such as we are, and to having a seat in the Eternal City, to adding our collaboration in the renewal of the Church; we have never desired to break with the Successor of Peter, nor to consider the Holy See as vacant, in spite of the trials this has caused for us.

We submit to you a project of reintegration and normalization of our relations with Rome. Considering what you now know of us and our works, you will not be surprised at our demands, which are founded solely on zeal for the good of the Church, and the salvation of souls, for the glory of God. Only in this spirit and taking into account these considerations can a solution be valid and stable.

If, in these conditions, a solution is impossible, then we will continue on our way as at present, "persevering in prayer and the preaching of the word," as we wait for more favorable circumstances.

No matter what happens, however, we will continue to have a profound gratitude for you, for your charity and kindness, your understanding and your patience. At this hour we pray Our Lady of Fatima to repay you in blessings for what you have done for us.

Deign to accept, Eminence, my respectful and fraternal salutations in Jesus and Mary.

† Marcel Lefebvre
Archbishop-Bishop Emeritus of Tulle
Founder of the Priestly Society of Saint Pius X

Proposal for an Arrangement Creating a Solution to the Problem of Institutions Favoring the Traditional Liturgy in the Church

Archbishop Lefebvre established this project to present it to Cardinal Gagnon. Noteworthy are the two demands made by His Grace for the unity and identity of the works of Tradition, in which their power lies: on the one hand, aside from the Cardinal President, the members of the Roman Secretariat will all be members of the Society, or at least presented by it; and, on the other hand, three members of the Society will be enabled to receive episcopal consecration.

A comparison of this proposal with the Protocol of May 5 is very

interesting. In his letter of May 24 to Cardinal Ratzinger, Archbishop Lefebvre did not ask for anything other than what was already asked for in this proposal to Cardinal Gagnon.

INTRODUCTION

1) Referring ourselves to the suggestion of the Council in the text *Presbyteriorum Ordinis,* §10, which says the following:

> Where a real apostolic spirit requires it, not only should a better distribution of priests be brought about but there should also be favored such particular pastoral works as are necessary in any region or nation anywhere on earth. To accomplish this purpose there should be set up international seminaries, special personal dioceses or prelatures (vicariates), and so forth, by means of which, and according to their particular statutes and always with respect for the rights of local Ordinaries.

—and referring also to the proposition of Cardinal Ratzinger in the letter of July 28, 1987, it appears that a solution can be found to the problem which preoccupies us.

2) In conformity with the proposition of Cardinal Ratzinger in the letter already quoted, a Visitor-Cardinal Gagnon accomplished a prolonged visit of the works of the Society from November 11 to December 7.

PRELIMINARY NOTE TO THE PROPOSITION

3) Without prejudging the conclusions of the Visit, but in the hope that they will be positive, it seems indispensable to us, before proceeding further in the talks with the Holy See, to express a condition *sine qua non,* in the name of all the priests and faithful attached to Tradition.

4) If the Holy See sincerely desires that we officially become efficacious collaborators for the renewal of the Church, under its authority, it is utterly necessary that we be received as we are, that we not be asked to modify our teaching or means of sanctification, which are those of the Church of all time.

5) Thus it seems absolutely necessary to us, if good relations are to be restored with the Holy See, that these relations be entrusted to persons who are respectful of and attached to the Holy See, but who are also convinced of the urgent necessity for the Church of favoring initiatives which maintain Tradition, and of doing nothing which would alienate them again.

6) Thus the Cardinal, the Secretary and the *minutanti* of the Roman Secretariat, if it is accepted, will have to be chosen according to the criteria expressed above, otherwise it will stifle the efforts of several months for an agreement.[14]

I. THE ROMAN SECRETARIAT

1. The Necessity of a Permanent Roman Organization

7) The rapid worldwide extension of the Priestly Society of Saint Pius X and the multiplication of similar works calls for an organization having its seat at Rome, patterned after a Secretariat or a Commission, for the maintenance and development of the Latin liturgy according to the prescriptions of John XXIII.

2. Composition of The Secretariat

8) Modeled after other secretariats and commissions of this nature, namely:
- A Cardinal Prefect, named by the Pope with the consent of the Superior General of the Society of Saint Pius X.
- An Archbishop or Bishop serving as secretary and president, and some *minutanti,* presented by the Superior General of the Society of Saint Pius X.

3. The Powers of This Secretariat

9) They would be similar to those of the Congregation of the Propagation of the Faith *vis-à-vis* mission territories, and the Congregation for the Eastern Church *vis-à-vis* the Eastern Rites.

4. Goal of These Powers

10) These powers would exist to normalize the works and initiatives in favor of Tradition and help them to fulfil their role in the Church in present circumstances, especially for the Priestly Society of Saint Pius X:
- to see to their continuation by granting the episcopate to several priest-members
- to see to their harmonious development, remaining at peace with the diocesan bishops
- to get the local Ordinaries to see the advantage of collaboration, for example, with their seminaries.

---

[14] Please note that this condition was put at the very beginning of the negotiations with Rome. On May 24, 1988, Archbishop Lefebvre *will stress it again.* On May 31, Cardinal Ratzinger *refused to grant it.*

5. Determination of Work and Initiatives by The Secretariat

11) Those which have always exclusively used the liturgical editions of John XXIII and prayed for the Pope, according to the public formulas of the Liturgy.

- those which are in accordance with the spirit of the Law of the Church, in their constitutions, spirit of the founders and original constitutions, for the choice of subjects, preparation, spirituality, doctrine, habit, community life, *etc....*

II. CANONICAL STATUTE OF VARIOUS SOCIETIES, ISOLATED PRIESTS, AND RELIGIOUS IN RELATION WITH THE ROMAN SECRETARIAT

Preliminary Note

12) Before proceeding to the study and normalization of all these societies and persons devoted to Tradition, which can take place over time, it is urgent to:

- *i.* Lift suspensions or condemnations.
- *ii.* Recognize again the statutes of the Priestly Society of Saint Pius X, as was done before 1975.
- *iii.* Modify some articles of its statutes to provide for the episcopal succession of Archbishop Lefebvre.
- *iv.* Canonically it seems that one could refer to what was decided on April 21, 1986, on the subject of Military Ordinariates.

13) The detailed application of these points could be left to a precise study undertaken by the Secretariat or the Cardinal Visitor and the Society.

The different stages to be followed might be the following:

14) 1. To consider the Society as the support of the Ordinariate for the Latin liturgy, stating in its Constitutions that the Superior General, if he is accepted by Rome through the Secretariat, will receive episcopal consecration, and will be able to designate two auxiliaries to assist him in his functions, and who could become auxiliary bishops.

15) By way of exception, however, for the first designation or presentation of names of those who are to become bishops, it will be done by Archbishop Lefebvre in accord with the Cardinal Visitor.

16) 2. Once this first stage is completed, a deeper study of the application of the general principles will be made, using the example of the Military Ordinariate in relation to the situation of the Society of Saint Pius X. Thus the application of cumulative jurisdiction seems very realistic and solves many problems.

17) 3. It does not seem that there is any disadvantage in the Superior General being a bishop; if he is not re-elected, he can become an auxiliary or be put in charge of a diocese, or be employed in other functions by the Roman Secretariat.

18) 4. The relations between the different works and initiatives on the one hand and the Society on the other would remain as they are now for ordinations, confirmations and other assistance: blessings, retreats, ceremonies of profession, *etc.*...but, everything which concerns the canonical statute and the dispensations to be submitted to Rome would go directly to the Roman Secretariat.

III. INCARDINATIONS[15] AND JURISDICTION
VIS-À-VIS THE FAITHFUL

19) The norms of the Apostolic Constitution *Spirituali militum curæ*,[16] on the subject of incardination can easily be applied to the Priestly Society of Saint Pius X, which has been entrusted with the spiritual care of a small army of those who maintain liturgical Tradition. *Servatis servandis*, in the future the possibility of incardination will apply to interested religious societies.

- Jurisdiction over the faithful is confirmed by Rome, meaning that the priests of the Society receive jurisdiction from Rome through the Superior General, while the others receive it directly from the Secretariat in Rome, at the request of the different Superiors.

It is obvious that these priests must observe the prescriptions of Law to confer the Sacraments according to the indications of the *Ritual* of 1962.

CONCLUSION

There seem to be no major difficulties from the canonical point of view, or from the standpoint of those faithful to Tradition, if the above stipulations are followed exactly.

For the episcopal consecrations, we wish that they not be delayed past Good Shepherd Sunday, April 17, 1988.

---

[15] Canon Law requires that each cleric in major orders be attached to a diocese or congregation; this is referred to as *incardination*. Thus Church forbids a cleric *vagus, i.e.,* not attached to any legitimate superior (*1917 Code of Canon Law*, Canon 111 and *1983 Code of Canon Law*, Canon 265).

[16] *On the Spiritual Care of the Soldiers*, Constitution of April 21, 1986 concerning Military Chaplains, incardinated in the Military Ordinariates; see *L'Osservatore Romano*, May 5-6, 1986.

DECEMBER 8, 1987

VISIT OF CARDINAL GAGNON

The visit started on November 11, at Ecône, and lasted for a whole month. Then Msgr. Perl went to our school in Eguelshardt, our priory in Saarbrucken, the Carmel in Quiévrain. On Saturday, November 21, he came to St. Nicolas du Chardonnet in Paris, and the Cardinal arrived the next day, though intentionally after the Mass; then together they visited the French Youth Group, (MJCF), our University (*Institut Universitaire Saint Pie X*), and met a large group of traditional priests of the region in Paris. On May 24, they arrived at our school in St. Michel of Niherne, then the Mother House of our Sisters at St. Michel en Brenne, and the nearby Carmel at Ruffec, the Fraternity of the Transfiguration of Fr. Lecareux. At Poitiers, he took part in a meeting with many traditional priests of the area, including Fr. Reynaud (the first chaplain of the MJCF), Fr. André (of the Association Noël Pinot), Fr. Coache, the Dominican foundation of Avrillé, the Benedictine foundation of nuns at Le Rafflay, the Little Sisters of St. Francis, *etc.* After this, they visited our retreat house at Le Pointet, our priory and school at Unieux, the Benedictine Monastery of Le Barroux, the Dominican school at St. Pré (Brignoles), and the other Dominican novitiate and school at Fanjeaux, our school at St. Joseph des Carmes, our church at Marseilles, our priory at Lyons and our main European publishing house (*Fideliter*). Then another priestly meeting at Dijon, the Dominican school of Pouilly, the seminary of the Holy Curé of Ars, and returned to Ecône for the Feast of the Immaculate Conception.

At the end of the visit, the following addresses were given.

ADDRESS OF FR. SCHMIDBERGER TO
HIS EMINENCE CARDINAL GAGNON

Eminence, Monseigneur, my dear brethren,

Eminence, it is a duty for us to thank you wholeheartedly for the visit you have done in the houses of the Society and friendly communities.

We have admired much you patience, your objectivity during these past four weeks. We are convinced you have found everywhere a profound spirit of faith and the ardent desire to serve Holy Church.

Of course, today with this feast, the first stage is accomplished, that of your visit. There is still a second which will follow in Rome and which shall probably be more difficult, I do not know.

In any case, you can be sure that, when you shall leave tomorrow morning, our thoughts and especially our prayers shall accompany you. This is what you have asked us many times during this visit: prayers to the Blessed Virgin Mary. And we shall do this from our whole heart and our whole spirit, knowing that it is just three years since we consecrated the Society, here at Ecône on this same Feast of the Immaculate Conception, to the Immaculate and Sorrowful Heart of the Blessed Virgin Mary, surrounded by all the superiors of the Society who signed this Act, which has been inserted in this altar upon which we celebrate the Holy Sacrifice of the Mass each morning.

Thus all our confidence is raised towards the Blessed Virgin Mary because she is the one who must prepare the words and who must still convert this or that heart, as you have said, so that we may come to a satisfying solution.

In any case, we have been very touched by and happy for this charity with which you have performed this visit. And I think that the Blessed Virgin shall reward you a hundredfold.

May I add, Eminence, a short word which is a personal testimony.

If I am a priest, it is thanks to Archbishop Lefebvre. It is he who has drawn us, Fr. Wodsack and myself especially, to enter Ecône, because we had found there the fidelity to the Tradition of the Church. This was what we wanted, this was what confirmed our vocation.

I would add that it was Archbishop Lefebvre who, during all these years, has confirmed our Faith, encouraged it and, through our priestly ordination, has truly become our father in Jesus Christ. And we have a somewhat infinite gratitude towards him. It is all our honor and dignity and our most profound joy to be able to work with him, to be in this little army of those who have but one desire: to spread day after day the Social Reign of Our Lord Jesus Christ, to be worthy dispensers of the grace of Jesus Christ in the whole world into the hearts who are so hungry and thirsty for the eternal truths.

Throughout all these years of apostolate, it was always Archbishop Lefebvre who has supported us, encouraged us, and who was by his own fidelity the model of our own fidelity to the priesthood. And I think he is the model of fidelity for many of the faithful and especially for those who are married.

You understand, Eminence, why we are so firmly convinced to remain strongly united with our Founder and to continue at all costs the work for which the Good Lord has raised him—we cannot see it otherwise—to fulfil this great mission for Holy Church which is also a great mission for the pope. We are absolutely convinced that one day it will be openly recognized that Archbishop Lefebvre has rendered very great service not only to the Church, but also to the pope, even though the evidence is often obscured and not readily acknowledged.

We have been able to witness the fruits of Tradition in our different houses. We have seen the work that has been undertaken. I dare then to express a desire, a wish: do all you can, Eminence, that we may have the concrete means to preserve these fruits, to continue this work and develop it. We do not want anything else than to be instruments in the hands of the Blessed Virgin to restore the reign of her Son, of His Cross, that He may reign thus through and by the Holy Mass in the world.

This is our desire and we would be happy if you could transmit this ardent desire to the Holy Father.

We thank you again wholeheartedly.

Fr. Schmidberger

ANSWER OF HIS EMINENCE CARDINAL GAGNON

Your Excellency and dear Friends,

I cannot let this occasion pass without first offering my respects and congratulations to the Superior General who celebrates today his 12th anniversary of priesthood, 12 years certainly well filled as he has just expressed all the gratitude he has for the one who led him to the priesthood.

I would also like with simplicity to thank you all for the charity and warmth with which we have been welcomed in all the houses of the Society and all the houses [with which] the priests of the Society exercise their apostolate, houses which are in the same "movement" as the Society, as the Abbot of Le Barroux has said.

Thus I thank you for all this and express also the admiration of Msgr. Perl, whom I must thank. We knew little of each other before this trip and had met but a few times; he has been for me an extraordinary support and help, as well as Fr. du Chalard, who has always been at our services.

Fr. du Chalard and the whole team of experienced drivers who are used to drive around the world this precious treasure which is Archbishop Lefebvre[17] has treated us very well...always a little better than we had thought.

---

[17]   Note this expression of Cardinal Gagnon himself.

But, to return to more serious thoughts on this Feast of the Immaculate Conception, I want to say that we have been struck everywhere by and keep a great admiration for the piety of the persons, for the relevance and importance of the works, especially with regards to catechesis, education, and the administration of the sacraments. We certainly have in hand all that is necessary to make a very positive report.

Thus we continue to pray to the Virgin and to pray with the Virgin during this time of Advent, so that Christmas may be the occasion of a new birth of Jesus, in all the senses of the word, and for the Society too.

Thank you again.

Edward Cardinal Gagnon
President of the Pontifical Council for the Family
Apostolic Visitor

HAND-WRITTEN INSCRIPTION BY CARDINAL GAGNON IN THE GUEST BOOK OF ECÔNE

May the Immaculate Virgin hear our fervent prayers so that the work of formation marvelously accomplished in this house may find its full radiation for the life of the Church.

Edward Cardinal Gagnon
Msgr. Camile Perl

COMMUNIQUÉ OF THE SUPERIOR GENERAL TO THE PRIESTS OF THE SOCIETY OF SAINT PIUS X AND TO THE FAITHFUL ON THE OCCASION OF THE END OF THE VISIT OF CARDINAL GAGNON

The visitation of the Society of Saint Pius X by His Eminence Cardinal Gagnon ended on the Feast of the Immaculate Conception of the Blessed Virgin Mary, December 8, 1987. The Cardinal attended the Pontifical Mass celebrated by Archbishop Lefebvre, during which 27 seminarians made their first Engagement into the Society. He shall return tomorrow to Rome, having already started writing his report, which he hopes to place before Christmas into the hands of the pope on the occasion of a private audience.

According to his own words, he has gathered an excellent impression of the seminaries, schools, priories, and friendly religious communities, as well as of the faithful who gather themselves around all these houses. We must now, in the weeks and months to come, accompany his efforts with our fervent prayers. There are indeed still many hearts to be converted by God before a satisfying solution can be found.

We sincerely thank all of you who, in the past days and in many ways, have given testimony to the fruitfulness of the tradition of the Catholic Church.

As He did for the Good Samaritan who showed compassion to the mortally wounded, so may God, through the intercession of the Blessed Virgin Mary, reward you a hundredfold for your acts of charity toward the Church.

Fr. Schmidberger
Superior General
Ecône
December 8, 1987

FEBRUARY 15, 1988

LETTER OF CARDINAL GAGNON
TO ARCHBISHOP LEFEBVRE

Very Dear Monseigneur,

After a long wait I was able to ask the Holy Father what had been done with regard to the Society of Saint Pius X and the wider problem of Tradition.

He has confirmed that he had attentively read my long report and the propositions that you had given me.

As usual, he had been very busy with problems of world-wide dimensions. But he has already requested some canonists to suggest juridical forms that could be applied to the Society. He should be able to present some projects for this and for the doctrinal problems before the end of April.

He has asked me to give you this assurance and to invite you to patience[18] He would also like you to request your collaborators to have a great discretion in public declarations, indeed those who do not desire the reconciliation are happy to take advantage of the least thing to raise up opposition.

No need to tell you how much I am near you, especially in prayer. May the Holy Virgin keep you in good health even long after this difficult period of a search for a solution.

Fraternally yours in Jesus and Mary,

Edward Cardinal Gagnon
President of the Pontifical Council for the Family

---

[18] Patience, yes; interminable delays, no. They wanted to postpone a solution until Archbishop Lefebvre would be dead.

FEBRUARY 20, 1988

LETTER OF ARCHBISHOP LEFEBVRE
TO POPE JOHN PAUL II

On January 5, 1988, Cardinal Gagnon submitted the report of his Apostolic Visitation to the Pope. In spite of the Cardinal's promises, Archbishop Lefebvre never received a copy of it. It happened exactly as after the Visitation in 1974.

After the Pope had read this detailed report Archbishop Lefebvre expected to hear soon from the Vatican. After a long wait he wrote to the Holy Father to express once again the requirements necessary for a happy solution: a Roman Secretariat composed exclusively of members chosen from within Tradition; consecration of several bishops to be decided on before June 30, 1988; exemption *vis-à-vis* the local Ordinaries.

Most Holy Father,

His Eminence Cardinal Gagnon has just sent me a letter in which he informs me of an audience he had with you, after he gave you the report of his visit.

In this regard, permit me to express the profound satisfaction this Visit caused for everybody who was the object of it, and to inform you of our profound gratitude.

It would be regrettable if the hopes raised by this Visit turned into disappointment, observing the continual delays in the application of even a temporary solution.

May I permit myself to propose some suggestions on the subject of this solution:

In the first place, to take up again the doctrinal problems right away seems to be excluded, since this would be returning to the point of departure, and would renew the difficulties which have endured for 15 years. The idea of a Commission intervening after the juridical arrangement appears the most suitable one if we really want to find a practical solution.

Since the Priestly Society of Saint Pius X had been recognized for five years by the diocese of Fribourg and by the Sacred Congregation for the Clergy from 1970 to 1975, there should be no difficulty in recognizing it once again; it would then be recognized as being "of pontifical right."

Three particular points seem necessary for a happy solution:

1. To establish at Rome an Office, a Commission—the term is not very important—which would have the same role *vis-à-vis* all the initiatives of Tradition, as the Congregation for the Missions has. This commission would be headed by a Cardinal, if at all possible Cardinal Gagnon,[19] aided by a secretary general and one or two collaborators, all chosen from Tradition.[20] This office would be charged with regulating all the canonical problems of Tradition, and would conduct relations with the Holy See, the dicasteries,[21] and the bishops.

The bishops exercising their ministry within Tradition would depend on this organism for their ministry.

It does not seem that the erection of this Roman organism would offer difficulties.

2. The consecration of bishops succeeding me in my apostolate appears indispensable and urgent.

For the first designation, and while waiting for the Roman office to assume its functions, it seems to me that you can entrust it to me, as is done with the Eastern patriarchs.

If this is agreed to in principle, I will present the names to Cardinal Gagnon.

This second point is the most urgent one to be resolved, given my age and my fatigue. It is now two years that I have not done any ordinations at the seminary in the United States. The seminarians ardently aspire to be ordained, but I no longer have the health to be crossing oceans.

This is why I entreat Your Holiness to resolve this point before June 30 of this year.

These bishops would be in the same situation *vis-à-vis* Rome and *vis-à-vis* their Society that the missionary bishops were *vis-à-vis* the Congregation for the Propagation of the Faith and their own Society. Instead of a territorial jurisdiction, they would have a jurisdiction over individuals.[22]

It goes without saying that the bishops would always be chosen from among the priests of Tradition.

3. The exemption *vis-à-vis* the local Ordinaries

The works and initiatives of Tradition would be exempt from the jurisdiction of the local Ordinaries.[23]

---

19 Not granted in the May 5 Protocol.
20 Not granted in the May 5 Protocol.
21 A *dicastery* is an organ of the Roman Curia, such as the Congregation for the Doctrine of the Faith.
22 Not granted in the May 5 Protocol.
23 Not granted in the May 5 Protocol.

For the resumption of good relations however, the superiors of traditional works would make a report on the houses existing in the dioceses and communicate it to the local Ordinaries; similarly, before founding a new center, they will submit a report to the Ordinary, but are not required to ask for authorization.

After examining these diverse points, I think that Your Holiness will recognize that the problem of Tradition can find a rapid and satisfactory solution.

We would be happy to renew normal relations with the Holy See, but without changing in any way what we are; for it is in this way that we are assured of remaining children of God and the Roman Church.

Deign to accept, Most Holy Father, the expression of my most respectful and filial devotion in Jesus and Mary.

† Marcel Lefebvre
Ecône
February 20, 1988

FEBRUARY 20, 1988

LETTER OF ARCHBISHOP LEFEBVRE TO CARDINAL GAGNON

Eminence,

Fr. du Chalard has faithfully transmitted to me the letter in which you let me know the dispositions of the Holy Father after you had communicated to him your report.

Surely I do not doubt that the Holy Father has not only our problem to solve. But I fear that the procedure chosen for a solution would prolong indefinitely and thus put me in a moral obligation to proceed with the episcopal consecrations without the authorization of the Holy See which should be able to be avoided.

Therefore I take the liberty to write to the Holy Father through your intermediary, giving you a copy of this letter, in order to encourage him to make a decision, even a temporary one, that would not engage the future and would allow the experience of the exercise of tradition, in a manner officially approved by the Church.

The doctrinal problems could be the object of discussions after the canonical solution, otherwise we would be back at the starting point.[24]

A positive thing was your friendly visit with Monsignor Perl, which certainly consoled and encouraged all those who had the advantage to come close to you and to listen to you. It would be sad that they be disappointed by the passivity of Rome.

By the way, I hope that we will be soon able to receive a copy of your report and that we will not be deprived of this as in the visit of 1974.

We put our hope in God and in Our Lady, but also in you, Eminence, who are the only one at the Vatican to understand our fight for the Faith and for the salvation of souls.

---

[24] In his letter of July 28, 1987, Cardinal Ratzinger did not ask for such a doctrinal declaration: that had pleased Archbishop Lefebvre and giving him hope that a solution could be found promptly. See October 1, 1987, p.28.

Deign to receive, Eminence, my very grateful and fraternal feelings in Jesus and Mary,

Monseigneur Lefebvre
Archbishop-Bishop Emeritus of Tulle.

After the first visitation in November 1974, which ended in the illegal suppression of the Society of Saint Pius X, no report of the visitation was given to Archbishop Lefebvre. Neither was the request of a copy of the report granted after the second visitation in December 1987 by Cardinal Gagnon. If the report was bad, the Vatican had all advantage to release it, so as to prove that it was right to condemn Archbishop Lefebvre. If the report was good, then why did it not grant the solution proposed by Archbishop Lefebvre in order to continue its good work?

It has been reported Cardinal Gagnon theorized that if Archbishop Lefebvre would proceed with the episcopal consecrations without the Pope's approval, 80% of the faithful attached to Tradition would abandon him. The attachment of the faithful to Rome and to the Pope, which Cardinal Gagnon had been able to witness in all traditional centers, probably made him say so. However, he had not sufficiently assessed the fact that the faithful were rightly attached to what the Pope represents more than to his own person. It is the magisterium of the popes of all times that the traditional faithful uphold, not the novelties of any single modern pope.

MARCH 18, 1988

LETTER OF CARDINAL RATZINGER TO ARCHBISHOP LEFEBVRE

The role of Cardinal Gagnon stops with this letter. Clearly the Pope removes him and replaces him with Cardinal Ratzinger. The latter takes the initiative of continuing the negotiations, and works out a plan of reconciliation, presenting the first stage of it to Archbishop Lefebvre. The removal of Cardinal Gagnon from the negotiations was the first of a long series of disappointments after hopes had been so high in the fall of 1987.

Strictly confidential

Excellency,

At the stage we have reached in the reflection undertaken following the Apostolic Visit to canonically regularize the situation of the Society of Saint Pius X, and considering your letter to the Holy Father dated last February 20, it appears extremely useful to be able to proceed to an exchange of views on the concrete propositions whose application can be envisaged.

To get it under way, Cardinal Gagnon and I would like to propose to you that a meeting take place between two experts (a theologian and a canonist) designated by the Holy See, and two experts (likewise, a theologian and a canonist) of the Society designated by yourself, presided over by a personality designated by the Holy Father in the role of "moderator." Obviously, this stage consisting of a mutual exchange of views would still not be the place for definitive decisions, but it would have to constitute an important step on the way to these decisions.

If, as we hope, you accept this proposition, please be kind enough to inform us of it. After this moment, the place and the conditions of this meeting could be fixed rapidly, of course in the conditions of the most rigorous discretion.

Deign to accept, Excellency, the assurance of my prayer, with the expression of my respectful and devoted sentiments in the Lord.

Joseph Cardinal Ratzinger

LETTER OF CARDINAL RATZINGER TO ARCHBISHOP LEFEBVRE

Confidential

Excellency,

Fr. du Chalard has let me know your favorable response to the proposition which I had made to you in my letter of March 18, of a meeting, as well as the names of the two experts which you have agreed to appoint. I thank you for this.

I am now in a position to indicate that this meeting is scheduled for Tuesday the 12th at Rome and if necessary on Wednesday, April 13. The Holy Father has appointed as moderator the Reverend Fr. Benoît Duroux, O.P.; as theologian, Don Fernando Ocariz and as canonist Don Tarcisio Bertone, SDB. All three are consultants for the Sacred Congregation for the Doctrine of the Faith.

During the coming week I will let Fr. du Chalard know by phone the exact location and timetable of this meeting. We foresee that participants will have to take their lunch there.

Giving you my best wishes for the holy feast of Easter, I assure you of my prayers and ask you to accept the expression of my respectful and dedicated feelings in the Lord.

Joseph Cardinal Ratzinger

APRIL 8, 1988

LETTER OF POPE JOHN PAUL II
TO CARDINAL RATZINGER

To my Venerable Brother Joseph Cardinal Ratzinger
Prefect of the Congregation for the Doctrine of the Faith

In this liturgical period, when we have relived through the Holy Week celebrations the events of Easter, Christ's words by which He promised the Apostles the coming of the Holy Spirit take on for us a special relevance: "And I will pray the Father, and he will give you another Counselor, to be with you for ever, even the Spirit of truth—whom the Father will send in my name, he will teach you all things, and bring to your remembrance all that I have said to you" (Jn. 14:16-17;26).

The Church at all times has been guided by faith in these words of her Teacher and Lord, in the certainty that thanks to the help and assistance of the Holy Spirit she will remain for ever in the divine Truth, preserving the apostolic succession through the College of Bishops united with their Head, the Successor of Peter.

The Church manifested this conviction of Faith also at the last Council, which met to reconfirm and reinforce the teaching of the Church inherited from the Tradition already existing for almost 20 centuries, as a living reality which progresses *vis-à-vis* the problems and needs of every age and deepens our understanding of what is already contained in the Faith transmitted once and for all (*cf.* Jude 3). We are profoundly convinced that the Spirit of truth who speaks to the Church (*cf.* Apoc. 2:7, 11, 17, *et. al.*) has spoken—in a particularly solemn and authoritative manner—through the Second Vatican Council preparing the Church to enter the third millennium after Christ. Given that the work of the Council taken as a whole constitutes a reconfirmation of the same truth lived by the Church from the beginning, it is likewise a "renewal" of that truth (an *aggiornamento* according to the well-known expression of Pope John XXIII), in order to bring closer to the great human family in the modern world both the way of teaching faith and morals and also the whole apostolic and pastoral work of the Church. And it is obvious how diversified and indeed divided this world is.

Through the doctrinal and pastoral service of the whole College of Bishops in union with the Pope, the Church took up the tasks connected with the implementation of everything which became the specific heritage of Vatican II. The meetings of the Synods of bishops are one of the ways in which this collegial solicitude finds expression. In this context the Extraordinary Assembly of the Synod in 1985, held on the 20th anniversary of the end of the Council, deserves special mention. It emphasized the most important tasks connected with the implementation of Vatican II, and it stated that the teaching of that council remains the path which the Church must take into the future, entrusting her efforts to the Spirit of truth. In reference to these efforts, particular relevance attaches to the duties of the Holy See on behalf of the universal Church, both through the *ministerium petrinum* of the Bishop of Rome and also through the departments of the Roman Curia which he makes use of for the carrying out of his universal ministry. Among the latter the Congregation for the Doctrine of the Faith led by Your Eminence is of particularly special importance.

In the period since the Council we are witnessing a great effort on the part of the Church to ensure that this *novum* constituted by Vatican II correctly penetrates the mind and conduct of the individual communities of the People of God. However, side by side with this effort there have appeared tendencies which create a certain difficulty in putting the Council into practice. One of these tendencies is characterized by a desire for changes which are not always in harmony with the teaching and spirit of Vatican II, even though they seek to appeal to the Council. These changes claim to express progress, and so this tendency is given the name "progressivism." In this case progress consists in an aspiration towards the future which breaks with the past, without taking into account the function of Tradition, which is fundamental to the Church's mission in order that she may continue in the Truth which was transmitted to her by Christ the Lord and by the Apostles and which is diligently safeguarded by the magisterium.

The opposite tendency, which is usually called "conservatism" or "integralism," stops at the past itself, without taking into account the correct aspiration towards the future which manifested itself precisely in the work of Vatican II. While the former tendency seems to recognize the correctness of what is new, the latter sees correctness only in what is "ancient," considering it synonymous with Tradition. But it is not what is "ancient" as such, or what is "new" *per se*, which corresponds to the correct idea of Tradition in the life of the Church. Rather, that idea means the Church's remaining faithful to the truth received from God throughout the changing circumstances of history. The Church, like that householder in the Gospel, wisely brings "from the storeroom both the new and the old" (Mt.

13:52), while remaining absolutely obedient to the Spirit of truth whom Christ has given to the Church as her divine Guide. And the Church performs this delicate task of discernment through her authentic magisterium (*cf. Lumen Gentium*, §25).

The position taken up by individuals, groups or circles connected with one or the other tendency is to a certain extent understandable, especially after an event as important in the history of the Church as the last Council. If, on the one hand, that event unleashed an aspiration for renewal (this also contains an element of "novelty"), on the other hand certain abuses in the realization of this aspiration, in so far as they forget essential values of Catholic doctrine on faith and morals and in other areas of ecclesial life, for example in that of the Liturgy, can and indeed must cause justified objection. Nevertheless, if by reason of these excesses every healthy kind of "renewal" conforming to the teaching and spirit of the Council is rejected, such an attitude can lead to another deviation which itself is in opposition to the principle of the living Tradition of the Church obedient to the Spirit of truth.

The duties, which in this concrete situation, face the Apostolic See require a particular perspicacity, prudence and farsightedness. The need to distinguish what authentically "builds up" the Church from what destroys her is becoming in the present period a particular demand of our service to the whole community of believers.

The Congregation for the Doctrine of the Faith is of key importance in the context of this ministry, as is shown by the documents which your Department has published in this matter of faith and morals during the last few years. Among the subjects which the Congregation for the Doctrine of the Faith has recently had to concern itself with, there also figure the problems connected with the "Society of Saint Pius X," founded and led by Archbishop Marcel Lefebvre.

Your Eminence knows very well how many efforts have been made by the Apostolic See since the beginning of the existence of the "Society," in order to ensure ecclesial unity in relation to its activity. The latest such effort has been the canonical visit made by Edward Cardinal Gagnon. Your Eminence is concerned with this case in a special way, as was your predecessor of venerable memory, Franjo Cardinal Seper. Everything done by the Apostolic See, which is in continual contact with the bishops and episcopal conferences concerned, has the same purpose: that in this case too there may be fulfilled the words of the Lord in his priestly prayer for the unity of all his disciples and followers. All the bishops of the Catholic Church, inasmuch as by the divine command they are solicitous for the unity of the universal Church, are bound to collaborate with the Apostolic

See for the welfare of the whole Mystical Body, which is also the body of the Church (*cf. Lumen Gentium*, 23).

For all these reasons I would assure Your Eminence once more of my desire that these efforts should continue. We do not cease to hope that—under the protection of the Mother of the Church—they will bear fruit for the glory of God and the salvation of men.

From the Vatican, on April 8, in the year 1988, the tenth of my pontificate.

In fraternal charity,

Joannes Paulus PP. II

This letter is quite important since it gives the whole spirit in which the negotiations were conducted by the Vatican. One can distinguish three parts in this letter: the first stresses the importance of Vatican II; the second opposes progressivism and conservatism; and the third draws some practical conclusions.

In the first part we notice the euphoria of Vatican II. No distinction is made, as if each and every word of Vatican II was directly inspired by the Holy Ghost. There are certainly many beautiful passages in the documents of Vatican II; yet, there are other passages directly inspired by Liberalism and Modernism.

This lack of distinction ignores the hijacking of the Council by a Modernist faction, a fact witnessed by both Cardinal Wojtyla and Fr. Ratzinger at the time. When the latter became Cardinal, he explicitly recalled it in his interview with Vittorio Messori: "After Pope John XXIII had announced its convocation, the Roman Curia worked together with the most distinguished representatives of the world episcopate[25] in the preparation of those schemata which were then rejected by the Council Fathers as too theoretical, too textbook-like and insufficiently pastoral. Pope John had not reckoned on the possibility of a rejection but was expecting a quick and frictionless balloting on these projects which he had approvingly read...."[26]

Archbishop Lefebvre, when recalling the same fact, says that the rest of the Council was spent trying to purge the worst passages from the new schemata proposed by the modernists. These two conflicting influences can be easily found in the texts of the Council. Many conservative priests try to draw only the good side of the Council, ignoring the other side; many modernists only refer to the bad side, despising the other. To be objective, one has to recognize both sides. Even Cardinal Ratzinger is no longer too euphoric about the fruits of the Council.

---

[25] In the Central Commission, whose task it was to oversee this whole preparatory work, there were 70 cardinals, 20 archbishops and bishops, and four superiors general, among whom Archbishop Lefebvre served.

[26] *The Ratzinger Report* (San Francisco: Ignatius Press, 1985), p.41.

"The Church took up the tasks connected with the implementation of everything which became the specific heritage of Vatican II...the teaching of that Council remains the path which the Church must take into the future...." These sentences, in the letter of April 8, 1988, were the stumbling block that made the negotiations fail.

The second part caricatures the attitudes of the faithful who are attached to Tradition, as if they were "stuck in the past." There may be no younger order in the Church than the Society of Saint Pius X. Archbishop Lefebvre is not attached so much to the letter but rather to the spirit of Tradition. When he drew up the rules of the Society of Saint Pius X he took care to adapt them to the necessities of the modern apostolate.

Regarding the accusation of an incorrect understanding of Tradition, please see the comments on the motu proprio, *Ecclesia Dei*.

The third part of this letter was perhaps the most noticeable. It stresses the confidence of the Pope in Cardinal Ratzinger. It also reminds all the bishops of the Catholic Church of their duty "to collaborate with the Holy See for the welfare of the whole mystical body."

This produced fear in some conciliar bishops but hope in members of the Society of Saint Pius X, including Fr. Schmidberger.

APRIL 15, 1988

MINUTES OF MEETINGS HELD
APRIL 12-14, 1988, AT THE VATICAN
CONCERNING THE SOCIETY OF SAINT PIUS X

The conversations took place at Rome, April 12-14. Present were Frs. Bernard Tissier de Mallerais and Patrice Laroche, named by Archbishop Lefebvre as the theologian and canonist representing the Society, and Frs. Bertone, Salesian, and Ocariz, of *Opus Dei*, under the direction of Fr. Benoît Duroux, O.P., moderator, as consultors of the Sacred Congregation for the Doctrine of the Faith. Subsequent to these discussions a preliminary protocol of accord was signed on April 15, 1988. These meetings took place in a discreet manner in order to avoid the insatiable curiosity of the journalists, thanks to Fr. du Chalard, priest of the Society of Saint Pius X in Rome.

I. DOCTRINAL QUESTION

The Commission has studied three possibilities for a formula of communion in the Faith.

1) The Profession of Faith (Appendix I, p.55), plus the Oath of Fidelity (Appendix II, p.56), plus a text on the acceptance of Vatican II (Appendix III, p.57).

2) The Oath of Fidelity (Appendix II), plus the text of Appendix III. The reason for not having the Profession of Faith comes from the fact that there is no doubt that H.E. Archbishop Lefebvre professes the Catholic Creed, and that the request of making this profession could be offensive.

3) A unique formula as brief and clear as possible, and corresponding to the concrete position of Archbishop Lefebvre and of the Society of Saint Pius X (see Appendix IV, p.57). This formula would contain:

   a) the points of the Oath of Fidelity concerning the position of Archbishop Lefebvre in particular,

   b) an adhesion to the magisterium of the Church, given as an acceptance of §25 of *Lumen Gentium,*

   c) the attitude which must be taken on the points of Vatican II which are not of Faith and which make difficulties for Archbishop Lefebvre, *d)* the recognition of the validity of the new liturgy.

The Commission favors this third solution:
- because it is reduced to the essential, in one document, and avoids the repetition of doctrinal points already admitted by Archbishop Lefebvre;
- because it signifies by itself an important doctrine of Vatican II in the Constitution *Lumen Gentium.*

APPENDIX I: PROFESSION OF FAITH[27]

This formula should be used instead of the Profession of Faith of the Council of Trent and of the Anti-Modernist Oath, in the cases in which the Law prescribes a Profession of Faith.

I, *N.,* believe with a firm faith and profess each and every point that is contained in the Symbol of Faith:

I believe in one God, the Father Almighty, Maker of heaven and earth, and of all things visible and invisible. And in one Lord Jesus Christ, the Only-begotten Son of God. Born of the Father before all ages. God of God; Light of Light, true God of true God. Begotten not made; consubstantial with the Father; by Whom all things were made. Who for us men, and for our salvation, came down form heaven. And was made Flesh by the Holy Ghost of the Virgin Mary: *and was made Man.* He was also crucified for us, suffered under Pontius Pilate and was buried. And on the third day He rose again according to the Scriptures. And ascending into heaven, He sits at the right hand of the Father. And He shall come again in glory to judge the living and the dead; and of His kingdom there shall be no end. And I believe in the Holy Ghost, Lord and Giver of life, Who proceeds from the Father and the Son. Who together with the Father and the Son is no less adored, and glorified: Who spoke by the Prophets. And I believe in One, Holy, Catholic and Apostolic Church. I confess one Baptism for the remission of sins. And I look for the resurrection of the dead. And the life of the world to come. Amen.

I firmly embrace and retain each and every point on the doctrine on Faith and Morals which have been either defined by the Church, through a solemn judgment or affirmed and declared through the Ordinary magisterium, as they have been proposed, especially what regards the mystery of the Church of Christ, her Sacraments, the Sacrifice of the Mass, and the primacy of the Roman Pontiff.

---

[27] The reader will see how short this Profession of Faith (original in Latin) is, compared with the Profession of Faith of the Council of Trent and the Anti-Modernist Oath. By removing these latter, Pope Paul VI took away an important barrier blocking the "auto-demolition" of the Church.

APPENDIX II: THE OATH OF FIDELITY
TO BE TAKEN BY THE BISHOPS

I, *N.*, promoted at the See of _____, shall always be faithful to the Catholic Church and to the Roman Pontiff as Supreme Shepherd, Vicar of Christ, Successor of the Blessed Apostle Peter in the primacy and headship of the College of Bishops.

I shall submit to the free exercise of the power of primacy of the Supreme Pontiff in the Universal Church, and I shall take care to defend and promote his rights and authority. I shall acknowledge and observe the prerogatives and rights of the legates of the Roman Pontiff who act in the name of the Supreme Shepherd.

I shall be careful to fulfil with the utmost diligence the apostolic responsibilities entrusted to the bishops, *viz.*, to teach, sanctify and to rule the people of God within the hierarchical communion with the head and members of the College of Bishops.

I shall support the unity of the Universal Church, therefore I shall work studiously so that the Deposit of Faith transmitted from the Apostles be kept in its purity and integrity, and that the truth to be held and applied in morals, as they are proposed by the magisterium of the Church, be given to all and illustrated. I shall show a fatherly affection to those who err in the Faith, and strive with all means possible that they reach the fullness of Catholic Truth.

Looking upon the Model of Christ, the Supreme and Eternal Priest, I shall act in a pious and holy manner, and fulfil the ministry entrusted to me in such a way that, being made a pattern of the flock from the heart, I may be able to confirm the faithful so that they reach Christian perfection.

I shall foster the common discipline of the whole Church, and the observance of all ecclesiastical laws, insisting especially on those that are contained in the Code of Canon Law, always vigilant lest evil practices creep in especially concerning the Ministry of the Word and the celebration of the Sacraments.

I shall show proper diligence in the administration of the temporal goods of the Church, especially those that have been given for the exercise of divine worship, for the honorable support of the clergy and the other ministers, and for the sacred apostolate and the works of charity.

I shall pursue with a special predilection all the priests and deacons, who are collaborators of the episcopal order for the fulfillment of the mandate given to me, and also the religious monks and nuns who participate in the one and same work. Also, I shall take the greatest care to promote holy vocations, in order to fittingly provide for the spiritual necessities of the whole Church.

I shall acknowledge and promote the dignity of the laity and their proper place in the mission of the Church. I shall care, with a particular solicitude, to foster the missionary works for the evangelization of the nations.

When called for councils or other legitimate collegial actions, I shall be personally present, unless I have impediments, and I shall respond in an opportune way.

At the set time, when there will be a good occasion, I shall give an account to the Holy See of my pastoral work, and I shall receive its comments and counsels with respect and fulfil them with the greatest efforts.

May God and these holy Gospels, which I touch with my hand, help me.

APPENDIX III: TEXT OF ACCEPTANCE OF VATICAN II

[This is composed §§ 1, 3, 4, 5 of Appendix IV below.]

APPENDIX IV: STATEMENT OF THE POSITION OF ARCHBISHOP LEFEBVRE AND OF THE SOCIETY OF SAINT PIUS X

I, Marcel Lefebvre, Archbishop-Bishop Emeritus of Tulle, as well as the members of the Priestly Society of Saint Pius X founded by me:

1) Promise to be always faithful to the Catholic Church and the Roman Pontiff, its Supreme Pastor, Vicar of Christ, Successor of Blessed Peter in his primacy and headship of the College[28] of bishops. (See Oath of Fidelity, Appendix II.)

2) We declare our acceptance of the doctrine contained in §25[29] of the dogmatic Constitution *Lumen Gentium* of Vatican Council II on the ecclesiastical magisterium and the adherence which is due to it.

3) Regarding certain points taught by Vatican Council II or concerning later reforms of the liturgy and law, which do not appear to us easily reconcilable with Tradition, we pledge that we will have a positive attitude of study and communication with the Apostolic See, avoiding all polemics.

4) Moreover, we declare that we recognize the validity of the Sacrifice of the Mass and the Sacraments celebrated with the inten-

---

[28] This word has been corrected in the May 5 Protocol to, "body."

[29] See p.77-79 for complete text of §25 of *Lumen Gentium*.

tion of doing what the Church does, and according to the rites indicated in the typical editions of the Roman Missal and the Rituals of the Sacraments promulgated by Popes Paul VI and John Paul II.

5) Finally, we promise to respect the common discipline of the Church and all[30] the ecclesiastical laws, especially those contained in the Code of Canon Law promulgated by Pope John Paul II, without prejudice to the special discipline granted to the Society by particular law.

II. JURIDICAL QUESTIONS

Considering the fact that the Priestly Society of Saint Pius X has been conceived for 18 years as a society of common life—and after studying the propositions formulated by H. E. Marcel Lefebvre and the conclusions of the Apostolic Visitation conducted by His Eminence Cardinal Gagnon—it seems that[31] the canonical form most suitable is that of a Society of apostolic life.

1. Society of Apostolic Life

This solution is canonically possible and suitable to the nature of the Priestly Society of Saint Pius X, with the advantage of eventually inserting into the clerical Society of apostolic life lay people as well (for example, coadjutor Brothers).

According to the Code of Canon Law promulgated in 1983, Canons 731-746, this Society enjoys full autonomy, can form its members, can incardinate clerics, and can insure the common life of its members.

In the proper Statutes, with flexibility and inventive[32] possibility in respect of the known models of these Societies of apostolic life, a certain exemption is foreseen with respect to the diocesan bishops (*cf.* Canon 591) for what concerns public worship, the *cura animarum*, and other apostolic activities, taking into account Canons 679-683. As for jurisdiction with regards to the faithful who have recourse to the priests of the Society, it will be conferred on these priests either by the Ordinaries of the place or by the Apostolic See.

---

[30] This word "all" has been suppressed in the Protocol, since Canons such as Canon 844 (of the *1983 Code of Canon Law*) are unacceptable.

[31] These three words have been suppressed, too.

[32] Please note the adjective.

2. Roman Commission

A commission to coordinate relations with the different dicasteries of the Roman Curia and diocesan bishops, as well as to resolve eventual problems and contentions, will be constituted through the care of the Holy See, and will be empowered with the necessary faculties to deal with the questions indicated above (for example, implantation at the request of the faithful of a house of worship where there is no house of the Society, *ad mentem,* Canon 683, §2).

Among other things this commission would have the function of exercising vigilance and lending assistance to consolidate the work of reconciliation, and to regulate questions relative to the religious communities having a juridical or moral bond with the Society.

a) The delegates of the Society recall here the requests presented to the Holy Father by Archbishop Lefebvre in his letter of February 20, 1988, *viz.,* that "this Commission be headed by a Cardinal, inasmuch as possible, Cardinal Gagnon, helped by a Secretary and one or two collaborators, all chosen from Tradition."

   1) For the relations with Roman dicasteries and the Cardinal President, the Holy Father could nominate one member not from Tradition, added to the other members of the Society.
   2) In any case, the contacts and relations with traditional religious communities would be assured by the members of the Commission taken from Tradition.

b) The members of the Commission nominated by the Holy Father make the following observations:

   1) Concerning the nomination of a Cardinal as President, it would be preferable that the Roman Commission depend upon Cardinal Ratzinger as Chairman, and guarantor of the works, especially by reason of the authority which he possesses as Prefect of the Congregation for the Doctrine of the Faith (see recent letter of the Holy Father to Cardinal Ratzinger).
   2) Concerning the composition of the Roman Commission, it would be opportune to widen the number of its members, taking them also from outside the Society or of persons linked with it, in order to foster the reconciliation with the whole Church.

3. Condition of Persons Connected to the Society:

1) The members of the clerical Society of apostolic life (priests and lay coadjutor brothers) are governed by the Statutes of the Society of Pontifical Right.

2) The oblates, both male and female, whether they have taken private vows or not, and the members of the Third Order connected with the Society, all belong to an association of the faithful connected with the Society according to the terms of Canon 303, and collaborate with it.

3) The Sisters (meaning the congregation founded by Archbishop Lefebvre) who make public vows: they constitute a true institute of consecrated life, with its own structure and proper autonomy,[33] even if a certain type of bond is envisaged for the unity of its spirituality with the Superior of the Society. This Congregation—at least at the beginning— would be dependent on the Roman Commission, instead of the Congregation for Religious.

4) The members of the communities living according to the rule of various religious institutes (Carmelites, Benedictines, Dominicans, *etc.*) and who have a moral bond with the Society. These are to be given, case by case, a particular statute regulating their relations with the respective Order.

Regarding the lay people who ask for pastoral assistance from the communities of the Society: they remain under the jurisdiction of the diocesan bishop, but—notably by reason of the liturgical rites of the communities of the Society—they can go to them for the administration of the sacraments (for which the usual notifications must still be given to their proper parish; *cf.* Canons 878, 896, 1122). The Commission draws attention to the particular complexity:

1) Of the question of reception by the laity of the Sacraments of Baptism, Confirmation, Marriage, in the communities of the Society.

2) Of the question of communities practicing the rule of such and such a religious institute, without belonging to it.

The Roman Commission will have the responsibility of resolving these problems.

---

[33] Note the desire to separate the unity that exists between traditional foundations.

4. Ordinations

For the ordinations, two phases must be distinguished:

1) In the immediate future. For the ordinations scheduled to take place in the immediate future, Archbishop Lefebvre would be authorized to confer them or, if he were unable, another bishop accepted by himself.

2) Once the Society of apostolic life is erected. As far as possible, the normal way is to be followed, that is, to send dimissorial letters to a bishop who agrees to ordain members of the Society.

In view of the particular situation of the Society, the ordination of a member of the Society as a bishop, who, among other duties, would also be able to proceed with ordinations.

N.B.: For the admission to the ordinations, especially in the first phase, given the judgement of fitness and the regular admission from the competent superiors of the Society, the candidates should make a promise of fidelity, which shall later be elaborated in the light of the formula presented above in the doctrinal part.

5. Problem of a Bishop

1) At the doctrinal (ecclesiological) level, the guarantee of stability and maintenance of the life and activity of the Society is assured by its erection as a Society of apostolic life of pontifical right, and the approval of its statutes by the Holy Father.

2) But, at the practical and psychological level, the utility of the consecration of a member of the Society as a bishop is considered. In this case, two hypothesis may be foreseen:

a) In the framework of the doctrinal and canonical solution of the project of reconciliation, the Holy Father would name a bishop chosen from within the Society, presented by Archbishop Lefebvre.

b) It would belong to the Roman Commission to propose to the Holy Father this nomination of a Bishop belonging to the Society.

This solution would solve the practical problems of the use of the Rite of St. Pius V, and in the celebration of the Mass of Ordination and in other circumstances (*e.g.,* Confirmations). Moreover, this bishop could represent the Society within the Roman Commission.

6. Particular Problems to be Resolved (By Decree or Declaration)

1) Lifting of the *suspensio a divinis* on Archbishop Lefebvre and dispensation from the irregularities incurred by the fact of the ordinations.

2) *Sanatio in radice*, at least *ad cautelam*, of the marriages already celebrated by the priests of the Society without the required delegation.

3) Provision for an "amnesty" and an accord for the houses and places of worship erected—or used—by the Society, until now without the authorization of the bishops.

Fr. Benoît Duroux, O.P.,
Don Tarcisius Bertone
Dom Fernando Ocariz
Fr. Bernard Tissier de Mallerais
Fr. Patrice Laroche

At the Vatican
April 15, 1988

III. NOTE CONCERNING THE EPISCOPATE IN THE SOCIETY

Referring themselves in particular to the letter addressed by Archbishop Lefebvre to the Holy Father on February 20, 1988, the delegates of the Society present insist on the fact that Archbishop Lefebvre sees in this point a very important element for the realization of the ecclesial communion. Here are the principal reasons:

a) necessity of bishops chosen from the Society:
- these episcopal consecrations are awaited by the seminarians who count upon being ordained by a bishop belonging to the same spiritual family.
- It will be psychologically difficult now to ask our faithful and seminarians to ask for the Sacraments of Confirmation and Order from bishops who did not cease to warn them against the Society, who approve catechisms such as *Pierres Vivantes*[34] or who have professed highly suspicious theological opinions.

---

[34] The current modernist French catechism. See *Apologia Pro Marcel Lefebvre*, Vol. III, available from the Angelus Press.

- It is very difficult in the present circumstances to find bishops knowing how to celebrate in the traditional rite the long ceremonies of the Roman Pontifical.
- These episcopal consecrations would be favorable to keep in the unity of the Church the faithful of Tradition, practically reducing to nought the inference of the many small sedevacantist groups, each one having its own "bishop."
- Moreover, there would be for Archbishop Lefebvre, the priests and the faithful of Tradition, the unequivocal sign of the sincerity of the Roman authorities, and of their will to give back an honorable place in the Church to the traditional rite.

From thence flows the following point:

b) Urgency of the nomination of a bishop from the Society within a very short space of time.[35]

- The great age of Archbishop Lefebvre and the physical exhaustion which he has been feeling for the past months do not allow him to continue to travel throughout the world.
- The good will of Archbishop Lefebvre which would have led to the normalization of the situation of the Society and of the works of tradition, would deserve that the Prelate sees while still living his episcopal ministry continued by one of his sons.
- Do the good fruits borne by the works of Tradition and which Cardinal Gagnon has witnessed during the course of his apostolic visit not merit such a gesture of acknowledgment from the Holy See at the very time of this agreement?
- the reception, within a short space of time, by Archbishop Lefebvre of the pontifical mandate enabling him to proceed to an episcopal consecration would be a delicate way to erase, in effect, the injustices endured by the Prelate for the past 15 years.

c) Necessity of several bishops taken from the bosom of Tradition.

- The development of the works of Tradition mean already from now at least 25 ceremonies of ordination per year throughout the whole world.

---

[35] See the letter of Archbishop Lefebvre to the Holy Father on February 20, 1988, p.42.

- The faithful addressing themselves to the Society for Confirmation in the traditional rite are more and more numerous.
  1) In 1987, Archbishop Lefebvre gave 2,500 Confirmations in France alone. This represents ceremonies three or four days per week for a whole month, often gathering children from great distances.
  2) In 1984, in Chile, Archbishop Lefebvre had to give, in one ceremony, the Sacrament of Confirmation to 1,527 faithful.
  3) In 1982, in Mexico, during one week's travel alone, he performed 2,500 Confirmations.
- The Society alone has opened, at the request of the faithful, 530 places of worship on five continents. The faithful would like to receive the visit of Archbishop Lefebvre, or of a bishop representing their spiritual family.
- Moreover, many ceremonies, blessings and consecrations,[36] must be accomplished by a bishop. One alone could not suffice for this work.

---

[36] Blessing of a church; consecration of an altar; of a chalice, *etc.*

APRIL 15, 1988

LETTER OF ARCHBISHOP LEFEBVRE TO CARDINAL RATZINGER

Eminence,

After having been able to follow the works of the Commission in charge of preparing an acceptable solution for the problem which preoccupies us, it seems that with the grace of God, we are coming closer to an agreement, which makes us very happy.

With this letter I attach the doctrinal declaration, modified slightly in such a way that I believe that I can sign it; I hope it will be agreeable to you.

Without doubt, there will be more precisions to add to the canonical document on the Roman Commission; I would like, at least in the beginning, to be able to play a part in it in order to facilitate the solutions for the diverse cases for those who have been at our side during these last years, and who also wish a happy ending of their problems.

On this occasion wouldn't it be desirable that the possibility[37] to use the liturgical books of John XXIII be granted for all the bishops and all priests?

The prospect of having a successor in the episcopate gives me great joy and I thank the Holy Father and yourself for it. Only one bishop will hardly suffice for the heavy work load; wouldn't it be possible to have two, or at the least, couldn't the possibility of raising its number in the next six months or a year be provided for?[38]

Please, Eminence, would you express to the Holy Father my deep gratitude on my behalf and on behalf of all those that I represent. Please believe in my respectful and fraternal sentiments, in *Christo et Maria.*

† Marcel Lefebvre
Archbishop Emeritus of Tulle

---

[37] The "wide application" of the 1984 Indult called for by Pope John Paul II in his motu proprio, *Ecclesia Dei,* does not fulfil this request, because the priest still depends upon a permission from modernist bishops to be allowed to have the traditional Mass. What is needed is to simply reaffirm the Indult granted by St. Pius V in *Quo Primum.*

[38] A conservative retired bishop, whom I know, asked the Pope in June [1988], after the failure of the negotiations, for this alternate possibility, which was not granted to him.

Formula

I, Marcel Lefebvre, Archbishop-Bishop Emeritus of Tulle, as well as the members of the Priestly Society of Saint Pius X founded by me:

1) Promise to be always faithful to the Catholic Church and the Roman Pontiff, its Supreme Pastor, Vicar of Christ, Successor of Blessed Peter in his primacy as head of the College of bishops. (see Oath of Fidelity, Appendix II).

2) We declare our acceptance of the doctrine contained in §25 of the dogmatic Constitution *Lumen Gentium* of Vatican Council II on the ecclesiastical magisterium and the adherence which is due to it.

3) Regarding certain points taught by Vatican Council II or concerning later reforms of the liturgy and law, and which do not appear to us easily reconcilable with Tradition, we pledge that we will have a positive attitude of study and communication with the Apostolic See, avoiding all polemics.

4) Moreover, taking into account what was said in §3, we declare that we recognize the validity of the Sacrifice of the Mass and the Sacraments celebrated with the intention of doing what the Church does, and according to the rites indicated in the typical editions of the Roman Missal and the Rituals of the Sacraments promulgated by Popes Paul VI and John Paul II.

5) Finally, here also taking into account what was said in §3, we promise to respect the common discipline of the Church and thus the disciplinary laws contained in the Code of Canon Law promulgated by Pope John Paul II, without prejudice to the special discipline granted to the Society by particular law.

Note that Archbishop Lefebvre inserted twice the words "taking into account what was said in §3," which stresses the reservations on the new liturgy and on the Canon Law, through which the liberal ideas of the Council were implemented.

Note also that "all the ecclesiastical laws" are changed into "thus the disciplinary laws..." Indeed some laws of the *1983 Code of Canon Law,* such as Canon 844 (on Eucharistic Hospitality) are in direct opposition with sound Catholic doctrine.

APRIL 28, 1988

LETTER OF CARDINAL RATZINGER TO ARCHBISHOP LEFEBVRE

Excellence,

I am now in a position to answer your last letter of April 15. Indeed I was able to submit it recently to the Sovereign Pontiff and to discuss with Him the results at which the Commission arrived during the sessions of April 12-14 last. It is thus with His agreement that I can communicate to you the following.

The Holy Father was satisfied with these results and He considers that they provide a valuable foundation to bring to a good end the work of reconciliation. This concerns in particular the juridical framework foreseen for the Priestly Fraternity of Saint Pius X.

As you have been able to observe, on certain points the document of the commission indicates alternate solutions or underlines a particular complexity. Several of these questions could be solved by the Roman Commission foreseen after the canonical erection of the Society but others should be solved as soon as possible. Now this requires common study and reflection and could take still more time. Thus definitive answer cannot be given to you for the moment but it will be at latest in the first half of June.

With regard to the nomination of a bishop[39] the Holy Father tends to regard your proposition taking into account the practical and psychological reasons for such a nomination. However this one could not happen right now, even if there were no other reason than the preparation and examination of the files according to the usual procedure of episcopal nominations.

Moreover, His Holiness has pointed out that which was marked in the document of the Commission, *viz.* that on the one hand the guarantee of stability and of the continuation of the life and activity of the Society would be assured by its erection as a Society of Pontifical Right and by the Pontifical approval of its Statutes and on the other hand it would be quite

---

[39] Note that Archbishop Lefebvre had asked for consideration for several bishops. Cardinal Ratzinger makes no reference at all to this.

possible to find a temporary solution for the ordinations which are already scheduled.

With regard to the doctrinal declaration, the Holy Father desires that the formula established as the outcome of the work of the Commission be kept without the addition of the three modifications which you proposed in your letter. It appears indeed that point No. 3 (see p.66) as it is in the formula sufficiently expresses with due precision the points of doctrine, of canon law and liturgical regulations which could present a difficulty and the engagement that you would take in their regard. But such a restriction cannot take place without regard to the very precise object of the adherence expressed at object No. 4 and of the promise formulated at No. 5.

At the end, allow me to assure you that though the definitive solution must wait some while because such an important problem cannot be resolved by being treated with precipitation, the desire of the Holy Father is however to reach it as soon as possible on the basis of the positive elements which already exist. This is the object of all our cares and of our common prayer.

In this spirit I beg you to accept, Excellence, the expression of my faithful and respectfully dedicated feelings in the Lord.

Joseph Cardinal Ratzinger

This letter manifests the intention of the Vatican to delay as much as possible the episcopal consecration. One can ponder the following expressions: "common study and reflection and could take still more time;" "definitive answer cannot be given to you for the moment;" "the Holy Father tends to regard your proposition;" "could not happen right now;" "even if there were no other reason than;" "the definitive solution must wait some while, *etc.*"

But the most alarming passage in this letter is the fifth paragraph. The whole intent of that paragraph is to say that, once the Society of Saint Pius X is recognized with a proper canonical situation, then there is no need of a Bishop, at least for a long time. This is what Archbishop Lefebvre feared the most: that after the approval of the Society, and a great increase of its number as the natural consequence which everyone could see, the Vatican would have said to him: "See you are going very well, you do not need a Bishop!" On the contrary, he saw the need of Bishops dedicated to Tradition, first as defenders of the Faith. Bishops, not priests, are part of the "Teaching Church," even if they do not have a flock assigned to them.[40]

There was need that the Bishops who would do the ceremonies of Ordinations or Confirmations be wholly attached to the tradition of the Church. Indeed to have these ceremonies performed by bishops who otherwise say the *Novus Ordo* would

be a danger. Their preaching and example would insinuate to the young priests or confirmands that the *Novus Ordo* is acceptable, as the current situation within the Fraternity of St. Peter proves.

---

[40] The Pope assigns the flock to the local bishops, thereby giving them jurisdiction on this flock. Archbishop Lefebvre never claimed to be able to assign flock to the four Bishops he consecrated. They are nonetheless successors of the Apostles and as such part of the Teaching Church.

MAY 3, 1988

LETTER OF ARCHBISHOP LEFEBVRE
TO CARDINAL RATZINGER

(This letter is confidential and will not be published.)

In this letter Archbishop Lefebvre proposed four names to Rome for its choice of one bishop. Of these four names, two were consecrated on June 30, 1988. The two others remained the secret of Archbishop Lefebvre.

MAY 5, 1988

LETTER OF ARCHBISHOP LEFEBVRE TO THE POPE

On May 3, Cardinal Ratzinger asked Archbishop Lefebvre that the consecrations be delayed indefinitely. After new meetings between Cardinal Ratzinger, Archbishop Lefebvre, and each's respective experts, a more precise Protocol of Accord was established on May 4. It was signed by Cardinal Ratzinger at the Vatican and counter-signed by Archbishop Lefebvre at Albano on May 5, Feast of St. Pius V.

Most Holy Father,

At the request of His Eminence Cardinal Ratzinger, I write you these few lines at the conclusion of the Visit of Cardinal Gagnon, and of the work of the Commission instituted by your care.

Through the grace of God, this initiative which you have deigned to take has reached a solution acceptable by both parties.

Thus, please find enclosed the declaration duly signed. If Your Holiness accepts it, it could be the starting point of the several measures which will give back to us a legal status in the Church: the legal recognition of the Society of Saint Pius X as a society of pontifical right, the use of the liturgical books of John XXIII, the constitution of a Roman Commission and the other measures indicated in the Protocol of Accord.

The members of the Society and all the persons who are morally united to it are rejoicing at this agreement and give thanks to God and to yourself.

Deign to receive, Most Holy Father, my respectful homage and my filial and respectful gratitude in Jesus and Mary.

† Marcel Lefebvre
Archbishop Emeritus of Tulle

This letter shows the goodwill of Archbishop Lefebvre. It was handed by him to Fr. Klemens, envoy of Cardinal Ratzinger, even before signing the Protocol. Fr. Klemens, after giving the Protocol to His Grace to sign, gave him the text of the

communication which Cardinal Ratzinger intended to be
released on May 8, and the draft of another letter to be addressed
to the Holy Father, which you will find after the text of the
Protocol (p.80). This letter of apology requested of the
Archbishop was the straw that broke the camel's back, and was
the cause of His Grace's letter to the Pope on May 6.

MAY 5, 1988

PROTOCOL OF ACCORD

This protocol contains a doctrinal declaration which Archbishop Lefebvre judged barely acceptable. Only two of the seven members of the proposed Roman Commission were to be upholders of Tradition, which was a grave handicap. Nevertheless, at that moment, His Grace saw fit to sign this Accord. In the Protocol Rome recognizes, in principle, that the episcopate is to be conferred on a member of the Society of Saint Pius X. Note how vague is left the date of an eventual consecration. Note also, that since the jurisdiction would come from the local bishop, the bishop proposed by Rome for the Society would be a powerless bishop, not able to protect the priests and faithful from modernist influences.

I. TEXT OF THE DOCTRINAL DECLARATION

I, Marcel Lefebvre, Archbishop-Bishop Emeritus of Tulle, as well as the members of the Priestly Society of Saint Pius X founded by me:

a) Promise to be always faithful to the Catholic Church and the Roman Pontiff, its Supreme Pastor, Vicar of Christ, Successor of Blessed Peter in his primacy as head of the body of bishops.

b) We declare our acceptance of the doctrine contained in §25[41] of the dogmatic Constitution *Lumen Gentium* of Vatican Council II on the ecclesiastical magisterium and the adherence which is due to it.

c) Regarding certain points taught by Vatican Council II or concerning later reforms of the liturgy and law, and which do not appear to us easily reconcilable with Tradition, we pledge that we will have a positive attitude of study and communication with the Apostolic See, avoiding all polemics.

d) Moreover, we declare that we recognize the validity of the Sacrifice of the Mass and the Sacraments celebrated with the intention of doing what the Church does, and according to the rites indicated in the typical editions of the Roman Missal and the Rituals of the Sacraments promulgated by Popes Paul VI and

---

[41] Complete text of §25 found at the end of this chapter, pp.77-79.

John Paul II.

e) Finally, we promise to respect the common discipline of the Church and the ecclesiastical laws, especially those contained in the *Code of Canon Law* promulgated by Pope John Paul II, without prejudice to the special discipline granted to the Society by particular law.

II. JURIDICAL QUESTIONS

Considering the fact that the Priestly Society of Saint Pius X has been conceived for 18 years as a society of common life—and after studying the propositions formulated by H. E. Marcel Lefebvre and the conclusions of the Apostolic Visitation conducted by His Eminence Cardinal Gagnon— the canonical form most suitable is that of a society of apostolic life.

1. Society of Apostolic Life

This solution is canonically possible, and has the advantage of eventually inserting into the clerical Society of apostolic life lay people as well (for example, coadjutor Brothers).

According to the Code of Canon Law promulgated in 1983, Canons 731-746, this Society enjoys full autonomy, can form its members, can incardinate clerics, and can insure the common life of its members.

In the proper Statutes, with flexibility and inventive possibility with respect to the known models of these Societies of apostolic life, a certain exemption is foreseen with respect to the diocesan bishops (*cf.* Canon 591) for what concerns public worship, the *cura animarum*, and other apostolic activities, taking into account Canons 679-683. As for jurisdiction with regards to the faithful who have recourse to the priests of the Society, it will be conferred on these priests either by the Ordinaries of the place or by the Apostolic See.

2. Roman Commission

A commission to coordinate relations with the different dicasteries and diocesan bishops, as well as to resolve eventual problems and disputes, will be constituted through the care of the Holy See, and will be empowered with the necessary faculties to deal with the questions indicated above (for example, implantation at the request of the faithful of a house of worship where there is no house of the Society, *ad mentem*, Canon 683, §2).

This commission will be composed of a president, a vice-president, and five members, of which two shall be from the Society.[42]

Among other things it would have the function of exercising vigilance and lending assistance to consolidate the work of reconciliation, and to regulate questions relative to the religious communities having a juridical or moral bond with the Society.

3. Condition of Persons Connected to the Society

1) The members of the clerical Society of apostolic life (priests and lay coadjutor brothers) are governed by the Statutes of the Society of Pontifical Right.

2) The oblates, both male and female, whether they have taken private vows or not, and the members of the Third Order connected with the Society, all belong to an association of the faithful connected with the Society according to the terms of Canon 303, and collaborate with it.

3) The Sisters (meaning the congregation founded by Archbishop Lefebvre) who make public vows: they constitute a true institute of consecrated life, with its own structure and proper autonomy, even if a certain type of bond is envisaged for the unity of its spirituality with the Superior of the Society. This Congregation—at least at the beginning—would be dependent on the Roman Commission, instead of the Congregation for Religious.

4) The members of the communities living according to the rule of various religious institutes (Carmelites, Benedictines, Dominicans, *etc.*) and who have a moral bond with the Society: these are to be given, case by case, a particular statute regulating their relations with the respective Order.

5) The priests who, on an individual basis, are morally connected with the Society, will receive a personal statute taking into account their aspirations and at the same time the obligations flowing from their incardination. The other particular cases of the same nature will be examined and resolved by the Roman Commission.[43]

Regarding the lay people who ask for pastoral assistance from the communities of the Society: they remain under the jurisdiction of the diocesan bishop, but—notably by reason of the liturgical rites of the communities of the Society—they can go to them for the administration of the

---

[42] This paragraph replaces the notes in the April 15 minutes. See how this does not correspond to the suggestions of the representatives of the Society, but rather gives full majority to the members from outside Catholic Tradition. This is perhaps the major point of failure in this whole Protocol.

[43] This whole paragraph is new. See again how it separates these priests from the moral support they were getting from their connection with the Society.

sacraments (for the Sacraments of Baptism, Confirmation and Marriage,[44] the usual notifications must still be given to their proper parish; *cf.* Canons 878, 896, 1122).

Note: There is room to consider the particular complexity:

1) Of the question of reception by the laity of the Sacraments of Baptism, Confirmation, Marriage, in the communities of the Society.

2) Of the question of communities practicing the rule of such and such a religious institute, without belonging to it.

The Roman Commission will have the responsibility of resolving these problems.

4. Ordinations

For the ordinations, two phases must be distinguished:

1) In the immediate future: For the ordinations scheduled to take place in the immediate future, Archbishop Lefebvre would be authorized to confer them or, if he were unable, another bishop accepted by himself.

2) Once the Society of apostolic life is erected:

- As far as possible, and in the judgment of the Superior General, the normal way is to be followed: to send dimissorial letters to a bishop who agrees to ordain members of the Society.

- In view of the particular situation of the Society (*cf. infra*): the ordination of a member of the Society as a bishop, who, among other duties, would also be able to proceed with ordinations.

5. Problem of a Bishop

1) At the doctrinal (ecclesiological) level, the guarantee of stability and maintenance of the life and activity of the Society is assured by its erection as a Society of apostolic life of pontifical right, and the approval of its statutes by the Holy Father.

2) But, for practical and psychological[45] reasons, the consecration of a member of the Society as a bishop appears useful. This is why, in the framework of the doctrinal and canonical solution of

---

[44] Here they allow the possibility to give these Sacraments.

[45] Please note the choice of words! As if the need for a bishop from among Tradition would not be, first of all, for a reason of Faith: to have an authority without any compromise with the errors of the day.

reconciliation, we suggest to the Holy Father that he name a bishop chosen from within the Society, presented by Archbishop Lefebvre. In consequence of the principle indicated above (*1*), this bishop normally is not the Superior General of the Society, but it appears opportune that he be a member of the Roman Commission.

6. Particular Problems to be Resolved (By Decree or Declaration)

1) Lifting of the *suspensio a divinis* on Archbishop Lefebvre and dispensation from the irregularities incurred by the fact of the ordinations.

2) *Sanatio in radice*, at least *ad cautelam*, of the marriages already celebrated by the priests of the Society without the required delegation.

3) Provision for an "amnesty" and an accord for the houses and places of worship erected—or used—by the Society, until now without the authorization of the bishops.

For the convenience of our readers, we put here the text of §25 of *Lumen Gentium* **(including footnotes found in the original), oftentimes referred to in these documents [Taken from, Flannery, Austin, O.P.,** *Vatican Council II, The Conciliar and Post Conciliar Documents* **(Collegeville, MN: The Liturgical Press, 1975), pp.379- 381]. The passage to which Archbishop Lefebvre refers in his conference of May 10 and which condemns all the modernist bishops is the following: "This infallibility, however, with which the divine redeemer wished to endow his Church in defining doctrine pertaining to faith and morals, is co-extensive with the deposit of revelation, which must be religiously guarded and loyally and courageously expounded." How many bishops in our days are "religiously guarding and faithfully expounding" the Deposit of Revelation?**

Lumen Gentium, §25

25. Among the more important duties of bishops that of preaching the Gospel has pride of place.[46] For the bishops are heralds of the faith, who draw new disciples to Christ; they are authentic teachers, that is, teachers endowed with the authority of Christ, who preach the faith to the people assigned to them, the faith which is destined to inform their thinking and direct their conduct; and under the light of the Holy Spirit they make that faith shine forth, drawing from the storehouse of revelation new

---

46 *Cf.* Council of Trent, *Decr. de reform.*, Session V, can. 2, n. 9, and Session XXIV, can. 4; *Conc. Oecr.* pp.645, 739.

things and old (*cf.* Mt. 13:52); they make it bear fruit and with watchfulness they ward off whatever errors threaten their flock (*cf.* II Tim. 4:14). Bishops who teach in communion with the Roman Pontiff are to be revered by all as witnesses of divine and Catholic truth; the faithful, for their part, are obliged to submit to their bishops' decision, made in the name of Christ, in matters of faith and morals, and to adhere to it with a ready and respectful allegiance of mind. This loyal submission of the will and intellect must be given, in a special way, to the authentic teaching authority of the Roman Pontiff, even when he does not speak *ex cathedra* in such wise, indeed, that his supreme teaching authority be acknowledged with respect, and sincere assent be given to decisions made by him, conformably with his manifest mind and intention, which is made known principally either by the character of the documents in question, or by the frequency with which a certain doctrine is proposed, or by the manner in which the doctrine is formulated.

Although the bishops, taken individually, do not enjoy the privilege of infallibility, they do, however, proclaim infallibly the doctrine of Christ on the following conditions: namely, when, even though dispersed throughout the world but preserving for all that amongst themselves and with Peter's successor the bond of communion, in their authoritative teaching concerning matters of faith and morals, they are in agreement that a particular teaching is to be held definitively and absolutely.[47] This is still more clearly the case when, assembled in an ecumenical council, they are, for the universal Church, teachers of and judges in matters of faith and morals, whose decisions must be adhered to with the loyal and obedient assent of faith.[48]

This infallibility, however, with which the divine redeemer wished to endow his Church in defining doctrine pertaining to faith and morals, is co-extensive with the deposit of revelation, which must be religiously guarded and loyally and courageously expounded. The Roman Pontiff, head of the college of bishops, enjoys this infallibility in virtue of his office, when, as supreme pastor and teacher of all the faithful—who confirms his brethren in the faith (*cf.* Lk. 22:32)—he proclaims in an absolute decision a doctrine pertaining to faith or morals.[49] For that reason his definitions are rightly said to be irreformable by their very nature and not by reason of the assent of the Church, in as much as they were made with the assistance

---

[47] *Cf.* Vatican Council I, Const. Dogm. *Dei Filius*, 3: *Denzinger,* 1712 (3011). *Cf.* the note added to schema I *de Eccl.* (taken from St. Rob. Bellarmine): Mansi 51, 579C; also the revised schema of Const. *II de Ecclesia Christi*, with Kleutgen's commentary: Mansi 53, 313 AB. Pius IX, Letter *Tuas libenter*: *Denzinger,* 1683 (2879).

[48] Code of Canon Law, Canons 1322-1323.

[49] *Cf.* Vatican Council I, Const. Dogm. *Pastor aeternus*: *Denzinger,* 1839 (3074).

of the Holy Spirit promised to him in the person of blessed Peter himself; and as a consequence they are in no way in need of the approval of others, and do not admit of appeal to any other tribunal. For in such a case the Roman Pontiff does not utter a pronouncement as a private person, but rather does he expound and defend the teaching of the Catholic faith as the supreme teacher of the universal Church, in whom the Church's charism of infallibility is present in a singular way.[50] The infallibility promised to the Church is also present in the body of bishops when, together with Peter's successor, they exercise the supreme teaching office. Now, the assent of the Church can never be lacking to such definitions on account of the same Holy Spirit's influence, through which Christ's whole flock is maintained in the unity of the faith and makes progress in it.[51]

Furthermore, when the Roman Pontiff, or the body of bishops together with him, define a doctrine, they make the definition in conformity with revelation itself, to which all are bound to adhere and to which they are obliged to submit; and this revelation is transmitted integrally either in written form or in oral tradition through the legitimate succession of bishops and above all through the watchful concern of the Roman Pontiff himself; and through the light of the Spirit of truth it is scrupulously preserved in the Church and unerringly explained.[52] The Roman Pontiff and the bishops, by reason of their office and the seriousness of the matter, apply themselves with zeal to the work of enquiring by every suitable means into this revelation and of giving apt expression to its contents;[53] they do not, however, admit any new public revelation as pertaining to the divine deposit of faith.[54]

[50] *Cf.* Gasser's explanation of Vatican Council I: Mansi 52, 1213 AC.
[51] Gasser, *ibid.*: Mansi 1214 A
[52] Gasser, *ibid.*: Mansi 1215 CD, 1216-1217 A.
[53] Gasser, *ibid.*: Mansi 1213
[54] Vatican Council II Const. Dogm. *Pastor Aeternus, 4: Denzinger,* 1836 (3070).

MAY 5, 1988

PRESS RELEASE

The following press release was given to Archbishop Lefebvre on May 5 at the same time as the Protocol, and was due to be published on May 8. Cardinal Ratzinger cancelled its publication. The date written on it at the bottom was May 7, 1988.

Following the Apostolic Visit of His Eminence Edward Cardinal Gagnon to the Priestly Society of Saint Pius X, in conformity with the will of the Holy Father expressed in the letter to Cardinal Ratzinger dated April 8, 1988, meetings with the interested parties took place recently in Rome. The dialogue was concluded with the participation of His Eminence Joseph Cardinal Ratzinger, Prefect of the Congregation for the Doctrine of the Faith, and of His Excellency Archbishop Marcel Lefebvre, Founder of the Society. An agreement on the essential points was reached which allows us to foresee in the near future a formal act of reconciliation with the relative canonical consequences.

In the meantime, the Holy See shall make opportune contacts with the competent and especially interested ecclesiastical authorities.

May 7, 1988

MAY 5, 1988

DRAFT OF A LETTER GIVEN TO ARCHBISHOP LEFEBVRE FOR THE HOLY FATHER

Fr. Klemens, secretary to Cardinal Ratzinger, gave to Archbishop Lefebvre, with the Protocol, a draft of the following letter which the Cardinal wanted Archbishop Lefebvre to write to the Pope:

Most Holy Father,

I have learned with joy that you have favorably received the declaration made in my name and in the name of the Priestly Society of Saint Pius X—in which is expressed our adhesion to the Church and to the Roman Pontiff—as well as the proposals drafted during the recent dialogues between Cardinal Ratzinger and myself, in order to give to the Society a regular canonical status in full communion with the Apostolic See.

It seems to me that the moment has arrived to present to Your Holiness the humble but pressing request that the agreement which we reached be now implemented so that my personal situation and that of the Society be normalized for the good of holy Church.

Most Holy Father, it is this good of the Church that I have pursued in all conscience in the sight of God during these past years through much suffering. However, I know that even in good faith, one can make mistakes. Therefore, I humbly ask you to forgive all that in my behavior or that of the Society may have hurt the Vicar of Christ or the Church, and on my part, I forgive from the depth of my heart what I had to suffer.

Lastly, I wish to express my gratitude for the intention that you manifested to take into account the particular situation of the Society, proposing to nominate a bishop chosen from its members, and especially in charge of providing for its specific needs. Of course, I leave to Your Holiness the decision concerning the person to be chosen and the opportune moment. May I just express the wish that this be not in the too distant future?

With confidence putting all these matters into your hands, please, would you deign to receive the homage of my filial and deeply respectful sentiments in Jesus and Mary.

In his own hand writing, Archbishop Lefebvre corrected the third and fourth paragraphs of this draft but never sent even the corrected letter. The two questionable paragraphs were corrected as follows:

"Most Holy Father, it is this good of the Church that I have pursued in all conscience in the sight of God during these past years. However, if in my behavior or that of the Society we may have pained *you,* we are deeply sorry."

"Lastly, I wish to express my gratitude for the intention that you manifested to take into account the particular situation of the Society, proposing to nominate a bishop chosen from its members, and especially in charge of providing for its specific needs. Of course, I leave to Your Holiness the decision concerning the person to be chosen *from among the names submitted to your judgment."*

You will notice that, by upholding the Tradition of the Church, His Grace does not consider that he hurt the Successor of Peter as such. It is only as a private person that Pope John Paul II may have been pained by the strong stand of Archbishop Lefebvre. You will also notice that the vague expression regarding the date has been deleted (*i.e.*, "May I just express the wish that this be not in the too distant future?").

MAY 6, 1988

LETTER OF ARCHBISHOP LEFEBVRE
TO CARDINAL RATZINGER

On the very evening the Protocol was signed, May 5, 1988, after mature reflection and, he says, by a grace of the Most Holy Virgin Mary, Archbishop Lefebvre clearly perceived that, in spite of the principle recognized by Rome that the episcopate was to be conferred on a member of the Society, this Accord was not satisfactory; thus the very next day, May 6, he wrote to Cardinal Ratzinger to express his misgivings, on the grounds that Rome was not willing to fix a date for the episcopal consecration.

Eminence,

Yesterday it was with real satisfaction that I put my signature on the Protocol drafted during the preceding days. However, you yourself have witnessed my deep disappointment upon the reading of the letter which you gave me,[55] bringing the Holy Father's answer concerning the episcopal consecrations.

Practically, to postpone the episcopal consecrations to a later undetermined date would be the fourth time that it would have been postponed.[56]

The date of June 30 was clearly indicated in my previous letters as the latest possible.

I have already given you a file concerning the candidates. There are still two months to make the mandate.

---

[55] This sentence would seem to indicate that there was a letter from the Pope to Archbishop Lefebvre given on May 5. There was no such letter. It rather refers to the "Draft of a Letter Given to Archbishop Lefebvre for the Holy Father" (See previous document, p.81); it refers in particular to the two sentences: "*Of course, I leave to Your Holiness the decision concerning the person to be chosen and the opportune moment. May I just express the wish that this be not in the too distant future.*" The vagueness of such expression naturally aroused the fears of Archbishop Lefebvre.

[56] The first date had been set for the 40th anniversary of his episcopal consecration (Oct. 3, 1987). Late September, upon the report of some improvement of attitude in Rome with the hope of a proper visit of the Society, it was postponed to the Feast of St. John the Evangelist (Dec. 27, 1987); at the time of the visit, with the new hope of a true solution, it was postponed to Good Shepherd Sunday (Apr. 17, 1988), and later, due to the slowness of the negotiations to St. Paul's Commemoration (June 30, 1988).

Given the particular circumstances of this proposal, the Holy Father can very well shorten the procedure so that the mandate be communicated to us around mid-June.

In case the answer will be negative, I would find myself in conscience obliged to proceed with the consecrations, relying upon the agreement given by the Holy See in the Protocol for the consecration of one bishop member of the Society.

The reticence expressed on the subject of the episcopal consecration of a member of the Society, either by writing or by word of mouth, gives me reason to fear delays. Everything is now prepared for the ceremony of June 30: hotel reservations, transportation, rental of a huge tent to house the ceremony.

The disappointment of our priests and faithful would be extreme. All of them hope that this consecration will be realized with the agreement of the Holy See; but being already disappointed by previous delays they will not understand that I would accept a further delay. They are aware and desirous above all of having truly Catholic bishops, transmitting the true Faith to them, and communicating to them in a way that is certain the graces of salvation to which they aspire for themselves and for their children.

In the hope that this request shall not be an insurmountable obstacle to the reconciliation in process, please, Eminence, accept my respectful and fraternal sentiments in *Christo et Maria.*

† Marcel Lefebvre
Former Archbishop-Bishop of Tulle

Recalling the evening of May 5 to a reporter for *30 Days* magazine,[57] the Archbishop himself described how he came to write the preceding letter:

Yes, I signed the accord, but with extreme distrust. The same distrust I had when I came to Rome. I had made an effort in order to see whether something had changed in Rome, if they had decided to return to Tradition.

But all the disillusionments of these years kept coming back into my mind. The climate of distrust that characterized the meetings first with Cardinal Seper, then with Cardinal Ratzinger. The immense, laborious exchange of correspondence, and then all the things that happened against Tradition, in France and elsewhere. And the tricks that were played on us: Fr. Augustine at Flavigny forced to celebrate the Mass of Paul VI after he had returned to communion with Rome, the two seminaries set up in

---

[57]   *30 Days*, July 1988, pp.12-13.

Rome for the deserters from Ecône over the years. Both were closed, and the seminarians sent back to those bishops from whom they had fled. And the last attempt, the *Mater Ecclesiæ*, will close down next year. The letter that I received from the Abbé Carlo[58] is proof to me of the ill-will of Rome. And the apostolic visit of Cardinal Gagnon about which they obstinately refused to tell me anything. "These meetings are the result of that visit," Ratzinger's secretary said to me. But not a word about the report presented to the Pope. Just as it happened in 1974 after the visit of the two Belgian visitors. Still today I know nothing about the report they made.

And Assisi, the visit to the Synagogue,[59] the Cardinals who a few days before had gone to genuflect in front of Gorbachev. And now they were deceiving us again.

During the night between May 5 and May 6, I said to myself: "All this is impossible. I cannot accept Ratzinger's answer, which avoids fixing the date of the ordination." Then I thought that I should write a letter to the Pope and to Ratzinger: if they would not grant me the ordination on June 30, I would do it anyway. On the morning of May 6, I wrote the letter and I sent it to them.

Was this letter the cause of the cessation of the negotiations?

This May 5 Protocol had several flaws. In the present letter His Grace highlights one, the most urgent one, *i.e.*, the vagueness of the Protocol concerning the consecrations of bishops: No date was fixed, no candidate agreed upon.

Many accused Archbishop Lefebvre of having reneged on the Protocol by this letter. However, a careful reading of both cannot show any opposition between them. No date was mentioned in the Protocol, therefore he asked for a date. This was not to oppose the protocol, but rather to take steps to put it in practice. Archbishop Lefebvre did threaten in this letter, because, as he said, every step forward in the negotiation had only been obtained upon the pressure of such threats.

Such a threat did achieve its purpose, as Cardinal Ratzinger did give a date in his letter of May 30, 1988.

In that letter of May 30, 1988, by asking for "a greater number of dossiers on possible candidates," Cardinal Ratzinger practically rejected all the candidates proposed by Archbishop Lefebvre. That was the real cause of the break of negotiations. Indeed what guarantee that the new names His Grace would have proposed, would be accepted by August 15? By rejecting the candidates proposed by Archbishop Lefebvre, Cardinal Ratzinger made clear that the Vatican was not sincere in fulfilling its promises for a Bishop.

---

[58] One of the seminarians at Ecône staying at *Mater Ecclesiæ*. See his letter of June 2, 1988, in Part II, p.167.

[59] *i.e.*, the ecumenical day of prayer held in Assisi on October 27, 1986 and the Pope's visit to the synagogue of Rome on April 13, 1986.

MAY 6, 1988

LETTER OF CARDINAL RATZINGER
TO ARCHBISHOP LEFEBVRE

Excellency,

I have attentively read the letter which you just addressed to me, in which you tell me your intentions concerning the episcopal consecration of a member of the Society on June 30 next.

Since these intentions are in sharp contrast with what has been accepted during our dialogue on May 4, and which have been signed in the Protocol yesterday, I wish to inform you that the release of the press communiqué has to be deferred.

I earnestly wish that you reconsider your position in conformity with the results of the dialogue, so that the communiqué[60] may be released.

In this hope, please Excellency,...

Joseph Cardinal Ratzinger

---

[60] See *Press Release*, May 5, 1988, p.80.

MAY 10, 1988

CONFERENCE OF ARCHBISHOP LEFEBVRE AT ST. NICOLAS DU CHARDONNET

In this conference less than a week after the crucial moments in the relations between himself and the Vatican, Archbishop Lefebvre gives to his priests gathered at St. Nicolas du Chardonnet (Paris, France), for their monthly meeting, a detailed account of these moments. The text of this conference is appropriately included here.

If there is no agreement with Rome, we shall just have to continue our work. But supposing that there is an agreement with Rome, we would find ourselves in a different atmosphere. This would be a new period in the Society, a new period for Tradition, that will require infinite precautions.

Why do I say, "if" there is an agreement? It is not difficult; I shall explain it to you in a few words.

Thus I have signed the Protocol; I have it here. It contains five pages. The first is on doctrinal questions, and the others on disciplinary questions.

On the doctrinal questions the discussion was a little difficult. They prepared this text; we did not. They put it on the table. We corrected some omissions. It is always the same question: a few sentences on the Pope saying that we recognize the Pope, that we submit ourselves to the Sovereign Pontiff, that we acknowledge his primacy.

And they had added that we acknowledge him as "the head of the college of bishops." I said "I don't like that. It is an ambiguous notion. The best proof of this is that an explanatory note had to be included in the Council, to explain what 'college' meant in this sense, saying that it was not a true college." So I said, "You should not put that. It will give the impression that we accept Collegiality." So they said, "Let's put 'the body of bishops.'" The Pope is the head of the episcopal body.

Then they said we had to accept the paragraph in *Lumen Gentium* which deals with the magisterium of the Church, §25. When you read this paragraph, you understand it condemns them, not us; they would have to sign it because it is not so badly written and it contains a whole paragraph stressing the immutability of doctrine, the immutability of the Faith, the immutability of the formulas. We agree with that. There are those who need to sign this. Thus there is no difficulty in accepting this paragraph which expresses traditional doctrine.

Then they added a Number Three which made us swallow the pill that followed. It was not easy to accept but with this Number Three, we were "saved from the waters." In this Number Three they recognized that there were some points in the Council and in the reform of the liturgy and of the Canon Law, which we considered irreconcilable with Tradition. They agreed to speak of this, which they had always refused before. Every time that we had said something was not reconcilable with Tradition, such as Religious Liberty, they used to say, "You can't say that; there is nothing in the Council opposed to Tradition. Let us change the expression. We cannot say that there is anything irreconcilable with Tradition."

Then came the question of the liturgy. We recognized that "the validity of the Sacrifice of the Mass and the Sacraments celebrated with the intention of doing what the Church does, and according to the rites indicated in the typical editions of the Roman Missal." It was maybe too much, but since they had put that there were some points in the liturgy that were eventually against Tradition—I wanted to add, "taking into account what was stated in §3..." but they did not accept it.

Number Five was on Canon Law. We promised "to respect the common discipline of the Church and the ecclesiastical laws, especially those contained in the Code of Canon Law promulgated by Pope John Paul II." They wanted to say "*all* ecclesiastical law." I objected, it would have been to recognize *all* the new Canon Law.[61] So they took away the word "all." As you see, it was a constant fight.

At the conclusion of Number Three they put "we pledge that we will have a positive attitude of study and communication with the Apostolic See, avoiding all polemics," as we had done on Religious Liberty (with the *Dubia*). "Without polemics," I said, "We never did any polemics!" "Oh, no. See what you did to the Pope." They were referring to the little drawings which the Pope looked at attentively—and maybe they were looking at them with a little smile—So I said, "This was not polemics; it was a catechism lesson! Indeed, who is responsible for these actions? It is not us, it is the Pope. If the Pope would not do reprehensible things, we would say nothing. But since he does things which are absolutely unbelievable, unacceptable, therefore, we react; it is absolutely natural. Let the Pope stop doing these reprehensible things, incomprehensible, unthinkable, and we will stop reacting." They said nothing They did not answer.

Then we spoke of the juridical questions.

---

[61] *i.e.*, including Canon 844. See Part II of this volume, p.150.

The first was on the Roman Commission. There we lost some points. We wanted all the members of the Roman Commission to be members of Tradition. It did not matter whether they would be of the Society or not, but they should be members of Tradition in order to be able to judge of the things of Tradition. But they said, "No, this is not an embassy. We must be present, too." Thus the President would be Cardinal Ratzinger. There would be a Vice-President, too; but they did not want to release his name, but he probably would not be from Tradition. Then there would be other members from Rome and only two from Tradition. I said, "Well! That's very few."

Please note that. You shall see that throughout the discussions, and already you found that on the doctrinal discussions, their intentions have clearly appeared. I suspected they had such intentions but I did not expect them to manifest them so clearly. Their intention is clear. They want to put their hands on the Roman Commission. For the Society of Saint Pius X its recognition would not raise any difficulty, but all the other foundations which surround the Society would have to deal directly with the Roman Commission. They would have no more relations with the Society. They put "the members of the community living according to the rules of various religious institutes...are to be given case by case a particular statute regulating their relations with their respective order." One can see their intentions, separating these traditional communities from the Society and putting them under their (modernist) superiors general, making them defend themselves.

Then they agreed to recognize the Society as of pontifical right with some exemptions in the pastoral domain for the administration of the sacraments. This would be good only for the existing houses.

Then came the question of the bishops. They said very clearly, "You do not need a bishop. As soon as the Society is recognized with a canonical status with the Holy See, you can ask any bishop to perform your ordinations and confirmations. There are 3,000 bishops in the world ready to give you ordinations and confirmations...even Cardinal Gagnon and Cardinal Oddi are ready to give you confirmations and perform your ordinations!" I said, "This is impossible. This is condition *sine qua non.* The faithful will never accept this. Indeed, what would these bishops preach?" With the intentions that we can see among them, their preaching will always be, "you must accept the Council, you must accept what the Pope does, you must accept the novelties. We respect your Tradition, you must respect our new rights. No difference."

So, we have been very severe. So, they have put a little paragraph, "for psychological reasons, the consecration of a member of the Society appears useful."

What procedure to follow? After signing the Protocol, they wanted me to write a letter to the Pope, asking for the re-establishment of a normal situation for the Society, for the pontifical right, the suppression of the canonical penalties, exemptions, and privileges—so-called privileges—on the liturgy. Thus, I have signed, I have written that letter.

I signed it on Thursday, Feast of St. Pius V. They did not know it was the Feast of St. Pius V because they have relocated his feast to another date....

Thus I have said, "We must know where to stand concerning June 30; it's coming soon." So, with these thoughts, I did not sleep all night. I told myself, "They are going to get us." Indeed, the Cardinal had made a few frightening reflections. "Well! There is only one Church....As we respect your feelings, you must also respect Religious Liberty, the New Mass, the sacraments. It is inconceivable that you turn the faithful away from these new sacraments, from the New Mass...For example, if there is an agreement, it is evident that in churches such as St. Nicolas du Chardonnet, Cardinal Lustiger shall ask that a New Mass be said there. This is the one Church, in it there is the Tradition that we shall grant you but there are also the new rites that you must accept for the faithful of your parish who do not want Tradition." I said, "Well! Go and tell that to our parishioners and see how they receive you!"

They call all this a "reconciliation." This means that we accept what they do and they accept what we do. Thus, we have to align ourselves on Dom Augustin[62] and Fongombault.[63]

This is not possible. All this makes me hesitate. We have asked the Cardinal when shall we be able to consecrate a bishop. On June 30? He said, "No, this is much too early. It takes time to make a bishop. In Germany it takes nine months to make a bishop." When I told that to Cardinal Oddi, he said, "That must be a beautiful baby then!" I said, "Well, give us a date. Let's be precise. The 15th of August?" "No, on August 15 there is no one in Rome. It is the holidays from July 15 to September 15." "What about November 1?" "I can't tell you." "What about Christmas?" "I don't know."

---

[62] Dom Augustin had founded a traditional Benedictine monastery in the early 1970's. In 1985, after the Indult, he had secret meetings with the Vatican to make a special arrangement from himself. The Vatican required: 1) the New Mass as the Community Mass, 2) the new Breviary, 3) new rites of Ordination, 4) unconditional submission to the local bishop, who even for a while forbade them to preach the Exercises of St. Ignatius, which had been the main apostolic work of this monastery.

[63] A conservative Benedictine monastery in France which accepted the New Mass only in the mid-1970's, under pressure from the local bishop.

I said to myself, "Finished. I have understood. They do not want to give us a bishop." They put it on the paper because we were ready to quit the negotiations without it, but they will maneuver. They are convinced that when the Society is acknowledged we don't need a bishop.

So, I took my pen on Friday morning and wrote to the Cardinal: "It was with real satisfaction that I put my signature on the Protocol drafted during the preceding days. However, you yourself have witnessed my deep disappointment upon the reading of the letter which you gave me, bringing the Holy Father's answer concerning the episcopal consecrations." Indeed, in that letter—I do not have it here—which he brought me from the Holy Father, there is an astonishing sentence. It goes like, "It is possible that we consider one day granting you a consecration," as if it was something very vague, a mere possibility, an eventuality. I cannot accept that.

[Here, the Archbishop read the rest of the letter dated May 6, 1988. See pp.83,84.]

So, I immediately received an answer. On Friday morning I took my letter to the Cardinal before my departure from Rome. And, on that very evening, Fr. du Chalard was given the answer of the Cardinal, even before the Cardinal saw the Pope at 7:30 p.m. He should have waited to see the Pope and tell him, "Look what I just received from Archbishop Lefebvre. What shall we do?" He did not even wait.

[Here, the Archbishop read the Cardinal's letter of May 6, 1988. See p.86.]

Fr. du Chalard brought that letter to me at Ecône on Sunday morning. I said to him, "Tell the Secretary of the Cardinal that for me the whole thing is finished. I am not changing the date of June 30. It is the final date. I feel my strength diminishing. I even have difficulty in travelling by car.[64]

I think it would be to put in danger the continuation of the Society and the seminaries if I do not perform these consecrations." I think they will agree to that date. They are too anxious for this reconciliation.

Again, for them, this reconciliation means, "We shall give you this Tradition for a little while but, after two or three years when you will have understood that you must accept the reforms, then, your community

---

[64] Fr. Lorans, former Rector of the Seminary of Ecône (1983-88), told me that the health of the Archbishop was greatly affected by these negotiations. A choice between being strangled or shot is hard! But after the decision to proceed with the consecrations was made, without accepting the Protocol, a great peace and a better health in the Archbishop was noticeable to all those around him.

Masses will be the New Mass—as for Dom Augustin—you may be allowed to say the traditional Mass in private but no more. Vatican II happened; you must accept Vatican II and its consequences. It is inadmissible that there be in the Church people who do not accept the reforms and consequences of Vatican II."

One can see that this is their way of thinking. I want to remain firm. They are afraid. They think that if there is a bishop, he will lead all the faithful attached to Tradition, he will give strength to Tradition by his preaching. For confirmations, ordinations, any occasion, a bishop strengthens the faith of the faithful. So they say, "If there is a bishop we cannot stop it." They want none of this.

But their intention is very clear. If I write the letter they want to the Pope, we are officially recognized. They ask us to be patient for a little while, they do not give us any date. And after the summer holiday, they tell us, "Look, now, you have been living for three months with this official recognition. You do not need a bishop. You can address yourself to any bishop for ordinations." This is almost certain; otherwise, they would give us a date. If they were really sincere about giving us a bishop, it would not have been difficult for them to say, "For sure, at least by Christmas, you will have a bishop." But, no, they did not want that. It was clear that they had previously agreed among themselves on this: they were four in front of us, none of them said anything; not even one said to the Cardinal, "Eminence, couldn't we...?"

I think that by the end of this month they will call in Fr. du Chalard and say to him, "Well, let us settle. We shall give you a bishop."

I tell you that this makes a problem for me, given their will to impose Vatican II. After the Visit, they could have said a little word such as, "We can see that Tradition has brought a lot of good. We are happy to welcome you, and to allow you to continue." But, no, not even the least compliment.

One can feel very well that they want to hold us under their influence. I fear this influence. These Romans would go and visit the Dominicans, the Benedictines, the priories of the Society. All these traditional foundations will be isolated from the Society. They will send their superiors general, who will talk to these sisters and say, "Be open-minded. Don't be against the New Mass...." They will give conferences to the sisters....Above that, one has to reckon with the local bishops. What shall they say?...

We shall see what Providence shall manifest.

We are living through dramatic days. It is the whole of Tradition that is at stake. We must not make a mistake and let all these influences loose. There certainly are some advantages. It is like a bet: they bet that they shall "get us," and we bet that we will "get them!" They say that by having the upper hand on us, they will have the last word. We say that with the authorization of Rome, there will be such a development of our works that they won't be able to do anything against us. This bet is difficult to calculate. They have some flushes; we have some flushes.

I did tell them, we really wish to have the authorization of Rome. Everyone wishes to have it, but we cannot remain in limbo.

[At this point, a priest interrupted the Archbishop to ask two pertinent questions.]

Fr. Boivin[65]: "Shall there be one or several bishops?"

Archbishop Lefebvre: If there is no authorization from Rome, there shall be several bishops. Personally, I think that some important events shall come. Europe was invaded twice and cut from America, from Africa—no more communication. So I think it will be useful to have several bishops. I did insist and ask the Cardinal for two or three, also because of the immensity of the work. He has never accepted, or one at the most...

Fr. Boivin: "What about the churches?"

Archbishop Lefebvre: The existing places of worship will be ratified. They would ask the local bishops to consider them as regular places of worship in their diocese. But for any new one, there would be need of an agreement. It would be the duty of the Roman Commission to see what would be the conditions. It would certainly be more difficult. As they said for St. Nicolas du Chardonnet, if the bishops give us a parish—Cardinal Decourtray at Lyon has promised a beautiful church—they would require that one New Mass be said in that parish. Cardinal Decourtray did that with Fr. Cottin. He said to him, "I allow you to say the old Mass, but I request that at least one New Mass be said by the assistant priest." Thus there would be as much for the novelties as for Tradition. Of course, this is impossible. We have chosen Tradition because we deem the novelties to be bad and to hurt the Faith. It is the position of some conservative groups such as *Una Voce* who accept the New Mass. They would like to re-align us along these lines. This is not possible. This would be contrary to all that we have fought for.

---

[65] Fr. Claude Boivin, then District Bursar (Treasurer) of the District of France for the Society of Saint Pius X.

MAY 17, 1988

NOTE OF CARDINAL RATZINGER
TO ARCHBISHOP LEFEBVRE

Monseigneur,

Through the good services of Fr. du Chalard, I submit again to you the project of a final letter to the Holy Father more in conformity with requirements of the style of the Roman Curia. Your first letter was well received by the Holy Father who is now waiting with a paternal confidence for your final letter.

United in prayer with you I am very devotedly yours in Our Lord,

Joseph Cardinal Ratzinger

This "first letter" of May 5 must not have been as "well received" as Cardinal Ratzinger implied. Another was demanded of Archbishop Lefebvre.

SUGGESTIONS FOR A DEFINITIVE LETTER TO BE WRITTEN BY ARCHBISHOP LEFEBVRE TO THE ROMAN PONTIFF

I. General Considerations

1) It would be most convenient that this letter be such as to remove the barriers and allow the Holy Father not to ask for a solution of the problem other than the first one,[66] and to publish this solution in the first half of June, as planned.

2) To this end, apart from being accompanied by the Doctrinal Declaration (since it has already been sent to the Pope, it is not necessary to repeat it), this letter should have the following general characteristics:

a) It must be a *humble* request for the canonical regularization of the whole vicissitude, without entering into the details

---

[66] *i.e.*, not to negotiate another Protocol.

of the accord: this one remaining totally in force but being presented as a solution given by the Pope. In fact, it is not logical that the solution appear as the fruit of an agreement between two parties, in order to avoid as much as possible a negative reception from the other part of the Church. On the other hand, this letter shall be published simultaneously with the answer from the Pope, in which explicit reference to the concrete solution already stated would be made.

b) In the right way, which does not hurt the sensibilities of anyone, it would be most opportune that Archbishop Lefebvre—while reaffirming that he has always acted in good faith and pursuing the glory of God and the good of the Church—asks for pardon for anything in his actions which may have displeased the Holy Father.

c) Given the last letter of Archbishop Lefebvre to Cardinal Ratzinger in which he affirms his will to consecrate a bishop at the end of June, no matter what, in this new letter to the Pope it would be opportune to make a reference to this, but in a more humble tone, as a prayer or suggestion, without requesting a definite date.[67]

3) Summarizing: it is important to take into account the fact that the more humble and unconditional the letter shall be, the easier it will be for the Pope to accept it publicly, and to grant to Archbishop Lefebvre what he desires (as, after all, this is also the desire of the Roman Pontiff).

II. Suggestions for the Text of the Letter

Most Holy Father,

As I had the occasion to manifest to Your Holiness in one of my previous letters, the Apostolic Visit to the Society of Saint Pius X performed by His Eminence Cardinal Gagnon has raised in me and in all the members of the Society a great hope for a solution to the problem concerning the full union of the Society with the Holy See, being aware that such a union is a vital condition for all members of the Church.

This hope of ours has been further reinforced by the public letter of Your Holiness to His Eminence Cardinal Ratzinger of April 8 last, and was increased and made concrete after the recent intense meetings which were held with Cardinal Ratzinger.

---

[67] Please note that the vagueness of the date is *intentional,* not a "mistake."

It is with great confidence that I write this new letter to humbly ask Your Holiness to deign to provide the full canonical regularization of all the diverse aspects regarding my person and the entire Society of Saint Pius X. To this end, I delivered to Your Holiness, with my previous letter a formal declaration, signed in my own name and in the name of the Society, in which I express our full adhesion to the Church and to the Roman Pontiff.

Most Holy Father, through all the past years, through much suffering, I have always acted following my conscience in the sight of God, searching for the good of the Church. Nevertheless, I am aware that even in good faith, one can make mistakes. Yet, for this, I put in your hands all the questions and humbly ask pardon for all that, notwithstanding my good faith, may have caused displeasure to the Vicar of Christ.

Lastly, I would like to share with Your Holiness a special preoccupation of mine, which refers to my advanced age. Indeed, the canonical regularization of the Society does not provide for the consecration of a bishop who would take my place because it is not necessary, *per se*. However, paying attention above all to the practical need of one who would perform the pontifical functions according to the rite anterior to the liturgical reform, I would be most happy for Your Holiness to nominate a bishop who could, in a certain sense, succeed me.

Deign to accept, Most Holy Father, my most respectful homage and filial respects in Jesus and Mary.

MAY 20, 1988

LETTER OF ARCHBISHOP LEFEBVRE TO POPE JOHN PAUL II

After the previous letters, Cardinal Ratzinger went on retreat and the Pope went on a pastoral journey. After their return, Archbishop Lefebvre wrote the following letter to the Pope, insisting on the date of June 30, 1988, and more than one bishop to be consecrated.

May 20, 1988
Ecône

Most Holy Father,

While a certain hope was raised regarding a possible solution to the problem of the Society after the signing of the Protocol, a grave difficulty now arises with respect to the episcopacy granted to the Society, to succeed me in my episcopal function.

It clearly appears that this conferring of the episcopacy is a source of apprehensions and concern to the Holy See, for the following reasons:

- in the first place this episcopacy is superfluous. After the legal recognition of the Society as one of pontifical right, the Superior General can give dimissorial letters to a bishop of his choice.
- in the second place, this granting of the episcopacy might seem to be a distinct mark of disapproval of the bishops now in office, and might turn the bishops against the Holy See.
- finally, this episcopacy could eventually create difficulties in the dioceses, occasioned by the apostolate among the faithful.

No doubt these apprehensions are what provoke the delays, the evasive responses of the Holy See for over a year and which morally oblige me to put an end to this waiting, after having insisted several times on the urgent necessity of having several bishops, for the continuation and development of the work.

June 30 now appears to me as the final date to bring about this succession. Providence seems to have prepared this date. The accords have been signed, the names of the candidates have been proposed. If Cardinal Ratzinger is overworked and does not have time to prepare the mandates, perhaps Cardinal Gagnon could be entrusted with it.

Most Holy Father, deign to put an end to this sorrowful problem of priests, the faithful and your servant, who in keeping Tradition have had no other desire than to serve the Church, the Pope, and to save souls.

Permit me to add some considerations on the renewal of the Church, obtained by means of the Society and the episcopacy which would be granted to it.

In reporting the instances of Vienna in Austria, and Coire in Switzerland, regarding episcopal appointments, the press has alluded to a change of orientation on the part of the Holy See in the choice of bishops. This is a good sign, but the reactions show that these bishops will have enormous difficulties in the realization of their apostolate, and they will be forced to manifest their adherence to the modern spirit by ecumenism, as well as the charismatic movement, to calm people down.

Even if they observe a certain discipline and a greater piety, their seminaries will be imbued with this modern spirit, and only with difficulty will they contribute to the true renewal of the Church.

Henceforth this renewal can only be brought about by bishops who are free to revive Christian Faith and virtue by the means Our Lord entrusted to the Church for the sanctification of priests and the faithful.

Only an atmosphere entirely detached from modern errors and modern ways will permit this renewal. This atmosphere is the one encountered by Cardinal Gagnon and Msgr. Perl, an atmosphere made up of profoundly Christian families having many children, and from which come numerous and excellent vocations.

The development of this renewed atmosphere, encouraged by your decisions, Most Holy Father, will restore the dioceses through contacts with the bishops and the clergy. Certain bishops will entrust to us the formation of their seminarians and thus, by the grace of God, the Church will find a new youthfulness—and transform pagan society into Christian society.

You will easily understand why only one bishop will not suffice for such a vast field of the apostolate.

If I allow myself to submit these considerations to your judgment, it is in the most profound desire of coming to your aid in solving these grave problems which you are striving to resolve in the course of your apostolic journeys.

Deign to accept, Most Holy Father, the expression of my most respectful and filial sentiments in Jesus and Mary.

† Marcel Lefebvre
Archbishop-Bishop Emeritus of Tulle
Founder of the Society of Saint Pius X

MAY 24, 1988

LETTER OF ARCHBISHOP LEFEBVRE TO CARDINAL RATZINGER

On May 24, Archbishop Lefebvre met with Cardinal Ratzinger once again. He insisted once more on the necessity of consecrating several bishops and of having a majority of members on the Roman Commission, indispensable requirements for protecting Catholic Tradition from the deleterious influences of Modernist Rome and conciliarist bishops. He was asked by a reporter from the magazine *30 Days*: "A few weeks later, on May 24, the Holy See fixed the date of the ordination for August 15, as you had requested. Why didn't you accept?" His Grace replied: "I had lost faith. It was necessary to threaten continually in order to obtain something. No collaboration was any longer possible. The case of the Roman Commission, in which they wanted to put us in a minority, confirms this."[68]

The Archbishop gave to the Cardinal the following letter, insisting on the same requests he had already made to Cardinal Gagnon in November 1987.

Eminence,

It seems necessary to me to stress what I wrote to you on May 6 past.

Upon reflection, it appears clear that the goal of these dialogues is to reabsorb us within the Conciliar Church, the only Church to which you make allusion during these meetings.

We hoped that you would give us the means to continue and develop the works of Tradition, especially by giving us some coadjutors, at least three, and by giving a majority to Tradition in the Roman Commission.

Now, on these two points which we deem necessary to maintain our works outside of all progressivist and conciliar influence, we are not satisfied.

Therefore, with much regret we feel obliged to ask that, before the date of June 1, you indicate clearly to us what the intentions of the Holy See are on these two points: consecration of three bishops asked for June

---

[68] *30 Days*, July 1988, pp.13-14.

30, and a majority of members from Tradition in the Roman Commission.

Without an answer to this request, I shall proceed with the publication of the names of the candidates to the episcopacy whom I will consecrate on June 30 with the collaboration of His Excellency Bishop de Castro Mayer.

My health and the apostolic necessities for the growth of our work, do not allow for any further delay.

In the hope that these requests will be taken into consideration, please accept, Your Eminence, my respectful and fraternally devoted sentiments in Jesus and Mary.

† Marcel Lefebvre

MAY 30, 1988

LETTER OF CARDINAL RATZINGER
TO ARCHBISHOP LEFEBVRE

The Pope's reply to the previous letter came in a letter of Cardinal Ratzinger. The Holy Father granted the date of August 15, but refused a majority for Catholic Tradition on the Commission, and kept silence on the number of bishops. Moreover the names already presented by Archbishop Lefebvre were deemed insufficient, and other names are requested. There was no guarantee that any name would be accepted by August 15, 1988.

Excellency,

After having been received in audience by the Holy Father on Friday, May 27, as I had indicated to you during our conversation on the 24th, I am in a position to respond to the letter you had given to me the same day, concerning the problems of a majority of members of the Society on the Roman Commission, and the consecration of bishops.

Concerning the first point, the Holy Father deems it proper to adhere to the principles fixed in part II, section 2 of the Protocol (see p.74) which you accepted. This Commission is an organism of the Holy See in the service of the Society and the diverse instances which will have to be handled to establish and consolidate the work of reconciliation. Moreover, it is not the Commission, but the Holy Father who in the final analysis will make the decisions; thus the question of a majority does not arise; the interests of the Society are guaranteed by its representation within the Commission, and the fears which you have expressed with respect to the other members are groundless, since the choice of members will be done by the Holy Father himself.[69]

Regarding the second point, the Holy Father confirms what I had already indicated to you in his behalf, namely that he is disposed to appoint a member of the Society as a bishop (in the sense of part II, section 5, para. 2 of the Protocol [see pp.76, 77]),[70] and to accelerate the usual process of

---

[69] The book, *Peter, Lovest Thou Me?* (available from Angelus Press) offers the evidence that this was no sufficient guarantee the members of the Commission would be dedicated to upholding the Tradition of the Church.

[70] *i.e.,* a powerless bishop.

nomination, so that the consecration could take place on the closing of the Marian Year, this coming August 15.

From the practical point of view this requires that you present without delay to the Holy See a greater number of dossiers on possible candidates, to allow him to freely choose a candidate who corresponds to the profile envisaged in the accords and at the same time the general criteria of aptitude which the Church maintains for the appointment of bishops.

Finally, you know that the Holy Father awaits from you a letter containing essentially the points which we spoke of more particularly in our conversation of May 24. But, since you have recently once again announced your intention of ordaining three bishops with or without the permission of Rome on June 30, it is necessary that in this letter (*cf.* part II, section 4 of the Protocol, [see p.76]), you state clearly that you renounce the idea, and that you place yourself in full obedience to the decision of the Holy Father.

With this final step, accomplished in as little time as possible, the process of reconciliation will have been completed, and a public announcement of this fact can be given.

Excellency, as I conclude this I can only repeat to you as I did last Tuesday, and with still more gravity if possible: when one considers the positive content of the accord which the benevolence of Pope John Paul II has allowed us to reach, there is no proportion between the last few difficulties you have expressed and the damage which would be caused now by a break, a rupture with the Apostolic See on your part, for these motives only. You must have confidence in the Holy Father, whose goodness and understanding he has shown in your regard and with regard to the Society, and which constitutes the best guarantee for the future. Finally, you must—as must we all—have confidence in the Lord, who has allowed the way of reconciliation to be opened as it is open today, the conclusion of which is now in sight.

Deign to accept, Excellency, the expression of my fraternal and respectfully devoted sentiments in the Lord.

Joseph Cardinal Ratzinger

MAY 30, 1988

SUMMARY OF THE SITUATION

Here is the account of the situation written by the hand of Archbishop Lefebvre, which he gave to the superiors of traditional communities and to some priests with whom he met at the Society's retreat house of Le Pointet, France. Present were Benedictine monks and nuns (including Dom Gérard), Dominican monks and nuns, Franciscan monks and nuns, Carmelite nuns, Fr. Coache, Fr. André, Fr. Lecareu....

Explanation of the Situation Concerning What Rome Calls "Reconciliation"

- Fifteen years of opposition to the doctrinal deviations of the Council and the reforms issuing from this conciliar spirit, to remain faithful to the Faith and the sources of edifying grace.
- To abide in this fidelity we undergo the persecution of Rome and conferences of bishops, and religious congregations.
- Being involved in the same struggle, we have helped each other to consolidate and develop the works which Providence has put in our hands and which it has visibly blessed.
- Providence has permitted us to have a bishop, thanks to which we have had the grace of ordinations and confirmations, an indispensable aid to our fidelity.
- Fifteen years of traditional ecclesial life, 15 years of blessings, of life with the Eucharistic Sacrifice, prayers, reception of valid and fruitful sacraments, a bishop, priests, brothers, nuns, Christian families united in the Faith. Fervor, generosity, full spiritual and material growth in the midst of trials, crosses, scorn...*etc.*
- The bishop formed the moral bond and even the ecclesial bond with the present Modernist Rome.[71]
- It must be recognized that the efforts to correct the spirit and reforms of the Council were in vain, as well as requests to officially authorize the "experiment of Tradition."

---

[71] *i.e.,* Rome occupied by modernists.

However, a vital problem is posed for fidelity to Tradition with the disappearance of the bishop. As Rome refuses to agree to the permanence of Tradition, the necessity of the salvation of souls becomes the (supreme) law.

On June 29, 1987, the decision to create some bishops to ensure the episcopal succession is announced.

On July 14, 1987, a final request is made of Rome, both by letter and in person.

On July 28, 1987, a serious hope of a solution appears. Rome seems frightened by the threat of episcopal consecrations.

The response does not reject the idea of an episcopal succession, but after legal recognition of the Society, the liturgy, the traditional seminaries are authorized. They no longer speak of a doctrinal document. They will return to that. An Apostolic Visitor is envisaged. *What would we do?*

- The visit of Cardinal Gagnon is decided on and takes place from November 11 to December 9.
- The report is given to the Pope on January 5.
- A Commission is proposed on March 18.
- A Commission of experts meets April 13-15. Signature of a proposal takes place on April 15.
- Meeting of the Commission of experts, Archbishop Lefebvre and the Cardinal, May 3 and 4. Signing of the Protocol, May 5, Feast of St. Pius V.
- Procedure for putting into application. Question of the *date of the consecration?* Put off *sine die* (indefinitely). Letter of His Grace to the Pope of May 5, 1988.

The difficulties of putting into application begin:
- Letter of May 6 to the Cardinal. Threat to proceed with the consecrations on June 30.
- Response of the Cardinal on May 6.
- Project of the letter to the Pope asking pardon, the letter of May 5 being too administrative (brought by Fr. du Chalard).
- Fr. du Chalard confirms to the Cardinal that I intend to consecrate on June 30. The Cardinal asks that I come to Rome.
- Letter to the Pope and letter to the Cardinal on the subject of the date and number of bishops and membership of the Roman Commission, May 20 and May 24.
- Meeting with the Cardinal and the secretaries on May 24.
- The letters are delivered. Then the Cardinal mentions August 15 as the date for the consecration, but does not respond to the other problems. As for the secretaries, they allude to the other problems by

saying that the requests can be looked into! The Cardinal gives me another project of a letter to the Pope.
- On May 28, the Pope confirms the date of August 15.

The atmosphere of these contacts and talks, the reflections of both sides during the conversations, clearly manifests to us that the desire of the Holy See is to bring us back to the Council and to the reforms, also to place us back into the bosom of the Conciliar Church as a religious congregation:
- The Bureau at Rome will be provisional. (Special note)
- The Bishop is not necessary, and grudgingly conceded. Delays!
- The Catholic Church is the Church of Vatican Council II.
- Acceptance of the conciliar novelties. St. Nicolas! (Cardinal Ratzinger had asked for the celebration of a Mass of Paul VI each Sunday at St. Nicolas, in Paris.)
- The religious congregations are to be returned to their respective orders, with a special statute!
- We are given a doctrinal note to be signed.
- Again we are expected to ask pardon for our faults.

Our reintegration seems to be a political, diplomatic "trump card" to offset the excesses of others.

This poses the following moral problem, in which I do not feel entitled to act without your counsel, since you are directly concerned. (Recall of Fr. Schmidberger from America.)

We must realize that a new situation will appear after the application of the accord.

Let us state the advantages:
- Canonical normalization of our works. Renewal of relations with Rome for each one of our works.
- At the same time we retain a certain independence, for the safeguarding of Tradition,
    i)   through the Liturgy.
    ii) through the formation of our members and the faithful.
    iii) by relations with the bishops, and the conciliar world.

- suppression of apprehensions and reticences (to a certain extent).
- facilitation of relations with certain civil administrations.
- easier missionary contacts to convert priests and faithful to Tradition!
- a flow of vocations and the faithful to our works.
- a bishop consecrated with the approval of the Holy See.

Let us state the disadvantages:
- a limited but definite dependence on modernist and conciliar Rome through the Roman Commission directed by Cardinal Ratzinger.
- its principles are the same ones which alienated us from modern Rome.
- disassociation of our moral unity created around my person, which disappears, partly in favor of Cardinal Ratzinger, and partly in favor of the different superiors general who report directly to Rome, but who can continue to have recourse to the bishop consecrated for Tradition. We risk having less unity and less strength.
- Relations with the congregations and orders. They are to have a special statute, but in spite of everything a moral dependence, which Rome would like to see transformed as early as possible into a canonical dependence. Danger of contamination.
- Relations with the conciliar bishops, faithful and clergy. In spite of the broad exemption, as the canonical barriers disappear, there will necessarily be courtesy contacts and perhaps offers of cooperation, for the student unions—superiors' unions—priests' meetings—regional ceremonies, etc...This whole world of the conciliar spirit—ecumenical and charismatic.
- Only one bishop. Less protection, more danger.

Up until now we were naturally protected, the selection was assured by the necessity of a rupture with the conciliar world. From now on, continual caution is necessary, to keep us always on guard against the atmosphere in Rome, against the atmosphere in the dioceses.

This is why we want three or four bishops and the majority in the Roman Commission, but they turn a deaf ear. They have agreed to only one bishop, after continual threats, and delayed the date. They consider it inconceivable that we treat them as a contaminated atmosphere, after all they are granting us.

Thus, a moral problem is posed for all of us.
- Must we run the risk of contacts with this modernist atmosphere in the hope of converting some souls, and with the hope of fortifying ourselves beforehand with the grace of God and the virtue of prudence, and thus remain legally united to Rome according to the letter, as we are in reality and in spirit?
- Or must we, before all else, preserve the traditional family to maintain its cohesion and vigor in the Faith and in grace, considering that the purely formal tie with modernist Rome cannot be as important as the protection of this family, representing those who remain faithful to the Catholic Church?

- What do God and the Holy Trinity, and Our Lady of Fatima ask of us in response to this question?

It is clear that four bishops will fortify us better than just one. The decision must be taken within 48 hours.

Reflect. Pray. Please give me your opinion, even in writing if you wish, and it will be my duty, with the help of the Holy Ghost, and Our Lady the Queen, to make a decision.

Msgr. de Castro Mayer has promised to come June 30, for the episcopal consecrations, with three priests of his diocese.

JUNE 2, 1988

LETTER OF ARCHBISHOP LEFEBVRE
TO POPE JOHN PAUL II

Most Holy Father,

The conversations and meetings with Cardinal Ratzinger and his collaborators, although they took place in an atmosphere of courtesy and charity, persuaded us that the moment for a frank and efficacious collaboration between us has not yet arrived.

For indeed, if the ordinary Christian is authorized to ask the competent Church authorities to preserve for him the Faith of his Baptism, how much more true is that for priests, religious and nuns?

It is to keep the Faith of our Baptism intact that we have had to resist the spirit of Vatican II and the reforms inspired by it.

The false ecumenism which is at the origin of all the Council's innovations in the liturgy, in the new relationship between the Church and the world, in the conception of the Church itself, is leading the Church to its ruin and Catholics to apostasy.

Being radically opposed to this destruction of our Faith and determined to remain with the traditional doctrine and discipline of the Church, especially as far as the formation of priests and the religious life is concerned, we find ourselves in the absolute necessity of having ecclesiastical authorities who embrace our concerns and will help us to protect ourselves against the spirit of Vatican II and the spirit of Assisi.

That is why we are asking for several bishops chosen from within Catholic Tradition, and for a majority of the members on the projected Roman Commission for Tradition, in order to protect ourselves against all compromise.

Given the refusal to consider our requests, and it being evident that the purpose of this reconciliation is not at all the same in the eyes of the Holy See as it is in our eyes, we believe it preferable to wait for times more propitious for the return of Rome to Tradition.[72]

---

[72] Note the expression. The Society of Saint Pius X never departed from the Church. It remains united with 20 centuries of popes and saints. Those who need to "return" are those who have engaged themselves in new paths of doctrines and practices.

That is why we shall give ourselves the means to carry on the work which Providence has entrusted to us, being assured by His Eminence Cardinal Ratzinger's letter of May 30, that the episcopal consecration is not contrary to the will of the Holy See, since it was granted for August 15.[73]

We shall continue to pray for modern Rome, infested with Modernism, to become once more Catholic Rome and to rediscover its 2,000 year-old tradition. Then the problem of our reconciliation will have no further reason to exist and the Church will experience a new youth.

Be so good, Most Holy Father, as to accept the expression of my most respectful and filially devoted sentiments in Jesus and Mary.

† Marcel Lefebvre

---

[73] *L'Osservatore Romano* and others have objected to this sentence. Archbishop Lefebvre does not say here that the Holy See agrees with all the particular circumstances of the consecrations, merely to its principle.

JUNE 9, 1988

LETTER OF POPE JOHN PAUL II
TO ARCHBISHOP LEFEBVRE

Excellency,

It is with intense and profound affliction that I have read your letter dated June 2.

Guided solely by concern for the unity of the Church in fidelity to the revealed Truth—an imperative duty imposed on the Successor of the Apostle Peter—I had arranged last year an Apostolic Visitation of the Saint Pius X Society and its work, which was carried out by Edward Cardinal Gagnon. Conversations followed, first with experts of the Congregation for the Doctrine of the Faith, then between yourself and Cardinal Ratzinger. In the course of these meetings solutions had been drawn up, accepted, and signed by you on May 5, 1988. They permitted the Saint Pius X Society to exist and work in the Church in full communion with the Sovereign Pontiff, the guardian of unity in the Truth. For its part, the Apostolic See pursued only one end in these conversations with you: to promote and safeguard this unity in obedience to divine Revelation, translated and interpreted by the Church's magisterium, notably in the 21 Ecumenical Councils from Nicæa to Vatican II.

In the letter you sent me you appear to reject all that was agreed on in the previous conversations, since you clearly manifest your intention to "provide the means yourself to continue your work," particularly by proceeding shortly and without apostolic mandate to one or several episcopal ordinations, and this in flagrant contradiction not only with the norms of Canon Law, but also with the Protocol signed on May 5 and the directions relevant to this problem contained in the letter which Cardinal Ratzinger wrote to you on my instructions on May 30.

With a paternal heart, but with all the gravity required by the present circumstances, I exhort you, Reverend Brother, not to embark upon a course which, if persisted in, cannot but appear as a schismatical act whose inevitable theological and canonical consequences are known to you. I earnestly invite you to return, in humility, to full obedience to Christ's Vicar.

Not only do I invite you to do so, but I ask it of you through the wounds of Christ our Redeemer, in the name of Christ who, on the eve of

His Passion, prayed for His disciples "that they may all be one" (Jn. 17:20).

To this request and to this invitation I unite my daily prayer to Mary, Mother of Christ.

Dear Brother, do not permit that the year dedicated in a very special way to the Mother of God should bring another wound to her Mother's Heart!

Joannes Paulus PP. II
From the Vatican,
June 9, 1988.

Even after the letter of June 2, Archbishop Lefebvre and the Society of Saint Pius X were praying for a miracle. God could have changed the heart of the Pope and made him grant the requests of Archbishop Lefebvre. After this letter of the Pope, telegrams poured into Rome asking for this.

JUNE 17, 1988

CANONICAL WARNING

Congregation for Bishops to His Excellency Archbishop Marcel Lefebvre, Archbishop-Bishop Emeritus of Tulle

Since on June 15, 1988[74] you stated that you intended to ordain four priests to the episcopate without having obtained the mandate of the Supreme Pontiff as required by Canon 1013 of the *1983 Code of Canon Law*, I myself convey to you this public canonical warning, confirming that if you should carry out your intention as stated above, you yourself and also the bishops ordained by you shall incur *ipso facto* excommunication *latæ sententiæ* reserved to the Apostolic See in accordance with Canon 1382. I therefore entreat and beseech you in the name of Jesus Christ to weigh carefully what you are about to undertake against the laws of sacred discipline, and the very grave consequences resulting therefrom for the communion of the Catholic Church, of which you are a bishop.

Given at Rome, from the Office of the Congregation for Bishops, June 17, 1988.

By Mandate of the Supreme Pontiff,

Bernardin Card. Gantin
Prefect of the Congregation for Bishops

---

[74] At a press conference held at Ecône.

JUNE 23, 1988

TELEGRAM OF *KEEP THE FAITH* TO POPE JOHN PAUL II

This telegram was sent to His Holiness Pope John Paul II and to His Eminence Joseph Cardinal Ratzinger. A copy was sent to Archbishop Lefebvre. *Keep the Faith, Inc.* **(Fairfield, NJ), directed by Mr. Howard Walsh, is a leading US distributor of conservative Catholic media materials.**

We at *Keep the Faith,* as with millions of American Catholics, were deeply saddened by the sudden break in negotiations between your commission and the Society of Saint Pius X. Hopes were high for certain reconciliation.

Keep the Faith is the largest media center in the US. We produce over 500,000 tapes a year and are unreservedly loyal to the Holy Father. Our program, *The Pope Speaks,* is listened to by thousands and our *Catholic Newswire* features the Vatican Report bimonthly. We mailed out millions of catalogs highlighting the Holy Father's activities, and we have the largest customer base in the country. We reach thousands of priests, seminarians, and religious with tapes and books, and many of them are deeply disturbed by the turn of events.

We distributed over 70,000 videotapes on the Tridentine Mass narrated by Archbishop Sheen, which have reached countless homes and seminaries. The hunger for the Immemorial Mass is still very much present and growing. Are these millions to be denied fundamental pastoral care and consideration as their right?

We respectfully tell you this to indicate that we are keenly aware of the prevailing spirit in the Catholic community. It is presently one of shock and confusion over the break in negotiations. We speak for millions of souls who pray the negotiations will re-open.

Archbishop Lefebvre has become a symbol of orthodoxy and sanity to countless souls in a church now being denied by dissent and scandal. Those many will not understand his imminent excommunication.

For the good of the Church and the salvation of souls, this tragedy must not be permitted to happen. We implore you, Holy Father, to re-open negotiations with Ecône. Our prayers are with you in this most trying hour for Holy Mother Church and the faithful

Howard J. Walsh, Director
Keep the Faith, Inc.

Countless other telegrams and letters had been sent to the Vatican. This one was chosen just as a sample. Even a retired diocesan bishop from the United States wrote to the Pope asking him to grant at least one bishop on June 30, 1988 and guaranteeing others on pre-determined dates in the near future, but to no avail.

JUNE 29, 1988

TELEGRAM OF CARDINAL RATZINGER TO ARCHBISHOP LEFEBVRE

The Apostolic Nunciature was requested to deliver to Archbishop Marcel Lefebvre, Bishop Emeritus of Tulle, the text of the following telegram addressed by His Eminence Joseph Cardinal Ratzinger, Prefect for the Congregation of the Doctrine of the Faith, in the name of the Holy Father:

Dated: Vatican June 29, 1988 at 2:00pm

For the love of Christ and His Church the Holy Father asks you with paternal firmness to leave today for Rome without proceeding to the episcopal consecrations on June 30 which you have announced. He prays the Holy Apostles Peter and Paul to inspire you not to betray the episcopate the care of which you have received, nor the oath you have pronounced to remain faithful to the Pope, successor of Peter. He asks God to keep you from leading astray and scattering those whom Christ Jesus came to gather in unity. He entrusts you to the intercession of the most Holy Virgin Mary Mother of the Church.

Joseph Cardinal Ratzinger

Archbishop Lefebvre was willing to see the Holy Father at any time before, but not to play the delaying game for ever. It belongs to the virtue of prudence to choose the right time for action. Archbishop Lefebvre had already delayed the Consecrations four times.[75]

If the Holy Father would have made a concrete proposal for a concrete date in the near future, he would have undoubtedly accepted. But this telegram only seems to hinder the possibility of such a concrete solution.

---

[75] He had not made known which were the previous three dates he had fixed.

JUNE 30, 1988

CONSECRATION SERMON
OF ARCHBISHOP MARCEL LEFEBVRE

Your Excellency, dear Bishop de Castro Mayer,
my most dear friends, my dear brethren,

Behold, here we are gathered for a ceremony which is certainly historic. Let me, first of all, give you some information.

The first might surprise you a little, as it did me. Yesterday evening, a visitor came, sent from the Nunciature in Berne, with an envelope containing an appeal from our Holy Father the Pope, who was putting at my disposal a car which was supposed to take me to Rome yesterday evening, so that I would not be able to perform these consecrations today. I was told neither for what reason, nor where I had to go! I leave you to judge for yourselves the timeliness and wisdom of such a request.

I went to Rome for many, many days during the past year, even for weeks; the Holy Father did not invite me to come and see him. I would certainly have been glad to see him if some agreement would have been finalized. So here you have the information. I give it to you simply, as I myself came to know it, through the letter from the Nunciature.

Now, some indications concerning the ceremony and some relevant documents regarding its significance.

The future bishops have already sworn in my hands the oath which you find in the little booklet on the ceremony of consecration which some of you have. Thus, this oath has already been pronounced, plus the Anti-Modernist Oath, as it was formerly prescribed for the consecration of bishops, plus the Profession of Faith. They have already taken these oaths and this profession in my hands after the retreat which took place at Sierre during these last days. Do not, therefore, be surprised if the ceremony begins with the interrogations on the Faith, the Faith which the Church asks from those to be consecrated.

I also want to let you know that, after the ceremony, you will be able to ask the blessing of the bishops and kiss their rings. It is not the custom in the Church to kiss the hands of a bishop, as one kisses the hands of a newly-ordained priest, as you did yesterday. But the faithful may ask for their blessing and kiss their ring.

Lastly, you have at your disposal at the bookstall some books and fliers which contain all the elements necessary to help you better understand why this ceremony, which is apparently done against the will of Rome, is in no way a schism. We are not schismatics! If an excommunication was pronounced against the bishops of China, who separated themselves from Rome and put themselves under the Chinese government, one very easily understands why Pope Pius XII excommunicated them.[76]

There is no question of us separating ourselves from Rome, nor of putting ourselves under a foreign government, nor of establishing a sort of parallel church as the Bishops of Palmar de Troya have done in Spain. They have even elected a pope, formed a college of cardinals....It is out of the question for us to do such things. Far from us be this miserable thought of separating ourselves from Rome!

On the contrary, it is in order to manifest our attachment to Rome that we are performing this ceremony. It is in order to manifest our attachment to the Eternal Rome, to the Pope, and to all those who have preceded these last Popes who, unfortunately since the Second Vatican Council, have thought it their duty to adhere to grievous errors which are demolishing the Church and the Catholic Priesthood.

Thus you will find among these fliers which are put at your disposal, an admirable study done by Professor Georg May, President of the Seminary of Canon Law in the University of Mayence in Germany, who marvelously explains why we are in a case of necessity:[77] necessity to come and help your souls, to help you! Your applause a while ago was, I think, not a purely temporal manifestation; it was rather a spiritual manifestation, expressing your joy to have at last Catholic bishops and priests who are dedicated to the salvation of your souls, to giving to your souls the Life of Our Lord Jesus Christ, through good doctrine, through the Sacraments, through the Faith, through the Holy Sacrifice of the Mass. You need this Life of Our Lord Jesus Christ to go to heaven. This Life of Our Lord Jesus Christ is disappearing everywhere in the Conciliar Church. They are following roads which are not Catholic roads: they simply lead to apostasy.

---

[76] The media and especially the Catholic diocesan papers all conveniently forgot this schism of the national Chinese Church, which was the occasion at which an excommunication was put for episcopal consecrations without papal mandate. They claimed that the so-called schism of Archbishop Lefebvre was the first since the schism of Döllinger and the "Old Catholics" after Vatican I. This claim is inaccurate and their parallel does not stand in the face of history. However, comparing 1988 with the Chinese Church would have shown the dissimilarity, as Archbishop Lefebvre does here.

[77] See p.175.

This is why we do this ceremony. Far be it from me to set myself up as pope! I am simply a bishop of the Catholic Church who is continuing to transmit Catholic doctrine. I think, and this will certainly not be too far off, that you will be able to engrave on my tombstone these words of St. Paul: "*Tradidi quod et accepi*"—"I have transmitted to you what I have received," nothing else. I am just the postman bringing you a letter. I did not write the letter, the message, this Word of God. God Himself wrote it; Our Lord Jesus Christ Himself gave it to us. As for us, we just handed it down, through these dear priests here present and through all those who have chosen to resist this wave of apostasy in the Church, by keeping the Eternal Faith and giving it to the faithful. We are just carriers of this Good News, of this Gospel which Our Lord Jesus Christ gave to us, as well as of the means of sanctification: the Holy Mass, the *true* Holy Mass, the true Sacraments which truly give the spiritual life.

It seems to me, my dear brethren, that I am hearing the voices of all these Popes—since Gregory XVI, Pius IX, Leo XIII, St. Pius X, Benedict XV, Pius XI, Pius XII—telling us: "Please, we beseech you, what are you going to do with our teachings, with our preaching, with the Catholic Faith? Are you going to abandon it? Are you going to let it disappear from this earth? Please, please, continue to keep this treasure which we have given you. Do not abandon the faithful, do not abandon the Church! Continue the Church! Indeed, since the Council, what we condemned in the past the present Roman authorities have embraced and are professing. How is it possible? We have condemned them: Liberalism, Communism, Socialism, Modernism, Sillonism."[78]

"All the errors which we have condemned are now professed, adopted and supported by the authorities of the Church. Is it possible? Unless you do something to continue this Tradition of the Church which we have given to you, all of it shall disappear. Souls shall be lost."

Thus, we find ourselves in a case of necessity. We have done all we could, trying to help Rome to understand that they had to come back to the attitudes of the holy Pius XII and of all his predecessors. Bishop de Castro Mayer and myself have gone to Rome, we have spoken, we have sent letters, several times to Rome. We have tried by these talks, by all these means, to succeed in making Rome understand that, since the Council and since *aggiornamento*, this change which has occurred in the Church is not Catholic, is not in conformity to the doctrine of all times. This ecu-

---

[78] Please note that many reporters have misunderstood the Archbishop who did not say "Zionism," but "Sillonism," the error condemned by St. Pius X in 1910. (See *Our Apostolic Mandate*, by Pope St. Pius X, available from Angelus Press.)

menism and all these errors, this collegiality—all this is contrary to the Faith of the Church, and is in the process of destroying the Church.

This is why we are convinced that, by the act of these consecrations today, we are obeying the call of these Popes and as a consequence the call of God, since they represent Our Lord Jesus Christ in the Church.

"And why, Archbishop, have you stopped these discussions which seemed to have had a certain degree of success?" Well, precisely because, at the same time that I gave my signature to the Protocol, the envoy of Cardinal Ratzinger gave me a note in which I was asked to beg pardon for my errors. But if I am in error, if I teach error, it is clear that I must be brought back to the truth in the minds of those who sent me this note to sign. "That I might recognize my errors" means that, "if you recognize your errors we will help you to return to the truth." What is this truth for them, if not the truth of Vatican II, the truth of the Conciliar Church? Consequently, it is clear that the only truth that exists today for the Vatican is the conciliar truth, the spirit of the Council, the spirit of Assisi. That is the truth of today. But we will have nothing to do with this for anything in the world!

That is why, taking into account the strong will of the present Roman authorities to reduce Tradition to nought, to gather the world to the spirit of Vatican II and the spirit of Assisi, we have preferred to withdraw ourselves and to say that we could not continue. It was not possible. We would have evidently been under the authority of Cardinal Ratzinger, President of the Roman Commission, which would have directed us; we were putting ourselves into his hands, and consequently putting ourselves into the hands of those who wish to draw us into the spirit of the Council and the spirit of Assisi. This was simply not possible.

This is why I sent a letter to the Pope, saying to him very clearly: "We simply cannot [accept this spirit and proposals], despite all the desires which we have to be in full union with you. Given this new spirit which now rules in Rome and which you wish to communicate to us, we prefer to continue in Tradition; to keep Tradition while waiting for Tradition to regain its place at Rome, while waiting for Tradition to re-assume its place in the Roman authorities, in their minds." This will last for as long as the Good Lord has foreseen.

It is not for me to know when Tradition will regain its rights at Rome, but I think it is my duty to provide the means of doing that which I shall call "Operation Survival," operation survival for Tradition. Today, this day, is Operation Survival. If I had made this deal with Rome, by continuing with the agreements we had signed, and by putting them into practice, I would have performed "Operation Suicide." There was no choice, we must live! That is why today, by consecrating these bishops, I am convinced that I am continuing to keep Tradition alive, that is to say, the Catholic Church.

You well know, my dear brethren, that there can be no priests without bishops. When God calls me—this will certainly not be long—from whom would these seminarians receive the Sacrament of Orders? From conciliar bishops, who, due to their doubtful intentions, confer doubtful sacraments? This is not possible. Who are the bishops who have truly kept Tradition and the Sacraments such as the Church has conferred them for 20 centuries until Vatican II? They are Bishop de Castro Mayer and myself. I cannot change that. That is how it is. Hence, many seminarians have entrusted themselves to us, they sensed that here was the continuity of the Church, the continuity of Tradition. And they came to our seminaries, despite all the difficulties that they have encountered, in order to receive a true ordination to the Priesthood, to say the true Sacrifice of Calvary, the true Sacrifice of the Mass, and to give you the true Sacraments, true doctrine, the true catechism. This is the goal of these seminaries.

So I cannot, in good conscience, leave these seminarians orphaned. Neither can I leave you orphans by dying without providing for the future. That is not possible. It would be contrary to my duty.

This is why we have chosen, with the grace of God, priests from our Society who have seemed to us to be the most apt, whilst being in circumstances and in functions which permit them more easily to fulfil their episcopal ministry, to give Confirmation to your children, and to be able to confer ordinations in our various seminaries. Thus I believe that with the grace of God, we, Bishop de Castro Mayer and myself, by these consecrations, will have given to Tradition the means to continue, given the means to Catholics who desire to remain within the Church of their parents, their grandparents, of their ancestors. They built churches with beautiful altars, often destroyed and replaced by a table, thus manifesting the radical change which has come about since the Council regarding the Holy Sacrifice of the Mass which is the heart of the Church and the purpose of the priesthood. Thus we wish to thank you for having come in such numbers to support us in the accomplishment of this ceremony.

We turn to the Blessed Virgin Mary. You well know, my dear brethren, you must have been told of Leo XIII's prophetic vision revealing that one day "the See of Peter would become the seat of iniquity." He said it in one of his exorcisms, called "The Exorcism of Leo XIII." Has it come about today? Is it tomorrow? I do not know. But in any case it has been foretold. Iniquity may quite simply be error. Error is iniquity: to no longer profess the Faith of all time, the Catholic Faith, is a grave error. If there ever was an iniquity, it is this. And I really believe that there has never been a greater iniquity in the Church than Assisi, which is contrary to the First Com-

mandment of God and the First Article of the Creed. It is incredible that
something like that could have ever taken place in the Church, in the eyes
of the whole Church—how humiliating! We have never undergone such a
humiliation! You will be able to find all of this in Fr. LeRoux's booklet
which has been especially published in order to give you information on
the present situation in Rome.

It was not only the good Pope Leo XIII who said these things, but Our
Lady prophesied them as well. Just recently, the priest who takes care of the
Society priory in Bogota, Colombia, brought me a book concerning the
apparition of Our Lady of "*Buen Suceso,*"—of "Good Fortune," to whom
a large church in Quito, Ecuador, was dedicated. They were received by a
nun shortly after the Council of Trent, so you see, quite a few centuries
ago. This apparition is thoroughly recognized by Rome and the ecclesiastical authorities; a magnificent church was built for the Blessed Virgin Mary
wherein the faithful of Ecuador venerate with great devotion a picture of
Our Lady, whose face was made miraculously. The artist was in the process
of painting it when he found the face of the Holy Virgin miraculously
formed. And Our Lady prophesied for the 20th century, saying explicitly
that during the 19th century and most of the 20th century, errors would
become more and more widespread in Holy Church, placing the Church
in a catastrophic situation. Morals would become corrupt and the Faith
would disappear. It seems impossible not to see it happening today.

I excuse myself for continuing this account of the apparition, but she
speaks of a prelate who will absolutely oppose this wave of apostasy and
impiety—saving the priesthood by forming good priests. I do not say that
prophecy refers to me. You may draw your own conclusions. I was stupe-
fied when reading these lines but I cannot deny them, since they are re-
corded and deposited in the archives of this apparition.

Of course, you well know the apparitions of Our Lady at La Salette,
where she says that Rome will lose the Faith, that there will be an "eclipse"
at Rome; an eclipse, see what Our Lady means by this.

And finally, closer to us, the Secret of Fatima. Without a doubt, the
Third Secret of Fatima must have made an allusion to this darkness which
has invaded Rome, this darkness which has invaded the world since the
Council. And surely it is because of this, without a doubt, that John XXIII
judged it better not to publish the Secret: it would have been necessary to
take measures, such steps as he possibly felt himself incapable of doing,
e.g., completely changing the orientations which he was beginning to take
in view of the Council, and for the Council.

There are the facts upon which, I think, we can lean.

We place ourselves in God's providence. We are convinced that God
knows what He is doing. Cardinal Gagnon visited us 12 years after the

suspension: after 12 years of being spoken of as outside of the communion of Rome, as rebels and dissenters against the Pope, his visit took place. He himself recognized that what we have been doing is just what is necessary for the reconstruction of the Church. The Cardinal even assisted pontifically at the Mass which I celebrated on December 8, 1987, for the renewal of the promises of our seminarians. I was supposedly suspended and, yet, after 12 years, I was practically given a clean slate. They said we have done well. Thus we did well to resist! I am convinced that we are in the same circumstances today. We are performing an act which apparently—and unfortunately the media will not assist us in the good sense. The headlines will, of course, be "Schism," "Excommunication!" to their heart's content—and, yet, we are convinced that all these accusations of which we are the object, all penalties of which we are the object, are null, *absolutely null and void,* and of which we will take no account. Just as I took no account of the suspension, and ended up by being congratulated by the Church and by progressive churchmen, so likewise in several years—I do not know how many, only the Good Lord knows how many years it will take for Tradition to find its rights in Rome—we will be embraced by the Roman authorities, who will thank us for having maintained the Faith in our seminaries, in our families, in civil societies, in our countries, and in our monasteries and our religious houses, for the greater glory of God and the salvation of souls.

In the Name of the Father, and of the Son, and of the Holy Ghost. Amen.

JUNE 30, 1988

"MANDATUM"

At the beginning of the rite of the consecration the following dialogue takes place between the consecrating bishops and the Archpriest who presents the bishops-elect for consecration:

–Do you have the Apostolic Mandate?
–We have it!
–Let it be read.

We have this Mandate from the Roman Church, always faithful to the Holy Tradition, which She has received from the Holy Apostles. This Holy Tradition is the Deposit of Faith which the Church orders us to faithfully transmit to all men for the salvation of their souls.

Since the Second Vatican Council until this day, the authorities of the Roman Church are animated by the spirit of modernism. They have acted contrary to the Holy Tradition, "they cannot bear sound doctrine, they turned their ears from the Truth and followed fables" as says St. Paul in his second Epistle to Timothy (4:3-5). This is why we reckon of no value all the penalties and all the censures inflicted by these authorities.

As for me, "I am offered up in sacrifice and the moment for my departure is arrived" (II Tim 4:6). I had the call of souls who ask for the Bread of Life, Who is Christ, to be broken for them. "I have pity upon the crowd" (Mk. 8:2). It is for me therefore a grave obligation to transmit the grace of my episcopacy to these dear priests here present, in order that in turn they may confer the grace of the priesthood on other numerous and holy clerics, instructed in the Holy Traditions of the Catholic Church

It is by this Mandate of the Holy Roman Catholic Church, *semper fidelis* (always faithful), then that we elect to the rank of Bishop in the Holy Roman Church the priests here present as auxiliaries of the Priestly Society of Saint Pius X:

Fr. Bernard Tissier de Mallerais
Fr. Richard Williamson
Fr. Alfonso de Galarreta
Fr. Bernard Fellay

JUNE 30, 1988

DECLARATION OF BISHOP ANTONIO DE CASTRO MAYER

After the Consecration Sermon given by Archbishop Lefebvre, the co-consecrating bishop, Bishop Antonio de Castro Mayer, retired bishop of the Diocese of Campos, Brazil, gave a short allocution which was very warmly applauded. He read it in Portuguese and it was translated afterwards into French and then into German and English.

My presence here at this ceremony is caused by a duty of conscience: that of making a profession of Catholic Faith in front of the whole Church and more particularly in front of His Excellency Archbishop Marcel Lefebvre and in front of all the priests, religious, seminarians and faithful here present.

St. Thomas Aquinas teaches that there is no obligation to make a profession of faith at every moment. But when the Faith is in danger it is urgent to profess it, even if it be at the risk of one's own life.

Such is the situation in which we find ourselves. We live in an unprecedented crisis of the Church, a crisis that attacks her inner essence, in her very substance which is the Holy Sacrifice of the Mass and the Catholic priesthood, two mysteries essentially united because without priesthood there is no sacrifice of the Mass and therefore no form of worship. It is also on this foundation that the social reign of Our Lord Jesus Christ is built.

For this reason, because the conservation of the priesthood and the Holy Mass is at stake, and in spite of the requests and pressures of many, I am here in order to accomplish my duty: to make a public profession of faith.

It is painful to witness the deplorable blindness of so many confrères in the episcopate and in the priesthood who do not see or do not want to see the present crisis nor the necessity to resist the reigning modernism in order to be faithful to the mission entrusted to us by God.

I want to manifest here my sincere and profound adherence to the position of His Excellency Archbishop Lefebvre, dictated by his fidelity to the Church of all centuries. Both of us, we have drunk at the same spring which is that of the Holy Catholic Apostolic and Roman Church.

May the Most Holy Virgin Our Mother, who at Fatima has warned us in her motherly love with regard to the gravity of the present situation, give us the grace to be able by our attitude to help and enlighten the faithful in such a way that they depart from these pernicious errors of which they are the victims, deceived by many persons who have received the fullness of the Holy Ghost.

May God bless Archbishop Lefebvre and his work!

JULY 1, 1988

DECREE

Note that the decree from Rome regarding the episcopal consecrations is not the sentence of a judge, but rather a declaration that Canons 1364 and 1382 (of the *1983 Code of Canon Law*) apply. It does not add to the motives brought forth in these Canons. Thus, if these motives do not apply in the present case because of the necessity in which the modernists have put the Church, then this decree is insufficient to make these Canons apply, since it does not remove the state of necessity.

Monsignor Marcel Lefebvre, Archbishop-Bishop Emeritus of Tulle, notwithstanding the formal canonical warning of June 17 last and the repeated appeals to desist from his intention, has performed a schismatical act by the episcopal consecration of four priests, without pontifical mandate and contrary to the will of the Supreme Pontiff, and has therefore incurred the penalty envisaged by Canon 1364 §1, and Canon 1382 of the Code of Canon Law.

Having taken account of all the juridical effects, I declare that the above mentioned Archbishop Marcel Lefebvre, and Bernard Fellay, Bernard Tissier de Mallerais, Richard Williamson, and Alfonso de Galarreta have incurred *ipso facto* excommunication *latæ sententiæ* reserved to the Apostolic See.

Moreover, I declare that Archbishop Antonio de Castro Mayer, Bishop Emeritus of Campos, since he took part directly in the liturgical celebration as co-consecrator and adhered publicly to the schismatical act, has incurred excommunication *latæ sententiæ* as envisaged by Canon 1364 §1.

The priests and faithful are warned not to support the schism of Archbishop Lefebvre, otherwise they shall incur *ipso facto* the very grave penalty of excommunication.

From the Office of the Congregation for Bishops, July 1, 1988.

Bernardinus Card. Gantin
Prefect of the Congregation for Bishops

JULY 2, 1988

APOSTOLIC LETTER OF POPE JOHN PAUL II
ECCLESIA DEI

With great affliction the Church has learned of the unlawful episcopal ordination conferred on June 30 last by Archbishop Marcel Lefebvre, which has frustrated all the efforts made during the previous years to ensure the full communion with the Church of the Priestly Society of Saint Pius X founded by the same Archbishop Lefebvre. These efforts, especially intense during recent months, in which the Apostolic See has shown comprehension to the limits of the possible, were all to no avail.[79]

This affliction was particularly felt by the Successor of Peter to whom in the first place pertains the guardianship of the unity of the Church, even though the number of persons directly involved in these events might be few, since every person is loved by God on his own account and has been redeemed by the blood of Christ shed on the Cross for the salvation of all.

The particular circumstances, both objective and subjective in which Archbishop Lefebvre acted, provide everyone with an occasion for profound reflection and for a renewed pledge of fidelity to Christ and to His Church.

In itself, this act was one of disobedience to the Roman Pontiff in a very grave matter and of supreme importance for the unity of the Church, such as is the ordination of bishops whereby the apostolic succession is sacramentally perpetuated. Hence such disobedience—which implies in practice the rejection of the Roman primacy—constitutes a schismatic act. In performing such an act, notwithstanding the formal canonical warning sent to them by the Cardinal Prefect of the Congregation for Bishops on June 17 last, Archbishop Lefebvre and the priests Bernard Fellay, Bernard Tissier de Mallerais, Richard Williamson and Alfonso de Galarreta, have

---

[79] This paragraph would give the impression that the Vatican has been as generous and sincere in their "efforts" as possible. This impression was not at all shared by Archbishop Lefebvre, who said in an interview with *30 Days*: "It was necessary to threaten continually in order to obtain something. No collaboration was any longer possible" (*30 Days*, July 1988, pp.13-14).

incurred the grave penalty of excommunication envisaged by ecclesiastical law.

The root of this schismatic act can be discerned in an incomplete and contradictory notion of Tradition. Incomplete, because it does not take sufficiently into the account the living character of Tradition, which, as the Second Vatican Council clearly taught, "comes from the apostles and progresses in the Church with the help of the Holy Spirit. There is a growth in insight into the realities and words that are being passed on. This comes about in various ways. It comes through the contemplation and study of believers who ponder these things in their hearts. It comes from the intimate sense of spiritual realities which they experience. And it comes from the preaching of those who have received, along with their right of succession in the episcopate, the sure charisma of truth."

But especially contradictory is a notion of Tradition which opposes the universal magisterium of the Church possessed by the Bishop of Rome and the body of bishops. It is impossible to remain faithful to the Tradition while breaking the ecclesial bond with him to whom, in the person of the Apostle Peter, Christ himself entrusted the ministry of unity in His Church.[80]

Faced with the situation that has arisen I deem it my duty to inform all the Catholic faithful of some aspects which this sad event has highlighted.

a) The outcome of the movement promoted by Archbishop Lefebvre can and must be, for all the Catholic faithful, a motive for sincere reflection concerning their own fidelity to the Church's Tradition, authentically interpreted by the ecclesiastical magisterium, ordinary and extraordinary, especially in the ecumenical councils from Nicæa to Vatican II. From this reflection all should draw a renewed and efficacious conviction of the necessity of strengthening still more their fidelity by rejecting erroneous interpretations and arbitrary and unauthorized applications in matters of doctrine, liturgy and discipline.

To the bishops especially it pertains, by reason of their pastoral mission, to exercise the important duty of a clear-sighted vigilance full of charity and firmness, so that this fidelity may be everywhere safeguarded.

---

[80] Unity in the Church is first of all a unity of Faith: *One Faith, one Lord, one Baptism.* Peter has the ministry of unity first of all because he has the duty to safeguard this One Faith intact, undefiled. Keeping the Tradition certainly does not oppose this unity of the Church; on the contrary, introducing novelties undermines the unity of the Church.

However, it is necessary that all the pastors and the other faithful have a new awareness, not only of the lawfulness but also of the richness of the Church of a diversity of charisma, traditions of spirituality and apostolate, which also constitutes the beauty of unity in variety: of that blended "harmony" which the earthly Church raises up to Heaven under the impulse of the Holy Spirit.

b) Moreover, I should like to remind theologians and other experts in the ecclesiastical sciences that they should feel called upon to answer in the present circumstances. Indeed, the extent and depth of the teaching of the Second Vatican Council call for a renewed commitment to deeper study in order to reveal clearly the Council's continuity with Tradition, especially in points of doctrine which, perhaps because they are new, have not yet been well understood by some sections of the Church.[81]

c) In the present circumstances I wish especially to make an appeal both solemn and heartfelt, paternal and fraternal, to all those who until now have been linked in various ways to the movement of Archbishop Lefebvre, that they may fulfil the grave duty of remaining united to the Vicar of Christ in the unity of the Catholic Church, and of ceasing their support in any way for that movement. Everyone should be aware that formal adherence to the schism is a grave offence against God and carries the penalty of excommunication decreed by the Church's law.

To all those Catholic faithful who feel attached to some previous liturgical and disciplinary forms of the Latin tradition I wish to manifest my will to facilitate their ecclesial communion by means of the necessary measures to guarantee respect for their rightful aspirations. In this matter I ask for the support of the bishops and of all those engaged in the pastoral ministry in the Church.

Taking account of the importance and complexity of the problems referred to in this document, by virtue of my Apostolic Authority, I decree the following:

a) A Commission is instituted whose task it will be to collaborate with the bishops, with the departments of the Roman Curia and with the circles concerned, for the purpose of facilitating full ecclesial communion of priests, seminarians, religious communi-

---

[81] Note the acknowledgment that these doctrines are "new."

ties or individuals until now linked in various ways to the Society founded by Archbishop Lefebvre, who may wish to remain united to the Successor of Peter in the Catholic Church, while preserving their spiritual and liturgical traditions, in the light of the Protocol signed on May 5 last by Cardinal Ratzinger and Archbishop Lefebvre;

b) this Commission is composed of a Cardinal President and other members of the Roman Curia, in a number that will be deemed opportune according to the circumstances;

c) moreover, respect must everywhere be shown for the feelings of all those who are attached to the Latin liturgical tradition, by a wide and generous application of the directives already issued some time ago by the Apostolic See, for the use of the Roman Missal according to the typical edition of 1962.

As this year specially dedicated to the Blessed Virgin is now drawing to a close, I wish to exhort all to join in unceasing prayer which the Vicar of Christ, through the intercession of the Mother of the Church, addresses to the Father in the very words of the Son: "That they all may be one!"

Joannes Paulus II
Given at Rome, at St. Peter's, July 2, 1988,
in the tenth year of the pontificate.

In this letter the Pope makes three objections against Archbishop Lefebvre: disobedience, an incomplete, and a contradictory notion of Tradition.

Disobedience? No!

Firstly, he accuses him of disobedience. However, obedience is the response in the subject to the proper use of authority in a superior. The Pope received his authority "unto edification and not unto destruction" (II Cor. 13:10). The Pope received his power to eradicate evil and promote the good of the Church. Archbishop Lefebvre asked from him nothing other than the means necessary to promote the good of the Church and, thus, deserved his support, not his opposition.

We have included in Part II a sermon delivered by Archbishop Lefebvre on September 3, 1977, on the subject of obedience which explains very well real and apparent disobedience.

But one would say: "Archbishop Lefebvre could keep Tradition without consecrating a bishop." The duty of the faithful is different from the duty of a bishop; the faithful must keep the Faith for themselves and pass it on to their children; a bishop has not only the duty to keep the Faith for himself, but also to assure its transmission to future generations. The Pope received his

power "to feed the Lord's sheep," not to let them starve. At a time when so many bishops not only let the good faithful starve but are poisoning them by their bad doctrine and example, it is a strict duty of charity to provide the faithful with the spiritual food, with the doctrine, with the Sacraments, and with the priests to administer these Sacraments. St. Thomas teaches that obedience cannot forbid us to fulfil a necessary duty.[82]

The true life of Tradition

The second objection is that of an incomplete notion of Tradition. As if Archbishop Lefebvre's notion of Tradition did "not take sufficiently into account the living character of Tradition." The fallacy of this objection comes from an ambiguity on "life": what is the true life of Tradition?

In his book, *The Reshaping of Catholicism*[83] (p.78), Fr. Avery Dulles makes a similar criticism of Archbishop Lefebvre's notion of Tradition: "It is evident that the conflicting evaluations of Vatican II turn upon different concepts of Tradition. For Imbelli, Tradition is not so much content as process–a process that is, in his own words, living, creative and community based. What Lefebvre dismisses as 'Modernist influence' can therefore be defended by Imbelli as a rediscovery of an ancient and precious heritage–The objectivist authoritarian concept still dominant in contemporary traditionalism is widely criticized in our days." Thus, there are two conflicting notions of Tradition: on the one hand, you have a living, creative and community based *process*; but what process? A transmission of a changing personal religious experience empty of content? Unrelated to the objective truth? On the other hand, you have the authentic notion of Tradition as the faithful transmission of the Deposit of Faith by the popes and bishops. The first concept is living of a human life; the second concept is living of the Divine Life! The life of Tradition is the life of the Church, which is the life of Christ, the Divine Life communicated to men.

Tradition is, first of all, related to an Object: the Immutable, Divine Truth. To lose sight of this is certainly an incomplete notion of Tradition. In my editorial in *The Angelus*, July 1988, I wrote:

"What is the life of Tradition? It is not a life of change. It is not a life such as that of a plant or an animal, which changes constantly. No! It is a sharing in the Life of God, Who is Immutable. For minds accustomed to the modern, materialistic atmosphere, it is hard to understand a life without any change. Yet it is clear that what is proper to life is not movement alone: when one pushes with one's foot the body of a dead animal, one gives it movement...but not life. What is proper to life is rather the immanence of the movement; when Our Lord said: "Lazarus, come out!" the dead came out without anyone pushing him. His

---

[82] *Summa Theologica,* IIa IIæ Q.104, A.3, ad.3.

[83] Dulles, Avery, *The Reshaping of Catholicism: Current Challenges in the Theology of Church* (San Francisco: Harper and Row, 1988).

movement was from within: he had come back to life.

"As for the life of the Church, one must first of all distinguish the life of each one of the faithful, and the life of the Church as a whole. Each one of the faithful passes from the ignorance of the Faith (before he became faithful) to the knowledge of it, and must always deepen his Faith. But the object of this Faith is One, Immutable; it is the Eternal Truth: Jesus Christ, the Word of God made flesh.

"Each faithful passes from the state of sin (before he became faithful) to the state of grace. He must constantly fight against temptation and the residue of sin; he must purify his soul more and more in the Blood of the Lamb; he must become closer and closer to God in Our Lord Jesus Christ, "walking in charity": this is spiritual progress. Thus it is clear that there is movement in the life of the faithful. But this is a spiritual movement: the deepening of the knowledge of the Truth and the strengthening of virtues. It is not the abandonment of what he believed and strove to practice yesterday!

"Now for the Church there is even less movement. Christ has given to His Church the complete Deposit of Faith. Each individual may deepen his knowledge of this Deposit, but the Church had it all since its beginning. The Church may teach it, explain it and defend it more and more explicitly against the negators and the heresies,[84] but *neither adds to it, nor loses* any parcel of this Eternal Truth.

"Concerning the life of virtue, the Church possesses from her Divine Founder the Seven Sacraments—seven fountains of the life of holiness. The Church cannot add a new one (as some Pentecostals would like to do), nor subtract another (some would like to take away Confession, or Confirmation). The Church possesses, from the beginning, the Perfect Example of Virtue: the Life of Our Lord Jesus Christ. All the saints have imitated Him; we have to follow in their footsteps. The way to heaven is not to be invented; there is one, and only one; it is Our Lord Jesus Christ: 'I am the Way, the Truth and the Life. No one comes to the Father but by Me.'

"Therefore there can be no change in the Church's morals, which are all summed up in these words of Our Lord: 'Be ye perfect as your heavenly Father is perfect' (Mt. 5:48). The Divine Perfection is eternal and immutable. In heaven the saints 'rest' in God, thus without changes, sharing divine eternity.[85] On the contrary, in hell

---

[84] In this way some truths may be put in greater light, and more explicitly and precisely defined, such as the Immaculate Conception, but these are not "new" truths. Moreover, in order to show the conciliation of some points of doctrine that may appear to conflict, the Church may develop the doctrine: thus the notion of sacramental character was developed as a solution in the conflict between on the one hand St. Cyprian, Bishop of Carthage, holding the Dogma *Outside the Church no salvation* and thus rebaptizing those baptized outside the church, and on the other hand St. Stephen, Pope, holding that *nothing should be innovated except that which is in conformity with Tradition* and thus refusing to rebaptize because it was a novelty. This is called the *homogenous evolution of the dogma,* which is not a change but rather a drawing of conclusion from unchangeable principles of Faith.

the damned will be tormented by unrest: *But the wicked are like the troubled sea, when it cannot rest, whose waters cast up mire and dirt. There is no peace for the ungodly, saith the Lord God;*[86] by the unceasing succession and changes of torments, one worse than the other. Folly of those who love change for the sake of change! They might have an eternity of changes–in hell!

"If there is some change in the Church as such, it is her wonderful capability of *putting into practice her eternal principles* to meet the needs of each era.[87] This is particularly manifested in the many religious orders which have sprung up throughout the whole history of the Church. All of them follow the same Model: Jesus Christ, and the same principles of Faith and morals, but adapt them to their particular circumstances. In this regard, *one can see Tradition living in the work of Archbishop Lefebvre and all the other traditional foundations*. They have all come to the Eternal Principles to receive Eternal Life from them.

"In one word, the life of Tradition is a life of contemplation of the Eternal Truth and love of the Eternal Good–not constant change!"

We might add that this life is manifested in its fruitfulness: in the many vocations, and also in the large families resolutely Catholic which abound among the faithful attached to Tradition.

One can also see the *fruits of death* in the departure from Tradition: seminaries and novitiates closed, almost no more religious teachers in schools, or nurses in hospitals, churches closed for lack of priest, thousands of priests and nuns who abandoned their holy vocation, millions of faithful who abandoned the Faith, such as in South America.

In the Liturgy too, one can see the difference of concepts of "life." The modernist concept leads to constant changes in the Liturgy, as the last 30 years have witnessed. The core of the Liturgical reform has been to remove from the Liturgy [almost] all the profession of Faith on the points which displeased the modern world, and the Protestants in particular. Thus many genuflections, mention of sin, penance, punishments, sacrifice, detachment from the things of this world, the Devil, *etc*...have been greatly removed. Now one of the important purposes of the Liturgy is to feed the Faith by professing it; the new Liturgy makes the faithful starve, when it does not poison them by some personal innovation of the celebrant. This is not to foster the true spiritual life of the faithful! On the contrary, the Traditional Liturgy, living the truth, loving the Truth, professes it and thus feeds the soul of the faithful with the food of true spiritual life.

In the light of the above considerations, does Archbishop Lefebvre "not take sufficiently into account the living character of Tradition"? Or does he rather defend the true life of Tradition by keeping its most solemn expression which is the Traditional Liturgy?

---

[85] This is life everlasting.

[86] Is. 57:20-21.

[87] Pope Pius XII gave a great example in applying the eternal principles to the new challenges of our times in his teaching. This is true "progress."

Contradictory notion of Tradition?

The third objection to Archbishop Lefebvre was that of a "contradictory notion of Tradition, which opposes the universal magisterium of the Church possessed by the Bishop of Rome and the body of bishops." Here, again, one must not forget that the magisterium of the Church is essentially related to the Deposit of Faith. Pope Pius IX and the Fathers of the First Vatican Council said: "For the Holy Ghost was not promised to the Successors of Peter that by His revelation they might disclose new doctrine, but that by His help they might guard sacredly the revelation transmitted through the Apostles and the Deposit of Faith, and might faithfully set it forth."[88]

Archbishop Lefebvre received this Deposit of Faith from the Popes. Fr. Le Floch[89] explained the Popes' encyclicals to all his students, a practice which Archbishop Lefebvre has introduced in his seminaries. He even taught the course on the "Acts of the Magisterium" by himself when there was a lack of teachers for two years at Ecône.

Archbishop Lefebvre's fidelity to the constant teaching of the previous Popes, far from undermining the authority of the Pope, is its best guarantee. Remember that Fr. Avery Dulles linked the "objectivist" notion of Tradition with the "authoritarian" notion, and rejected both as "traditional" notion. Without the pejorative endings, it is true that the traditional notion of Tradition insists on its object, the Deposit of Faith, to be religiously handed down by those who have received authority from Our Lord for this end: to insist on the unchangeable object of Tradition is to defend the "authoritarian" notion of Tradition, thus the authority of the Pope. He holds the place of authority to keep the Tradition, which notion of authority is rejected by the modernist, not by Archbishop Lefebvre! If authority is only there to approve any new modern "study of believer," then it destroys itself, it is exactly what St. Pius X describes in *Pascendi*,[90] as the modernist notion of authority. If, on the contrary, authority is to keep the Deposit of Faith, which is "complete with the Apostles,"[91] and unchangeable, then this notion of authority in Tradition is fully accepted by Archbishop Lefebvre.

St. Pius X asked every priest and bishop to swear the following: "I accept sincerely the doctrine of faith transmitted from the Apostles through the orthodox fathers, *always in the same sense and interpretation*, even to us; and so I reject *the heretical invention of the evolution of dogmas*, passing from one meaning to another, different from that which the Church first had..."[92]

If there is any opposition between Archbishop Lefebvre and

---

[88] Vat. I, Sess. IV, chap. 4.

[89] Rector of the French Seminary in Rome where Archbishop Lefebvre received his priestly training.

[90] *Pascendi Gregis.* (See, Denzinger, *The Sources of Catholic Dogma*, 2093.)

[91] *Lamentabili,* July 3, 1907, §21.

[92] The *Oath Against Modernism,* Sept. 1, 1910, which was sworn by Karol Wojtyla before he received the priesthood and, later, the episcopacy in 1958.

today's teaching of "the Bishop of Rome and the body of Bishops," it is because they are no longer teaching what their predecessors have taught, they are no longer teaching the Syllabus, the Anti-modernist Oath, the social Kingship of Our Lord Jesus Christ, etc....They are trying to teach a NEW doctrine (otherwise there would be no such opposition) and to impose it with an authority that is made "not to teach a new Revelation, but to keep entirely and expose faithfully the Deposit of Faith."

The present crisis of the Church comes from a crisis of authority: those who have the authority foster a new doctrine.[93]

Every novelty introduced or approved by the Pope tends to undermine his authority. Indeed if yesterday altar girls were forbidden and today they are permitted, today women priests are forbidden but why not tomorrow permitted? Once one accepts the principle of changes in doctrine[94] there is no limit to it, and no doctrinal authority can stand it.

Thus it appears that these three criticisms of Archbishop Lefebvre are not justified. If the reasons for a censure are false or undeserved, then the censure is void.

The Pope's letter finishes with beautiful promises which have been received with joy and extensively quoted by many conservatives. I wish these promises were reliable, but how can we trust them when they come with the refusal to grant to the best representative of Tradition the means he deemed necessary for its continuation? Without bishops dedicated to Tradition, how can the faithful trust such promises? Shall the sheep expect good food from the wolves?

The two most important points of the Protocol were the granting of a bishop and of two members in the Commission. These two points so necessary for the defense of Tradition have never been granted.

---

[93] See *The Ratzinger Report* in Part II, pp.211-217.

[94] The practice of employing "altar girls" is connected with doctrine since the service at the altar is the proper act of the Acolyte, one of the Minor Orders, which is soley reserved to males since it is a step culminating in ordination to the priesthood.

JULY 6, 1988

OPEN LETTER TO CARDINAL GANTIN PREFECT OF THE CONGREGATION FOR BISHOPS

Ecône, July 6, 1988

Eminence,

Gathered around our Superior General, the Superiors of the Districts, Seminaries and autonomous houses of the Priestly Society of Saint Pius X think it good to respectfully express to you the following reflections.

You thought it good, by your letter of July 1st, to inform Their Excellencies Archbishop Marcel Lefebvre, Bishop Antonio de Castro Mayer, and the four Bishops whom they consecrated on June 30, at Ecône, of the excommunication *latæ sententiæ.* We let you judge for yourself the value of such a declaration, coming from an authority who, in its exercise, breaks with all its predecessors down to Pope Pius XII, in worship, teaching and government of the Church.

As for us, we are in full communion with all the Popes and Bishops before the Second Vatican Council, celebrating precisely the Mass which they codified and celebrated, teaching the Catechism which they drew up, standing up against the errors which they have many times condemned in their encyclicals and pastoral letters. We let you judge on which side the rupture is to be found. We are extremely saddened by the blindness of spirit and the hardening of heart of the Roman authorities.

On the other hand, we have never wished to belong to this system which calls itself the Conciliar Church, and defines itself with the *Novus Ordo Missæ,* an ecumenism which leads to indifferentism and the laicization of all society. Yes, we have no part, *nullam partem habemus,* with the pantheon of the religions of Assisi; our own excommunication by a decree of Your Eminence or of another Roman Congregation would only be the irrefutable proof of this. We ask for nothing better than to be declared out of communion with this adulterous spirit which has been blowing in the Church for the last 25 years; we ask for nothing better than to be declared outside of this impious communion of the ungodly. We believe in the One God, Our Lord Jesus Christ, with the Father and the Holy Ghost, and we will always remain faithful to His unique Spouse, the One Holy Catholic Apostolic and Roman Church.

To be publicly associated with this sanction which is inflicted upon the six Catholic Bishops, Defenders of the Faith in its integrity and wholeness, would be for us a mark of honor and a sign of orthodoxy before the faithful. They have indeed a strict right to know that the priests who serve them are not in communion with a counterfeit church, promoting evolution, pentecostalism and syncretism. In union with these faithful, we make ours the words of the Prophet: "*Præparate corda vestra Domino et servite Illi soli: et liberabit vos de manibus inimicorum vestrorum. Convertimini ad Eum in toto corde vestro, et auferte deos alienos de medio vestri*—Open your hearts to the Lord and serve Him only: and He will free you from the hands of your enemies. With all your heart return to Him, and take away from your midst any strange gods" (I Kings 7:3).[95]

Confident in the protection of Her who has crushed all the heresies in the world, we assure Your Eminence of our dedication to Him Who is the only Way of salvation.

Fr. Franz Schmidberger, *Superior General*
Fr. Paul Aulagnier, *District Superior, France*
Fr. Franz-Josef Maessen, *District Superior, Germany*
Fr. Edward Black, *District Superior, Great Britain*
Fr. Anthony Esposito, *District Superior of Italy*
Fr. François Laisney, *District Superior, United States*
Fr. Jacques Emily, *District Superior of Canada*
Fr. Jean Michel Faure, *District Superior of Mexico*
Fr. Gerard Hogan, *District Superior of Australasia*
Fr. Alain Lorans, *Superior, Seminary of Ecône*
Fr. Jean Paul André, *Superior, Seminary of France*
Fr. Paul Natterer, *Superior, Seminary of Germany*
Fr. Andrès Morello, *Superior, Seminary of Argentina*
Fr. William Welsh, *Superior, Seminary of Australia*
Fr. Michel Simoulin, *Rector, St. Pius X University*
Fr. Patrice Laroche, *Vice-Rector, Seminary of Ecône*
Fr. Philippe François, *Superior, Belgium*
Fr. Roland de Mérode, *Superior, Netherlands*
Fr. Georg Pflüger, *Superior, Austria*
Fr. Guillaume Devillers, *Superior, Spain*

---

[95] Antiphon at Matins, read in the beginning of July.

Fr. Philippe Pazat, *Superior, Portugal*
Fr. Daniel Couture, *Superior, Ireland*
Fr. Patrick Groche, *Superior, Gabon*
Fr. Frank Peek, *Superior, Southern Africa*

No answer was received.

PART II

ADDITIONAL DOCUMENTATION

1976

EXTRACT FROM TWO CONFERENCES PREACHED BY CARDINAL WOJTYLA TO POPE PAUL VI IN 1976

Important milestones on the theological journey of John Paul II
to Assisi are the retreat conferences which Karol Wojtyla, in 1976,
preached to Pope Paul VI and a few of his most intimate
colleagues in the Vatican. They were published under the title of
the original Italian work: *Segno di contradizzione, Meditazoni*
(Milan, 1977). The English translation: *Sign of Contradiction*
appeared in 1979 from the Seaburg Press,[96] thus after the
election of Karol Wojtyla as Pope. A commentary by Fr. Johannes
Dörmann on these conferences in particular and the thinking of
Pope John Paul II in general is available in English.[97] The
recommendation for the book makes an accurate observation:
"Here one gets to know [the new Pope] most intimately."
Theology and spirituality are so mutually related that they make
up a unified body.

The retreat conferences are no mere pious exhortations, but an
extensive theological and spiritual meditation which opens with
the very essence of religion, the encounter between God and
man, and then strives to realize this encounter or, as the Cardinal
puts it: "to get as close as possible to God and to be penetrated
by his Spirit."

I. A NATURAL THEOLOGY OF RELIGIONS

"The *itinerarium mentis in Deum* (*journey of the human spirit to God*)
emerges from the depths of created things and from a man's inmost being.
The modern mentality as it makes its way finds its support in human experience, and in affirmation of the transcendence of the human person. Man
goes beyond himself, man must go beyond himself. The tragedy of atheistic humanism—so brilliantly analyzed by Fr. de Lubac (*Atheisme et sens de
l'homme*, Paris, 1969) is that it strips man of his transcendental character,
destroying his ultimate significance as a person. Man goes beyond himself

---

[96] Karol Wojtyla, *Sign of Contradiction* (New York: The Seaburg Press, 1979), p.2.
[97] Available from Angelus Press, currently in three volumes (*Pope John Paul II's Theological Journey to the Prayer Meeting of Religions in Assisi*).

by reaching out towards God, and thus progresses beyond the limits imposed on him by created things, by space and time, by his own contingency. The transcendence of the person is closely bound up with responsiveness to the one who himself is the touchstone for all our judgments concerning being, goodness, truth and beauty. It is bound up with responsiveness to the one who is nevertheless totally Other, because He is infinite.

"The concept of infinity is not unknown to man. He makes use of it in his scientific work, in mathematics, for instance. So there certainly is room in him, in his intellectual understanding, for Him Who is infinite, the God of boundless majesty, the one to Whom Holy Scripture and the Church bear witness saying: 'Holy, holy, holy, God of the universe, heaven and earth are full of your glory.' This God is professed in His silence by the Trappist or the Camaldolite. It is to him that the desert Bedouin turns at his hour for prayer. And perhaps the Buddhist, too, rapt in contemplation as he purifies his thought, preparing the way to Nirvana. God in His absolute transcendence, God who transcends absolutely the whole of creation, all that is visible and comprehensible."[98]

Rev. Fr. Joannes Dörmann comments: "This is a natural theology of all religions in a nutshell." This is a way of immanence which neglects the theodicy [*i.e.*, that part of metaphysics by which through the natural light of human reason we can know with certitude attributes of God] recommended by the Church (Vatican I, Denzinger, *The Sources of Catholic Dogma*, 1806), which starts from the mirror of the creatures to reach up to the Creator. It is akin to the vital immanence condemned by St. Pius X (*Pascendi Gregis*, Denzinger, *The Sources of Catholic Dogma*, 2074). It presents itself as a common denominator between the revealed Faith and human false religions which are concocted by human minds.

II. THE THEOLOGY OF REDEMPTION
OF CARDINAL WOJTYLA

Teaching of the Council on Redemption and the Interpretation of the Cardinal

From the Pastoral Constitution, *Gaudium et Spes*, of Vatican II, Cardinal Wojtyla chooses a key text on Christ (§10) to base his thesis of universal redemption.

---

[98] *Pope John Paul II's Theological Journey to the Prayer Meeting of Religions in Assisi*, Part I, pp.49-50.

The conciliar text says: "The Church believes that Christ, who died and was risen for the sake of all (II Cor. 5:15), can show man the way and strengthen him through the Spirit in order to be worthy of his destiny:...."

Cardinal Wojtyla says: "Thus the birth of the Church at the time of the messianic and redemptive death of Christ coincided with the birth of 'the new man'—whether or not man was aware of such a rebirth and whether or not he accepted it. At that moment, man's existence acquired a new dimension, very simply expressed by St. Paul as 'in Christ'" (*cf.* Rom. 6:23; 8:39; 12:5; 15:17; 16:7 *et al.*).

"Man exists 'in Christ,' and he had so existed from the beginning in God's eternal plan; but it is by virtue of Christ's death and resurrection that this 'existence in Christ' became historical fact, with roots in time and space" (p.91*ff.*).[99]

Fr. Dörmann comments: "Everything speaks in favor of the fact that the Cardinal teaches the objective and subjective universality of Redemption."[100] Does the Cardinal formulate a thesis of the objective and subjective universality of redemption?...that is, by the Cross of Christ all men are not only objectively redeemed[101] but also subjectively justified.[102]

The answer to this question is found in the following passage from Cardinal Woytyla's retreat to Pope Paul VI in which he dealt with the realization of the divine plan of salvation in history:

"This is the point of history when all men are, so to speak, 'conceived' afresh and follow a new course within God's plan–the plan prepared by the Father in the truth of the Word and in the gift of Love. It is the point at which the history of mankind makes a fresh start, no longer dependent on human conditioning–if one may put it like that. This fresh starting point belongs in the divine order of things, in the divine perspective on man and the world. The finite, human categories of time and space are almost completely secondary. All men, from the beginning of the world until its end, have been redeemed and justified (*giustificati*) by Christ and His cross."[103]

In the above passages, and in the talks on the meeting at Assisi, there is a confusion between the goal to which every man is called, and the actual realization of this goal. Our Lord taught this difference very clearly: "Many are called, but few are chosen" (Mt. 22:14). At the beginning of his Gospel, St. John makes a clear

---

[99] *Ibid.*, p.60.

[100] *Ibid.*, p.63.

[101] *Objectively,* the sins of men are sufficiently paid for. Our Lord paid sufficiently for everyone.

[102] *Subjectively,* the sins of men are cleansed by the infusion of grace, but not everyone accepts the grace of Our Lord so they remain uncleansed.

[103] *Ibid.*, p.64-65.

distinction between souls which receive Christ and those which don't. "He came unto His own, and His own received Him not. But as many as received Him, He gave them power to be made the sons of God, to them that believe in His name" (Jn. 1:11,12). One becomes a child of God by the grace of Christ. The human nature common to men is absolutely unable to give us such a dignity.

SEPTEMBER 3, 1977

REAL AND APPARENT DISOBEDIENCE

Sermon delivered by Archbishop Lefebvre at Poitiers, France on the occasion of the first Mass of a newly ordained priest.[104]

Dear Father,

You have the joy today of celebrating Holy Mass in the midst of your dear ones, surrounded by your family, by your friends, and it is with great satisfaction that I find myself near to you today to tell you also of my joy and prayers for your future apostolate, for the good which you will do for souls.

We will pray especially to St. Pius X, our patron, whose feast it is today and who has been present during all your studies and your formation. We will ask him to give you the heart of an apostle, the heart of a saintly priest like him. And since we are right here in the city of St. Hilary, of St. Radegonde and the great Cardinal Pie, we shall ask of all those protectors of the city of Poitiers to come and aid you so that you may follow their example, so that you may defend, as they did in difficult times, the Catholic Faith.

You could have coveted an easy and comfortable life in the world. You had already begun the study of medicine. You could have gone in that direction. But no, you had the courage, even in times like these, to come and ask to be made a priest at Ecône. And why Ecône? Because there you found Tradition; you found that which corresponded to your faith. It was an act of courage that does you honor.

And that is why I would like, in a few words, to answer the accusations which have appeared in the local papers following the publication of the letter of Msgr. Rozier, Bishop of Poitiers. Oh, not in order to polemicize. I carefully avoid doing that. Generally, I do not answer these letters and I prefer to keep silent. However, since you as well as I are called into question it seems to me well to justify you here. We are not called into question because of our persons, but because of the choice we have made. We are incriminated because we have chosen the so-called way of disobedience. But we must understand clearly what this way of disobedience consists of.

---

[104] Printed in *The Angelus*, July 1979, pp.2-4 (available from Angelus Press).

I think we may truthfully say that if we have chosen the way of apparent disobedience, we have chosen the way of true obedience.

Then I think that those who accuse us have perhaps chosen the way of apparent obedience which, in reality, is disobedience, because those who follow the new way, who follow the novelties, who attach themselves to new principles contrary to those taught us by Tradition, by all the popes, by all the Councils—they are the ones who have chosen the way of disobedience.

One cannot say that one obeys authority today while disobeying all Tradition. Following Tradition is precisely the sign of our obedience. *Jesus Christus heri, hodie et in sæcula*—Jesus Christ yesterday, today and forever.[105]

One cannot separate Our Lord Jesus Christ. One cannot say that one obeys the Church of today but not the Christ of yesterday because then one does not obey the Christ of tomorrow. This is of vital importance. This is why we cannot say that we disobey the pope of today and that, for that reason, we cannot disobey the pope of yesterday. We obey the pope of yesterday, consequently, we obey the one of today; consequently, we obey the one of tomorrow. For it is not possible that the popes teach different things; it is not possible that the popes gainsay each other, that they contradict each other.

And this is why we are convinced that in being faithful to all the popes of yesterday, to all the Councils of yesterday, we are faithful to the pope of today, to the Council of today and to the Council of tomorrow. Again: *"Jesus Christus heri, hodie et in sæcula:"* and if today, by a mystery of Providence, a mystery which for us is unfathomable, incomprehensible, we are in apparent disobedience, in reality we are not disobedient but obedient.

How are we obedient? In believing in our catechism and because we always keep the same *Credo*, the same Ten Commandments, the same Mass, the same Sacraments, the same prayer—the *Pater Noster* of yesterday, today and tomorrow. This is why we are obedient and not disobedient.

On the other hand, if we study what is taught nowadays in the new religion we realize that it is not the same Faith, the same *Creed*, the same Ten Commandments, the same Sacraments, the same *Our Father*. It is sufficient to open the catechisms of today to realize that. It is sufficient to read the speeches which are made in our times to realize that those who accuse us of disobedience are those who do not follow the Popes, who do not follow the Councils, who, in reality, disobey. They do not have the right to change our *Creed*, to say today that the angels do not exist, to change the

---

[105] Heb. 13:8.

notion of original sin, to say that the Holy Virgin was not always a Virgin, and so on.

They do not have the right to replace the Ten Commandments with the Rights of Man. Nowadays one speaks of nothing but the rights of man and no one speaks of his duties, which are in the Ten Commandments. We don't see that it is necessary to replace the Ten Commandments in our catechisms with the Rights of Man. And this is very grave. The Commandments of God are attacked and thus those laws defending the family disappear.

The most Holy Mass, for example, which is the synthesis of our Faith, which is precisely our living catechism, the Holy Mass has been deprived of its nature, it has become confused and ambiguous. Protestants can say it, Catholics can say it. Concerning this I have never said, and I have never followed those who say, that all the New Masses are invalid. I have never said anything of the sort but I believe that it is in fact very dangerous to make a habit of attending the New Mass because it no longer is representative of our Faith, because Protestant notions have been incorporated into the New Mass.

All the Sacraments have, to some extent, been deprived of their nature and have become similar to an invitation to a religious assembly. These are not Sacraments. The Sacraments give us grace and take away our sins. They give us divine and supernatural life. We are not simply part of a purely natural, purely human, religious collectivity.

This is why we keep to the Holy Mass. We keep to it also because it is the living catechism. It is not just lifeless words written and printed on pages which can disappear. Rather, it is our living catechism, our living *Credo.* This *Credo* is essentially this history, as it were, the "song" of the redemption of our souls by Our Lord Jesus Christ. We sing the praises of God, Our Lord, Our Redeemer, Our Savior who became man to shed His Blood for us and thus to give birth to His Church and the priesthood so that the Redemption might continue, so that our souls might be bathed in the Blood of Jesus Christ through Baptism, through all the Sacraments, in order that we might participate in the nature of Our Lord Jesus Christ Himself, in His divine nature by means of His human nature and so that we might be admitted eternally into the family of the Most Holy Trinity.

This is our Christian life. This is our Faith. If the Mass is not the continuation of the Cross of Our Lord, the sign of His Redemption, is no longer the reality of His Redemption, then it is not our *Credo.* If the Mass is nothing but a meal, a eucharist, a "sharing," if one can sit around a table and simply pronounce the words of the Consecration in the midst of a meal, it is no longer our Sacrifice of the Mass. And if it is no longer the

Holy Sacrifice of the Mass, the Redemption of Our Lord Jesus Christ is no longer accomplished.

We need the Redemption of Our Lord. We need the Blood of Our Lord. We cannot live without the Blood of Our Lord Jesus Christ. He came on earth to give us His Blood, to communicate to us His life. We have been created for this and it is the Holy Mass that gives His Blood to us. This sacrifice continues in all reality. Our Lord is really present in His Body, in His Soul, and in His Divinity.

That is why He created the priesthood and this is why there must be new priests. This is why we wish to make priests who can continue the Redemption of Our Lord Jesus Christ. All the greatness, the sublimity of the priesthood, the beauty of the priesthood, is the celebration of the Holy Mass, in the saving words of the Consecration. It is in the making Our Lord Jesus Christ descend upon the altar, continuing the Sacrifice of the Cross, shedding His Blood on souls through Baptism, the Eucharist, the Sacrament of Penance. Oh, the beauty, the greatness of the priesthood! A greatness of which we are not worthy, of which no man is worthy. Our Lord Jesus Christ wanted it. What greatness, what sublimity!

And our young priests have understood this. You can be certain they have understood. Throughout their seminary days they loved the Holy Mass. They will never penetrate the mystery perfectly even if God gives them a long life on earth. But they love their Mass and I think they have understood and will understand even better that the Mass is the sun of their life, the *raison d'être* of their priestly life so that they may give Our Lord Jesus Christ to the souls of the people and not simply so that they may break bread in friendship while Our Lord is absent. Because grace is absent from these new Masses which are purely a eucharist, a mere symbol of a sign and a symbol of a sort of charity among human beings.

This is why we are attached to the Holy Mass. And the Holy Mass is the expression of the Ten Commandments. And what are the Ten Commandments if not the way of love of God and of our neighbor? How better is this love fulfilled than in the Holy Sacrifice of the Mass? God receives all the glory through Our Lord Jesus Christ and His Sacrifice. There can be no greater act of charity for man than this Sacrifice. And, is there any act of charity greater than that of giving one's life for those whom one loves? Our Lord Himself asked that.

Consequently the Ten Commandments are fulfilled in the Mass, the greatest act of love which God could have from man, the greatest act of love that we could have from God. Here are the Ten Commandments. Here is our living catechism. All the Sacraments take their radiance from the Eucharist. All the Sacraments, in a certain sense, are like satellites of the Sacrament of the Eucharist. From Baptism right through to Extreme

Unction, the Sacraments are only reflections of the Eucharist since all grace comes from Jesus Christ, present in the Holy Eucharist.

Now sacrament and sacrifice are intimately united in the Mass. One cannot separate sacrifice from sacrament. The Catechism of the Council of Trent explains this magnificently. There are two great realities in the Sacrifice of the Mass: the sacrifice and the sacrament deriving from the sacrifice, the fruit of the sacrifice. This is our holy religion and this is why we hold to the Mass. You will understand now, perhaps better than you understood before, why we defend this Mass and the reality of the Sacrifice. It is the life of the Church and the reason for the Incarnation of Our Lord Jesus Christ. And it is the union with Our Lord in the Mass. Therefore, we cry out if they try to take away the nature of the Mass, to deprive us in any way of this Sacrifice! We are wounded. We will not have them separate us from the Holy Sacrifice of the Mass.

This is why we hold firmly to the Sacrifice of the Mass. And we are convinced that our Holy Father, the pope, has not forbidden it and that no one can ever forbid the celebration of the Mass of All Time. Moreover, Pope St. Pius V proclaimed in a solemn and definitive manner that, whatever might happen in the future, no one might ever prevent a priest from celebrating the Sacrifice of the Mass; and that all excommunications, all suspensions, all the punishments which a priest might undergo because he celebrated this Mass would be utterly null and void, *in futuro, in perpetuum*—in the future and forever.

Consequently, we have a clear conscience whatever may happen to us. If we are apparently disobedient, we are really obedient. This is our situation. And it is right for us to tell this, to explain it, because it is we who continue the Church. Really disobedient are those who corrupt the Sacrifice of the Mass, the Sacraments and our prayers, those who put the Rights of Man in the place of the Ten Commandments, those who transform our *Credo.* Because that is what the new catechisms do.

We feel deep pain at not being in perfect communion with the authors of those reforms. Indeed, we regret it infinitely. I would like to go at this very minute to Msgr. Rozier and tell him that I am in perfect communion with him, but it is impossible for me. If Msgr. Rozier condemns this Mass which we say, it is impossible. Those who refuse this Mass are no longer in communion with the Church of All Time.

It is inconceivable that bishops and priests, ordained for this Mass and by this Mass, men who have celebrated it for perhaps 20 or 30 years of their priestly lives, persecute it with an implacable hatred—that they hound us from the churches, that they oblige us to say Mass here, in the open air, when the Mass is meant to be said in the churches constructed for that purpose. And was it not Msgr. Rozier himself who told one of you that if we were heretics and schismatics he would give us churches in which to celebrate our Masses? This is something beyond belief. If we were no longer in communion with the Church but heretics or schismatics we could have the churches. It is quite evident that we are still in communion with the Church. There is a contradiction in their attitude which condemns them. They know perfectly well that we are in the right because we cannot be outside of truth when we simply continue to do what has been done for 2,000 years, believing what has been believed for 2,000 years. This is not possible.

Once again, we must repeat this sentence and continue to repeat it: *Jesus Christus heri, hodie et in sæcula.* If I am with the Jesus Christ of yesterday. I am with the Jesus Christ of today and of tomorrow. I cannot be with the Jesus Christ of yesterday without being with the Jesus Christ of tomorrow. And that is because our Faith is that of the past and that of the future. If we are not with the Faith of the past, we are not with the Faith of the present, nor yet of the future. This is what we must always believe. This is what we must hold to at any price—our salvation depends upon it. Let us ask this today of the guardian saints of Poitiers, ask it especially for these dear priests, for this new priest. Let us ask it of St. Hilary, of St. Radegonde who so loved the Cross—it was she who brought to this land of France the first relic of the True Cross and so loved the Sacrifice of the Mass; and finally, of Cardinal Pie, who was an admirable defender of the Catholic Faith during the last century. Let us ask these protectors of Poitiers to give us the grace of fighting without hatred, without rancor.

Let us never be among those who try to polemicise, to disrupt, to be unjust to their neighbors. Let us love them with all our hearts but let us hold to the Faith. At all costs let us keep our faith in the divinity of Our Lord Jesus Christ.

Let us ask this of the most Holy Virgin Mary. She can only have had a perfect faith in the divinity of her Divine Son. She was present at the Holy Sacrifice of the Cross. Let us ask of Him the faith that she had.

JANUARY 25, 1983

THE *1983 CODE OF CANON LAW*

Canon 844 (on Eucharistic Hospitality)[106]

This canon is the most scandalous of the whole *1983 Code of Canon Law*. It is the open door to active *communicatio in sacris*, *i.e.,* active religious participation with non-Catholics. Canon 1258 of the *1917 Code of Canon Law* very strictly prohibited such participation. Rev. Fr. Dominicus M. Prümmer, O.P., a Swiss professor at the University of Fribourg, gives the very simple reason: "It is indeed nothing else than the negation of the Catholic Faith and the acknowledgment of a heterodox worship." Participation in the Sacraments is the most important part of the worship, especially for Holy Communion. Now Christ has founded and espoused only one Church, and only the voice of the Bride is agreeable to the Bridegroom. Only the voice of the Son is agreeable to the Father. The active participation in non-Catholic worship is the practical denial of the nature of the Church.

§1 Catholic ministers may lawfully administer the sacraments only to Catholic members of Christ's faithful, who equally may lawfully receive them only from Catholic ministers, except as provided in §§2, 3, and 4 of this canon and in Canon 861, §2.

§2 Whenever necessity requires or a genuine spiritual advantage commends it, and provided the danger of error or indifferentism is avoided, Christ's faithful for whom it is physically or morally impossible to approach a Catholic minister, may lawfully receive the Sacraments of Penance, the Eucharist and Anointing of the Sick from non-catholic ministers in whose churches these Sacraments are valid.

§3 Catholic ministers may lawfully administer the Sacraments of Penance, the Eucharist and Anointing of the Sick to members of the eastern churches not in full communion with the Catholic Church, if they spontaneously ask for them and are properly disposed. The same applies to members of other churches which the Apostolic See judges to be in the

---

[106] *The Code of Canon Law* (London: Collins Liturgical Publishers, 1983) pp.156-157.

same position as the aforesaid eastern churches so far as the Sacraments are concerned.

§4 If there is a danger of death or if, in the judgment of the diocesan bishop or of the episcopal conference, there is some other grave and pressing need, Catholic ministers may lawfully administer these same Sacraments to other Christians not in full communion with the Catholic Church, who cannot approach a minister of their own community and who spontaneously ask for them, provided that they demonstrate the Catholic Faith in respect of these Sacraments and are properly disposed.

§5 In respect of the cases dealt with in §§2, 3 and 4, the diocesan bishop or the episcopal conference is not to issue general norms except after consultation with the competent authority, at least at the local level, of the non-Catholic church or community concerned.

The only sacraments which the Church allows to be given by non-Catholic ministers are those which are absolutely required for salvation, that is, Baptism and Penance. In danger of death and in the absence of a Catholic capable of baptizing, one should ask for this Sacrament even from a non-Catholic. In danger of death, a Catholic who has fallen into mortal sin after his Baptism, in the absence of a Catholic priest, should ask even a non-Catholic priest for the sacrament of Penance.

For the sacraments not necessary for salvation, the Church never allowed the faithful to go to a non-Catholic minister.

This is particularly required for the sacrament of Holy Eucharist, which is the Sacrament of the unity of the Church. To participate in this Holy Sacrament with someone who does not belong to this unity is to introduce "a lie" in the sacrament, depriving it of its signification. One wonders what "genuine spiritual advantage" can be obtained at such a price! Everyone can see on the contrary the havoc wrought by these so-called "inter-celebrations."

A Catholic priest cannot give the Sacraments to a non-Catholic, for he is outside the unity of the Church, with the sole exception of the Sacraments of Penance or Baptism, given precisely that he might become a Catholic.

The condition put here: "provided that they demonstrate the Catholic Faith in respect of these Sacraments and are properly disposed," does not render this Canon acceptable. Indeed, either one requires in them the real Catholic Faith, therefore the repudiation of their errors and their return to the Unity of the Church, and thus there is no more need of such a Canon, or one requires only that they agree with the Catholic Church on the one particular point of Faith in question. But this latter alternative is insufficient, since the Faith is not divisible, it is one theological virtue. One cannot accept it on one point and reject it on another point.

AUGUST 15, 1984

EXCERPTS FROM *THE RATZINGER REPORT*

In 1984, Joseph Cardinal Ratzinger, Prefect of the Sacred Congregation for the Doctrine of the Faith, granted an interview to journalist Vittorio Messori on the state of the Catholic Church. The interview was published in English in 1985 as *The Ratzinger Report*. In it, Cardinal Ratzinger forcefully reaffirms his opinion of the immense and positive work of Vatican II, whose genuine fruits he provides a guideline for achieving. He speaks specifically of Archbishop Lefebvre. The following excerpt is taken from Chapter Two, "A Council to Be Rediscovered."[107]

Two Counterposed Errors

In order to get to the heart of the matter we must, almost of necessity, begin with the extraordinary event of Vatican Council II, the 20th anniversary of whose close will be celebrated in 1985. Twenty years which by far have brought about more changes in the Catholic Church than were wrought over the span of two centuries.

Today no one who is and wishes to remain Catholic nourishes any doubts—nor can he nourish them—that the great documents of Vatican Council II are important, rich, opportune and indispensable. Least of all, naturally, the Prefect of the Congregation for the Doctrine of the Faith. To remind him of this would not only be superfluous but ridiculous. Oddly enough, nevertheless, some commentators have obviously considered it necessary to advance doubts on this matter.

Yet, not only were the statements in which Cardinal Ratzinger defended Vatican II and its decisions eminently clear, but he repeatedly corroborated them at every opportunity.

Among countless examples, I shall cite an article he wrote in 1975 on the occasion of the tenth anniversary of the close of the Council. I reread the text of that article to him in Brixen, and he confirmed to me that he still wholly recognized himself therein.

Thus ten years before our conversation, he had already written: "Vatican II today stands in a twilight. For a long time it has been regarded by

---

[107] *The Ratzinger Report* (San Francisco: Ignatius Press, 1985), pp.27-33.

the so-called progressive wing as completely surpassed and, consequently, as a thing of the past, no longer relevant to the present. By the opposite side, the 'conservative' wing, it is, conversely, viewed as the cause of the present decadence of the Catholic Church and even judged as an apostasy from Vatican I and from the Council of Trent. Consequently demands have been made for its retraction or for a revision that would be tantamount to a retraction."

Thereupon he continued: "Over against both tendencies, before all else, it must be stated that Vatican II is upheld by the same authority as Vatican I and the Council of Trent, namely, the Pope and the College of Bishops in communion with him, and also with regard to its contents, Vatican II is in the strictest continuity with both previous councils and incorporates their texts word for word in decisive points."

From this Ratzinger drew two conclusions. First: "It is impossible ('for a Catholic') to take a position *for* or *against* Trent or Vatican I. Whoever accepts Vatican II, as it has clearly expressed and understood itself, at the same time accepts the whole binding tradition of the Catholic Church, particularly also the two previous councils. And that also applies to the so-called 'progressivism,' at least in its extreme forms." Second: "It is likewise impossible to decide *in favor* of Trent and Vatican I, but *against* Vatican II. Whoever denies Vatican II denies the authority that upholds the other two councils and thereby detaches them from their foundation. And this applies to the so-called 'traditionalism,' also in its extreme forms." "Every partisan choice destroys the whole (the very history of the Church) which can exist only as an indivisible unity."

Let Us Rediscover the True Vatican II

Hence it is not Vatican II and its documents (it is hardly necessary to recall this) that are problematic. At all events, many see the problem—and Joseph Ratzinger is among them, and not just since yesterday—to lie in the manifold interpretations of those documents which have led to many abuses in the post-conciliar period.

Ratzinger's judgment on this period has been clearly formulated for a long time: "It is incontestable that the last ten years have been decidedly unfavorable for the Catholic Church." "Developments since the Council seem to be in striking contrast to the expectations of all, beginning with those of John XXIII and Paul VI. Christians are once again a minority, more than they have ever been since the end of antiquity."

He explains his stark remark (which he also repeated during the interview—but that should not cause any surprise, whatever judgment we might make of it, for he confirmed it many times) as follows: "What the Popes and the Council Fathers were expecting was a new Catholic unity, and instead one has encountered a dissension which—to use the words of Paul VI—seems to have passed over from self-criticism to self-destruction. There had been the expectation of a new enthusiasm, and instead too often it has ended in boredom and discouragement. There had been the expectation of a step forward, and instead one found oneself facing a progressive process of decadence that to a large measure has been unfolding under the sign of a summons to a presumed 'spirit of the Council' and by so doing has actually and increasingly discredited it."

Thus, already ten years ago, he had arrived at the following conclusion: "It must be clearly stated that a real reform of the Church presupposes an unequivocal turning away from the erroneous paths whose catastrophic consequences are already incontestable."

On one occasion he also wrote: "Cardinal Julius Döpfner once remarked that the Church of the post-conciliar period is a huge construction site. But a critical spirit later added that it was a construction site where the blueprint had been lost and everyone continues to build according to his taste. The result is evident."

Nevertheless, the Cardinal constantly takes pains to repeat, with equal clarity, that "Vatican II in its official promulgations, in its authentic documents, cannot be held responsible for this development which, on the contrary, radically contradicts both the letter and the spirit of the Council Fathers."

He says: "I am convinced that the damage that we have incurred in these twenty years is due, not to the 'true' Council, but to the unleashing *within* the Church of latent polemical and centrifugal forces; and *outside* the Church it is due to the confrontation with a cultural revolution in the West: the success of the upper middle class, the new tertiary bourgeoisie,' with its liberal-radical ideology of individualistic, rationalistic and hedonistic stamp."

Hence his message, his exhortation to all Catholics who wish to remain such, is certainly not to *"turn back"* but, rather, "to *return to the authentic texts of the original Vatican II."*

For him, he repeats to me, "to defend the true tradition of the Church today means to defend the Council. It is also our fault if we have at times provided a pretext (to the 'right' and 'left' alike) to view Vatican II as a 'break' and an abandonment of the tradition. There is, instead, a continuity that allows neither a return to the past nor a flight forward, neither anachronistic longings nor unjustified impatience. We must remain faithful to the *today* of the Church, not the *yesterday* or *tomorrow.* And this today of the Church is the documents of Vatican II, without *reservations* that amputate them and without *arbitrariness* that distorts them."

A Prescription Against Anachronism

Although critical of the "left," Ratzinger also exhibits an unmistakable severity toward the "right," toward that integralist traditionalism quintessentially symbolized by the old Archbishop Marcel Lefebvre. In a reference to it, he told me: "I see no future for a position that, out of principle, stubbornly renounces Vatican II. In fact in itself it is an illogical position. The point of departure for this tendency is, in fact, the strictest fidelity to the teaching particularly of Pius IX and Pius X and, still more fundamentally, of Vatican I and its definition of papal primacy. But why only the popes up to Pius XII and not beyond? Is perhaps obedience to the Holy See divisible according to years or according to the nearness of a teaching to one's own already-established convictions?"

The fact remains, I observe, that if Rome has intervened with respect to the "left," it has not yet intervened with respect to the "right" with the same vigor.

In reply, he states: "The followers of Archbishop Lefebvre assert the very opposite. They contend that whereas there was an immediate intervention in the case of the respected retired Archbishop with the harsh punishment of suspension, there is an incomprehensible toleration of every kind of deviation from the other side. I don't wish to get involved in a polemic on the greater or lesser severity toward the one or the other side. Besides, both types of opposition present entirely different features. The deviation toward the 'left' no doubt represents a broad current of the contemporary thought and action of the Church, but hardly anywhere have they found a juridically definable common form. On the other hand, Archbishop Lefebvre's movement is probably much less broad numerically, but it has a well-defined juridical organization, seminaries, religious houses, *etc.* Clearly everything possible must be done to prevent this movement from giving rise to a schism peculiar to it that would come into being whenever Archbishop Lefebvre should decide to consecrate a bishop, which, thank God, in the hope of a reconciliation he has not yet done. In the ecumenical sphere today one deplores that not enough was done in the past to prevent incipient divisions through a greater openness to reconciliation and to an understanding of the different groups. Well, that should apply as a behavioral maxim for us too in the present time. We must commit ourselves to reconciliation, so long and so far as it is possible, and we must utilize all the opportunities granted to us for this purpose."

But Lefebvre, I object, has ordained priests and continues to do so.

"Canon law speaks of ordinations that are illicit but not invalid. We must also consider the human aspect of these young men who, in the eyes of the Church, are 'true' priests, albeit in an irregular situation. The point of departure and the orientation of individuals are certainly different.

Some are strongly influenced by their family situations and have accepted the latter's decision. In others, disillusionment with the present-day Church has driven them to bitterness and to negation. Others still would like to collaborate fully in the normal pastoral activity of the Church. Nevertheless they have let themselves be driven to their choice by the unsatisfactory situation that has arisen in the seminaries in some countries. So just as there are some who in some way have put up with the division, there are also many who hope for reconciliation and remain in Archbishop Lefebvre's priestly community only in this hope."

His prescription for cutting the ground from under the Lefebvre case and other anachronistic resistances seems to re-echo that of the last popes, from Paul VI to today: "Similar absurd situations have been able to endure up to now precisely by nourishing themselves on the arbitrariness and thoughtlessness of many post-conciliar interpretations. This places a further obligation upon us to show the true face of the Council: thus one will be able to cut the ground from under these false protests...."

In these passages Cardinal Ratzinger stresses his view of the importance of the Council, stating that it is upheld by the same authority as Vatican Council I and the Council of Trent. This is a false premise. The Cardinal fails to distinguish between persons and their actions. The persons possess the same authority, but they do not always engage their full authority in every one of their actions. By refusing to be a dogmatic council, the Fathers of the Second Vatican Council did not invest this Council with the same authority as all the previous ecumenical Councils.

It is highly doubtful that Cardinal Ratzinger sees those who uphold Tradition to be on "the erroneous path whose catastrophic consequences are already incontestable." He blames havoc of this kind only on the so-called false interpretation of the Council. However, he is not able to show where the Council has been properly implemented. Can he cite one diocese in which a proper implementation has brought about good fruits?

Cardinal Ratzinger insinuates that Archbishop Lefebvre is dividing obedience to the Holy See "according to the nearness of the teaching to one's own already established convictions." The convictions of Archbishop Lefebvre are not his own. He recalls that he had to change some of his conceptions when he arrived at the Seminary in Rome, realizing that they were not in conformity with the teachings of the Popes. From that day on he has remained attached to these convictions which the constant teachings of the Pope had built in his soul.

The problem springs forth from the desire of the present authorities to give a place in the Church to values which are foreign to her. Cardinal Ratzinger admits:

"Vatican II was right in its desire for a revision of the relations between the Church and the world. There are in fact values, which, even though they originated outside the Church, can find their place–provided that they are clarified and corrected–in her perspective. This task has been accomplished in these years. But whoever thinks that these two realities can meet each other without conflict or even be identical would betray that he understands neither the Church nor the world."[108]

To try to clarify and correct the false principles of the French Revolution is to try to convert the devil!

The fact that this new doctrine is incompatible with the past is manifested by the Cardinal himself when he refuses any return to the past, opposing it to the present. "We must remain faithful to the today of the Church, not to the yesterday or tomorrow. *And this today of the Church is the documents of Vatican II*, without <u>reservations</u> that amputate them and without <u>arbitrariness</u> that distorts them."[109]

There should be no opposition between the today of the Church, its past or its future: "Jesus Christ yesterday, today and the same forever" (Heb. 13:8). This opposition which, according to Ratzinger, is in the documents of Vatican II, is, in itself, the strongest condemnation of these documents.

---

[108] *The Ratzinger Report*, p.36.
[109] *ibid.*, p.31.

FOUR NON-CATHOLIC
"EPISCOPAL CONSECRATIONS"

It is permissible to have heretic Lutheran or Methodist "episcopal consecrations" in Catholic churches, as these news stories prove, yet the consecration of traditional Catholic bishops are disallowed. In the mentality of the Conciliar Church ecumenism has come to have more value than the continuation of Catholic Tradition.

ST. LOUIS

"Lutherans to Use New Cathedral"
St. Louis Post-Dispatch (May 28, 1987)

In a highly symbolic ecumenical step, Lutherans here will use the Roman Catholic St. Louis Cathedral this fall for a worship service to mark the merger of three Lutheran denominations.

The Rev. Vincent Heier, the Catholic priest in charge of ecumenical relations for the Archdiocese of St. Louis, described the Lutherans' choice of the cathedral, at Lindell Boulevard and Newstead Avenue, as "a watershed" in Catholic-Lutheran relations here.

"This shows how far we have come," Heier said.

The Rev. Samuel Roth, pastor of Zion Lutheran Church in Ferguson and chairman of the event, said the service, scheduled for Nov. 22, will be a major celebration sponsored by 45 Lutheran congregations. Bishop Herbert W. Chilstrom, recently elected head of the new 5.3 million member Lutheran church, will preside over the service...

Many ecumenical leaders here recall when relations between Catholics and Lutherans were strained and on occasion marked by deep hostility. The tensions date as far back as the 16th century Reformation in Europe, but they have gradually diminished since the mid-1960's after the Second Vatican Council in the Roman Catholic Church.

Lutherans trace their roots to Martin Luther, a Catholic monk whose conflicts with Church leaders led to his excommunication from the Catholic Church and the birth of Protestantism. Historic barriers between Catholics and Lutherans began to erode with the Second Vatican Council's exhortations to Catholics to work for Christian unity.

Roth said he hopes the service will be "quite spectacular. We think it speaks volumes that we're holding the service at the cathedral and that they have been open to our being there."

The Rev. Martin Rafanan, pastor of Resurrection Lutheran Church, said the symbolism of the event extends beyond Lutheran-Catholic relations.

"We are doing the service at the cathedral as a sign that our new church is going to be more open to a variety of ecumenical endeavors in the future," he said.

The Rev. Robert Betram, a participant in recent dialogues between Lutherans and Catholics in the United States, said the choice of the cathedral is "doubly significant" because the service is to be a Eucharist.

"For Lutherans to conduct a service in a sanctuary consecrated for eucharistic services of the Roman Catholic communion, that can't help but mean a lot to Lutherans and Catholics alike."

Bertram, of University City, is a professor at the Lutheran School of Theology in Chicago.

Ecumenical leaders, including Roman Catholic Archbishop John L. May, will be invited to participate.

Heier said the cathedral has been used by the United Church of Christ for a prayer service about 15 years ago. But that was not a communion service, he said.

"Lutherans in Our Cathedral"
by Archbishop May
St. Louis Review (June 12, 1987)

It was my intention to announce to you that the new Evangelical Lutheran Church in America would celebrate its birth in their first solemn liturgy in our Cathedral, but another local paper beat me to it. It will not occur until Nov. 22, so I was a bit surprised to have them break the news. Perhaps some background will help.

In January of 1988 one church body to be known as the Evangelical Lutheran Church in America will come into being officially. It is being created from three church bodies which were formerly independent. They were the Association of Evangelical Lutheran Churches, the American Lutheran Church and the Lutheran Church in America. There are 47 congregations in the St. Louis area who will be part of this one new church body. We thank God for this step toward the day when we will be "one body, one spirit in Christ." We pray, too, that this one step will be one of many prompted by the Holy Spirit so that the prayer of Jesus at the Last Supper will be realized: "That all may be one."

When representatives of those who are involved in this church reconciliation began to meet to plan their celebration of their new unity in Christ, they wrote to me asking if it might be possible for them to gather in our Cathedral for this occasion. Among other reasons that they cited for their request one stands out. The Evangelical Lutheran Church in America is committed to seeking further unity with all brothers and sisters in Christ. Furthermore, they were seeking an appropriate setting with adequate seating capacity. They hoped to avoid a convention hall or sports arena.

We have agreed to extend the hospitality of our Cathedral to the congregations of the Evangelical Lutheran Church in America in the St. Louis area for their celebration of unity and thanksgiving on the Feast of Christ the King, Sunday, Nov. 22, 1987. The newly elected Bishop of their church will preside at their eucharistic celebration and preach on that occasion. I plan to be present as a gesture of good will to give a word of welcome and congratulations.

In coming to this decision I was mindful of the commitment to Christian ecumenism in the teaching of Vatican Council II. More recently the example of our Holy Father was persuasive—especially in his approaches to Lutherans in his sermon in their church in Rome and during his two visits to Germany. In our country very fruitful Catholic-Lutheran theological dialogues have been going on over recent years thanks to our bishops' conference. The new emphasis on Eucharist in Lutheran worship has been noted in this dialogue and it is something we greet with joy.

This is not the first time for a gathering like this in our Cathedral. The United Church of Christ gathered in our Cathedral some years ago for a worship service. More recently the Methodist Church in Washington, D.C. gathered in the National Shrine of the Immaculate Conception there for a Eucharistic Celebration and the ordination of deacons for service in their church. Years ago in Springfield, IL, Bishop McNicholas hosted the installation liturgy of the new Episcopal bishop in Immaculate Conception Cathedral there. So this is really nothing so new or controversial.

Someone has said that this is a nice gesture, but 400 years too late. We may be latecomers in ecumenism but I hope we can make up for lost time.

NEW ORLEANS

"Methodists Make History at St. Louis Cathedral"
The Times Picayune (July 16, 1988)

For the first time in the long history of the St. Louis Cathedral—the most notable Catholic landmark in New Orleans—three Protestant ministers knelt at the altar Friday and were consecrated as bishops of the United Methodist Church.

As the cathedral's bells tolled at 10am and the Munholland United Methodist Church Choir of Metairie sang, a procession of twenty United Methodist bishops marched down the main aisle to the altar for the ecumenical ceremony.

The cathedral was packed, with some people standing in the back of the church.

Archbishop Philip M. Hannan and the cathedral pastor, the Rev. Gerard Barrett marched in the procession and took seats on the altar among the bishops, but didn't participate in the service. The Revs. William B. Oden of Enid, OK; Bruce P. Blake of Winfield, KS; and Dan E. Solomon of Corpus Christi, TX, knelt at the altar to be made bishops. Each of the participating bishops, about half of whom are retired, laid their hands on the heads of each for the consecration blessing.

"This is a historic event," said Mildred Koschel, a member of the Lake Vista United Methodist Church. "I wouldn't have missed it for the world..."

In 1985, the late Bishop Walter L. Underwood, the United Methodist Bishop for Louisiana, asked Hannan for permission for the next consecration of United Methodist bishops to take place at the cathedral. Underwood wanted an ecumenical service at the cathedral because of its beauty and history, said Marian Eggerton, a local United Methodist official.

Hannan happily accommodated the request, but Underwood died in April 1987.

"I know that Walter Underwood is smiling on us today," said Bishop Benjamin Oliphint of Houston, interim bishop of Louisiana since Underwood's death.

The consecration service was the climax of a conference of the United Methodists of the South Central Jurisdiction that opened Tuesday at the Marriott Hotel. Many of the people who packed the cathedral were delegates to the conference.

TWO CONSECRATIONS IN PHILADELPHIA
The Catholic Standard and Journal
(Sept. 29, 1988)

Archbishop Bevilacqua who will be in Rome at the time of Bishop Turner's consecration will appoint someone to give an official greeting on behalf of the Archdiocese of Philadelphia, according to Fr. Diamond.

The Philadelphia Inquirer
(Sept. 8, 1988)

The consecration of Bishop Turner was the second protestant celebration in the Catholic cathedral in recent months. Lawrence L. Hand was inaugurated as the first bishop of the Southeastern Pennsylvania Synod of the Evangelical Lutheran Church in America, at a ceremony in the cathedral in April.

Auxiliary Bishop Martin N. Lohmuller welcomed the Episcopalians to the cathedral on behalf of the Archdiocese of Philadelphia.

He said, Catholics were "complemented" that the Episcopal Diocese had asked to use the cathedral and extended "our congratulations, our very best wishes" to Bishop Turner.

ARCHBISHOP MAY
TO JOIN IN HINDU JUBILEE

That Archbishop May considers that these Hindus with their vague search for God will avoid hell, while they are still ignorant of Our Lord Jesus Christ, the only Savior, is tantamount to a practical denial of the Catholic Faith. "But without faith it is impossible to please God. For he that cometh to God must believe that He is, and is a reminder to them that seek Him" (Heb. 11:6). St. Augustine explains very well that, though ignorance excuses from an additional sin against Faith, it is incapable of cleansing the original sin and other sins with which one's soul is burdened. Baptism of desire only applies to those who, by a special grace of the Holy Ghost, have received the virtues of the Catholic Faith, Hope and Charity. (See St. Thomas Aquinas, *Summa Theologica*, IIIa, Q.66, A.11.) How Archbishop May can apply this doctrine to Hindus "in search of God" is a mystery of iniquity (II Thess. 2:7).

ST. LOUIS
The St. Louis Review (May 13, 1988)

Archbishop John L. May will take part in a golden jubilee celebration of the Vedanta Society of St. Louis on Sunday, May 22, at the Hindu Temple of Universal Philosophy and Religion, 205 S. Skinner Blvd. The program will begin at 8pm.

Archbishop May and Swami Chetanananda will speak on "Our Common Search for God." Fr. Vincent Heier, director for the Archdiocesan Office for Ecumenical and Interreligious affairs, will give the introduction.

Letter of Fr. Vincent Heier to *The Wanderer*[110]

Your *From the Mail* column of the latest issue of *The Wanderer* included erroneous information on Archbishop John May's participation at the Hindu Vedanta Society in St. Louis. To clarify the facts, the Archbishop

---

[110] *The Wanderer*, Sept. 8, 1988, pp.7,8 (published weekly from St. Paul, Minnesota).

was approached, through my office, by Swami Chetanananda to speak at the Vedanta Society on the occasion of their golden jubilee. It was patterned after a similar visit by Cardinal Manning to the Vedanta Society in Los Angeles a few years ago.

After much discussion, we decided to use the theme, "Our Common Search for God." This was to express Vatican II's teachings regarding non-Christian religions as they reflect, even imperfectly, the human longing for God. Certainly this was shown in the Holy Father's meeting on peace with world religious leaders (including the Vedanta Society) in Assisi in October 1986.

Unfortunately, after *The St. Louis Review* publicity, Archbishop May was called to Rome on urgent business and asked Auxiliary Bishop Terry Steib to speak in his place. I was asked to introduce Bishop Steib and then he gave a short talk on the subject mentioned above. The swami then gave a response, and after some music by their choir, including *Ave Maria,* the evening concluded.

The biased tone of your article, and especially the quotation by your unnamed correspondent that, "Archbishop May has not yet found God in the Catholic Church," reflect once again that your paper does not seek to publish the truth but innuendo. A simple phone call to the Archbishop's office, or mine, could have provided you with the facts. While I seldom see any retractions in your "infallible" paper, it would seem that one is called for in this regard

Fr. Vincent A. Heier, Director
Office for Ecumenical and Interreligious Affairs
Archdiocese of St. Louis

Letter of Archbishop May to Mr. Eugene St. Pierre

19 May 1988
Mr. Eugene J. St. Pierre
Depository of Sacred Music
Box 33046
St. Louis, Missouri 63119

Dear Mr. St. Pierre:

In reply to your recent letter I assure you that there is no violation of Canon Law in my attendance at the gold jubilee celebration of the Vedanta Society. Perhaps you have a specific canon in mind and I would appreciate your identifying it for me.

You may be sure that my address at this jubilee will be faithful to Catholic doctrine as taught by the magisterium. There is certainly no teaching of the Catholic Church that says that all the people in the world who are not Roman Catholics are automatically going to hell. You must remember your *Baltimore Catechism* which taught you of baptism by desire. That has always been part of our faith.

I just wonder how much you know about the Vedanta Society and what it teaches. You are wrong in saying that I am breaking one of God's commandments. I recall that our Holy Father joined in a celebration in which he prayed with people from the same Hindu background and with many other representatives of various world religions at the meeting in Assisi last year.

The bad example comes from the top! I know that the followers of the Lefebvre movement, whose bulletin you sent me, also oppose our Holy Father and consider him heretical in the same way.

Thank you for your prayers and I assure you also of mine.

Cordially in Christ,

Most Reverend John L. May
Archbishop of St. Louis

In the words of Archbishop May himself, the *1983 Code of Canon Law* does not forbid such practical denial of the Catholic Faith. The *1917 Code of Canon Law* clearly forbade any active participation in any non-Catholic "celebration" and held those who would participate to be suspect of heresy (Canons 1258, 2316).

In view of the different treatment of Archbishop May and Archbishop Lefebvre, there is only one conclusion: there is a double standard in the Church today!

The column of the same Fr. Vincent Heier in *The St. Louis Post-Dispatch* (July 15, 1988), which follows, manifests clearly that for Archbishop May, ecumenism is more important than upholding Catholic Tradition.

Religious Rifts

In a July 6 article on the Episcopalian compromise on women bishops, Bishop Michael Marshall of the Anglican Institute compared the situation with the recent schism of Archbishop Marcel Lefebvre from the Roman Catholic Church. He asked his fellow bishops, "Do we want to go down the road of Roman Catholicism? That's another way to handle conflict—cast it out of the body!"

How wrong Marshall is! If one read the correspondence between Rome and Lefebvre, one would note that the Vatican went out of its way to prevent a schism by the so-called traditionalists.

In the end, it was Lefebvre and his followers who would not bend. The theological conflict came not over the use of the Latin Tridentine Mass but over the ecumenical openness of Vatican II. Because that ecumenical openness has led to greater unity between Anglican and Roman Catholic Christians, it is unfortunate that a bishop of the Anglican Church could so misrepresent this latest wound within the body of Christ.

The Rev. Vincent A. Heier
Office for Ecumenical and Interreligious Affairs
Archdiocese of St. Louis

JUNE 2, 1988

ROME AND THE "RECONCILIATION"

"Could Rome have not been trusted?...Had not Rome given enough signs of goodwill, and of a sincere desire for reconciliation?" Such are the questions that many asked on the occasion of the episcopal consecrations of June 30, 1988.

It is not for us to judge men's intentions, so rather than question the goodwill of the Roman authorities we prefer to state the facts for which they are responsible.

That is why we are giving here below the extracts from a letter written by a seminarian who left Ecône to join the seminary *Mater Ecclesiæ*, at Rome, an establishment desired by the Holy Father and opened by him on Oct. 15, 1986, and protected by a commission of cardinals. *Mater Ecclesiæ* was designed to be a seminary to receive seminarians who left Ecône and any others with similar feelings.

How sorry I am! Yes! I have everything, absolutely everything to be sorry about in this "enterprise" of *Mater Ecclesiæ*. Firstly, my being sent away for having made insistent requests in favor, for example, of more frequent Tridentine Masses, the wearing of ecclesiastical dress, the correction within the seminary of the errors of the courses being taught us at the Angelicum University...

The reply to these requests, repeated many times, was silence, and above all, the steady and by now complete realigning of the house and of each of the seminarians on Modernist Rome. The whole enterprise is the laughing-stock of the Progressives, with the French bishops at their head, including some of the most traditional!

Day by day, we saw the situation growing worse: the seminarians taking off their habit, seminarians getting themselves accepted by the bishops by renouncing everything, being ready for anything—Then there came the time of sanctions when all those who had been given the task of helping us were ordered by the authorities to look after us no longer— Henceforth for anyone who wanted nothing to do with the bishops of France or anywhere else, there is absolutely no further solution... *Vagus*— Nomad....We are from now on wandering clerics, left hanging in the void.

And the Pope did nothing, and no doubt next year the house *Mater Ecclesiæ* will be closed, which may well be no bad thing.

Several times I had the occasion to say either to Cardinal Ratzinger or to certain monsignori of the Curia that, alas, we were forced to admit that Archbishop Lefebvre was right on most questions and that I was wrong.

It causes me much suffering to write you these lines as I think of my idiocy in having abandoned Ecône despite your advice, the cowardice of the authorities (I am weighing my words) when it comes to Tradition and their similar cowardice when it comes to "ecumenism" towards the others, the abandoning and denial on the part of almost all those who had undertaken never to let go—everything, yes, absolutely everything fills me with regret!

An ex-Seminarian
Rome

JUNE 1988

REPORTS FROM THE MEDIA

During the months of June and July (1988) many newspapers and magazines carried articles on Archbishop Lefebvre. The two which are excerpted here are especially notable.

30 Days (June 1988)

Cardinal Gagnon was interviewed by *30 Days* at the beginning of June. For him, many of the faithful who follow Archbishop Lefebvre were scandalized because:

Cardinal Gagnon: ...[M]any things have been done too fast and without taking time to explain to the people what was happening....I think there was a lack of patience and prudence as a result.

Interviewer: So you think that the implementation of the vernacular Mass was too swift...

Cardinal Gagnon: Oh, yes, sure. It was too swift. When we were in the Seminary, we were taught that changing a word in the Canon of the Mass was a mortal sin. And then, all of a sudden, all that is changed.

Thus, for Cardinal Gagnon, the only problem was the rapidity of the change. He does not see the Protestant spirit which permeates the new liturgy. The purpose of the "reconciliation" in his eyes was to give the time to traditional faithful to make the change at their own pace. This is unacceptable.

America (June 18, 1988)

William D. Dinges, Professor in the Department of Religion at the Catholic University of America in Washington, D.C., acknowledges that the faithful attached to Tradition are not slow-minded faithful, incapable of changing fast enough. He sees the problem at its proper level, the doctrinal level:

"Catholic traditionalism—is not a form of naivete. It does not arise unaware of a new intellectual or theological order; it stands in opposition to it, defending a world view and governing assumptions of religious experience that have lost much of their credibility and legitimacy in the wake of Vatican II. Traditionalism, especially among its intellectual and clerical elite, is a repudiation of the historical consciousness, the "anthropocentric turn" toward the subjective, and other hermeneutical, relativising and praxis tendencies that characterize contemporary consciousness and much modern theology, and that are reflected in one fashion or another in key documents of the Council."

The first characteristic of modern theology is its incomprehensibility! We have here a great concession. Modern theology is characterized by this "anthropocentric turn toward the subjective." What does that mean? It means that everything is centered on man (*anthropos*) rather than God, rather than Jesus Christ. Indeed, we do reject this anthropocentric turn! Modern theology subjectivizes everything. Faith is no longer the adherence to the objective Truths; it is the subjective expression of religious feelings. This is the Modernist faith condemned by St. Pius X. Professor William D. Dinges, who wrote the *America* article, witnesses that these new characteristics of modern theology "are reflected in one fashion or another in key documents of the Council." The Professor continues:

"Traditionalism manifests the classic tendency to absolutise the cognitive aspects of religions and to reify[111] the constituent symbols of religious identity....[It is] a strongly rationalistic (orientation) in which religion is based on a standardized objective knowledge of God...the emphasis on "correct belief" as the primary datum of religion and norm for all other forms of religious self-understanding animates all of Archbishop Lefebvre's writings and public pronouncements and is his real *casus belli*[112] with the Vatican....

"The causes of Catholic traditionalism lie in...the logical development and extension of anti-modernist theological trends; the reaction against new epistemological and hermeneutical frames of reference that decisively penetrated Catholicism—and that were legitimated within Vatican II...in particular, the de-objectification of the liturgy brought about by the reforms following Vatican II, like the de-objectification of Scripture accompanying Protestantism's earlier embrace of historical-critical methods..."

Definitely, modern theology is incomprehensible, but when one begins to understand this jargon one is horrified to find nothing less than the pure Modernism condemned by St. Pius X. The

---

[111] *i.e.,* to consider as real, *e.g.,* to consider God as a real being, not just a symbol.
[112] *i.e.,* the cause of the war.

Professor does not acknowledge any objective Truth, especially in religious matters. Faith is just the expression of a religious feeling, there is no objective "correct belief..." Yes! Archbishop Lefebvre and all true Catholics reject this Modernism "that was legitimated within Vatican II" and this is the real *casus belli* with the Vatican.

JUNE 19, 1988

A STATEMENT BY ARCHBISHOP LEFEBVRE

Archbishop Lefebvre authored this Letter from Ecône, Switzerland, on why there was a cessation of negotiations between Rome and the Society of Saint Pius X after the signing of the Protocol (May 5, 1988).

Indeed, it would be difficult to understand why the talks ceased if they are not placed in their historical context.

Although we never wanted to have a break in relations with Conciliar Rome, even after the first visit of Rome on Nov. 11, 1974, had been followed by measures which were sectarian and null—the suppression of our work on May 6, 1975, and the "suspension" in July, 1976—these relations could only take place in a climate of mistrust.

Louis Veuillot says that there is no one more sectarian than a Liberal; in effect, having made a compromise between error and Revelation, he feels condemned by those who remain in the Truth, and thus if he is in power, he persecutes them fiercely. This is the case with us and all those who are opposed to the liberal texts and liberal reforms of the Council.

They absolutely want us to have a "guilt complex" in relation to them, but it is they who are guilty of duplicity.

Thus it was always in a tense although polite atmosphere that relations took place with Cardinal Seper and Cardinal Ratzinger between 1976 and 1987, but also with a certain hope that as the auto-demolition of the Church accelerated, they would end up taking a benevolent attitude towards us.

Up until that time, the goal of the contacts for Rome was to make us accept the Council and the reforms, and to make us recognize our error. The logic of events had to lead me to ask for a successor, if not two or three, to assure the ordinations and confirmations. Faced with the persistent refusal of Rome, on June 29, 1987, I announced my decision to consecrate bishops.

On July 28, Cardinal Ratzinger opened up some new horizons which legitimately gave us reason to think that finally Rome looked at us more favorably. No longer was there any question of a doctrinal document to be signed, or asking for pardon, but an Apostolic Visitor was finally announced, the Society could be recognized, the Liturgy would be that of before the Council, the seminarians would retain the same spirit!

Thus we agreed to enter into this new dialogue, but on the condition that our identity would be well protected against liberal influences by bishops taken from within Tradition, and by a majority of members in the Roman Commission for Tradition. Now, after the visit of Cardinal Gagnon, of which we still know nothing, the disappointments piled up.

The talks which followed in April and May were a distinct disappointment to us. We were given a doctrinal text, the new Canon Law was added to it, Rome reserved for itself five out of seven members on the Roman Commission, among them a President (who will be Cardinal Ratzinger) and the Vice-President.

The question of a bishop was solved after much hemming and hawing; they insisted on showing us why we did not need one.

The Cardinal informed us that we would now have to allow one New Mass to be celebrated at St. Nicolas du Chardonnet. He insisted on the one and only Church, that of Vatican II.

In spite of these disappointments, I signed the Protocol on May 5th. But already the date of the episcopal consecration caused a problem. Then came the project of a letter asking the Pope for pardon, which was put into my hands.

I saw that I was obliged to write a letter threatening to do the episcopal consecrations to arrive at the date of August 15 for the episcopal consecration.

The atmosphere is no longer one of fraternal collaboration and pure and simple recognition of the Society—not at all. For Rome the goal of the talks is reconciliation, as Cardinal Gagnon says in an interview granted to the Italian journal *L'Avvenire*, meaning the return of the lost sheep to the flock. This is what I express in the letter to the Pope on June 2: "The goal of the talks has not been the same for you as for us."

And when we think of the history of relations of Rome with the traditionalists from 1965 to our own day, we are forced to observe that there has been an unceasing and cruel persecution to force us to submit to the Council. The most recent example is that of the Seminary *Mater Ecclesiæ* for drop-outs from Ecône, who in less than two years, have been made to serve the conciliar revolution, contrary to all promises!

The present conciliar and Modernist Rome can never tolerate the existence of a vigorous branch of the Catholic Church which condemns it by its very vitality.

No doubt we shall have to wait yet another few years, therefore, for Rome to recover her Tradition of two thousand years. As for us, we continue to prove, with the grace of God, that this Tradition is the only source of sanctification and salvation of souls, and the only possibility of renewal for the Church.

† Marcel Lefebvre
June 19, 1988
Ecône

JUNE 1988

CANONICAL CONSIDERATIONS REGARDING EPISCOPAL CONSECRATIONS

These canonical considerations are excerpted by Fr. Patrice Laroche from a study by Dr. Georg May, President of the Seminary of Canon Law at the University of Mainz, entitled *Notwehr, Widerstand, Notsand (Legitimate Defense, Resistance, Necessity)*, drawn up in 1984. These furnish interesting points for reflection regarding the canonical penalties incurred after the episcopal consecration administered in the "case of necessity."

State of Necessity

The *1917 Code of Canon Law* spoke of necessity in Canon 2205, §2 and §3; the *1983 Code of Canon Law* deals with it in Canon 1324, §4 and 1324, §1, 5. The law does not say what is meant by this term, it leaves to jurisprudence and doctors the task of giving it a precise meaning. But it is clear from the context that necessity is a state where goods necessary for life are put in danger in such a way that to come out of this state the violation of certain laws is inevitable.

Law of Necessity

The Code recognizes necessity as a circumstance which exempts from all penalties in case of violation of the law (*1983 Code of Canon Law,* Canon 1324, §4), provided that the action is not intrinsically bad or harmful to souls; in this latter case necessity would only mitigate the penalty. But no *latæ sententiæ* penalty can be incurred by anyone who has acted in this circumstance (*1983 Code of Canon Law,* Canon 1324, §3).

State of Necessity in the Church

In the Church, as in civil society, it is conceivable that there arrive a state of necessity or urgency which cannot be surmounted by the observance of positive law. Such a situation exists in the Church, when the endurance, order or activity of the Church are threatened or harmed in a considerable manner. This threat can bear principally on ecclesiastical teaching, the liturgy and discipline.

Law of Necessity in the Church

A state of necessity justifies the law of necessity. The law of necessity in the Church is the sum total of juridical rules which apply in case of a menace to the perpetuity or activity of the Church.

This law of necessity can be resorted to only when one has exhausted all possibilities of re-establishing a normal situation, relying on positive law. The law of necessity also includes the positive authorization to take measures, launch initiatives, create organisms which are necessary so that the Church can continue its mission of preaching the divine truth and dispensing the grace of God.

The law of necessity uniquely justifies the measures which are necessary for a restoration of functions in the Church. The principle of proportionality is to be observed.

The Church, and in the first place its organs, has the right but also the duty of taking all the measures necessary for the removal of dangers. In a situation of necessity the pastors of the Church can take extraordinary measures to protect or re-establish the activity of the Church. If an organ does not carry out its necessary or indispensable functions, the other organs have the duty and the right to use the power they have in the Church, so that the life of the Church is guaranteed and its end attained. If the authorities of the Church refuse this, the responsibility of other members of the Church increases, but also their juridical competence.

JUNE 30, 1988

PROGRAMS FOR PRIESTLESS SUNDAYS OUTLINED IN VATICAN DOCUMENT

As reported in *The Beacon* (July 7, 1988)

The document upon which this New Jersey (US) newspaper reports was issued on the same day as Archbishop Lefebvre was consecrating bishops at Ecône. While the Vatican was providing for the absence of priests, Archbishop Lefebvre was providing for the continuation of the priesthood.

Bishops with too few priests to celebrate the necessary Sunday Masses should develop programs by which deacons or appointed lay people lead Sunday prayer services, according to a new Vatican document.

The most preferable service is a Liturgy of the Word followed by distribution of Communion with previously consecrated hosts, says the document, prepared by the Vatican Congregation for Divine Worship.

The phenomenon of parishes and church centers without a priest to celebrate Sunday Mass is worldwide and affects mission countries as well as developed countries, said Msgr. Pere Tena, undersecretary of the congregation, at a June 30 Vatican press conference. The document, issued in Italian, was dated June 2.

Msgr. Tena said the directory was prepared at the request of numerous bishops' conferences asking for guidelines in the preparation of their programs.

It codifies programs already in existence in many countries. In the United States the situation is known as "priestless Sundays."

The 18-page directory gives local bishops or bishops' conferences the power to determine whether in their jurisdictions the priest shortage is leaving church communities without Sunday Masses for long periods of time. It is also up to the bishops to determine if the distance to the nearest Sunday Mass is too great for their priestless parishes and church centers.

The local bishop is also authorized to appoint and train lay people as acolytes, readers and special ministers of the Eucharist to aid the deacon or to conduct the service if no deacon is available.

Under the Vatican rules, lay people are not authorized to preach a homily. However, they can read homilies prepared by priests, the directory says.

People attending the service must be made aware that the Mass is still the primary church liturgical ceremony and that they should make every effort to attend Sunday Masses, the directory says.

To avoid confusion between the prayer service and the Mass, "there can be no insertion in the celebration of that which is proper to the Mass, above all the presentation of gifts and of the eucharistic hosts," it says.

The laity must be aware that the hosts distributed were consecrated by a priest during a Mass, it adds.

The Liturgy of the Word should use prayers and Bible readings from the corresponding Sunday Mass, it says. Bishops may substitute other church-approved prayer services such as vespers and have the power to make modifications in prayer services, but this should be kept to a minimum, the directory says.

JULY 3, 1988

EXTRACTS FROM THE LETTER OF MOTHER ANNE MARIE SIMOULIN TO MSGR. JACQUES DESPIERRE, BISHOP OF CARCASSONNE, FRANCE

I thank you for your letter of June 24....On my own, I read it with great attention and read it publicly to all the sisters of our congregation. But one letter, though it purports to be well-meaning, cannot blot out at once 25 years of silence, contempt, and condemnation on the part of our bishops.

We are not leaving the Church, Monseigneur, I mean the Catholic Church founded by Our Lord Jesus Christ; we are just set apart by those who have left it years ago, because they departed from the communion of the Church.

We acknowledge the Pope as legitimate...and we pray daily for him and for our bishops. You ask us "to renew our confidence in him." What confidence can we have in a Pope who:...

6) has dealings with Communist heads of state, and shakes their hands instead of denouncing them, reminding all that "Communism is intrinsically evil."...

8) presides over Lutheran ceremonies, and who, at Munich, just a few days ago, publicly asked for forgiveness from the Protestants for their being excluded from the Church.

9) received the red mark on the forehead from a Hindu priestess in India.

10) in Africa, had a priestess/sorcerer spread ashes or dust over his head, during a witchcraft service, or a fetishistic cult.

11) organizes, sometimes presides over, and always encourages scandalous ecumenical congresses such as Assisi, Kyoto, Rome...[113]

12) opens his heart and door to everyone except faithful Catholics.

---

[113] Full documentation of the foregoing scandals is in, *Peter, Lovest Thou Me?* available from Angelus Press.

I could go on with this list of public scandalous actions of the present Pope. I abridge it voluntarily because these examples suffice. Only those who work to safeguard and defend the Catholic Faith, who live a blameless life, are condemned, rejected, publicly declared schismatic and excommunicated. This is derision, Monseigneur, and it puts great shame on the visage of the Church.

We were surprised yesterday to read in the newspaper, *Midi-libre* of July 1, 1988, under the photograph of Archbishop Lefebvre that "Lutherans and Calvinists did not create a schism, properly speaking." What, then, did they do?

But we—who neither tear apart the Faith nor the charity of holy Church—are schismatic! Who is mocked, and who is mocking whom?

And behold, you push the irony, after the condemnation of Archbishop Lefebvre which was so much hoped for by the French episcopate, to grant us the same "just requests of the traditionalists" according to the very words and actions of falsely benevolent Cardinal Decourtray and Cardinal Lustiger.

Now, for which reason have we been rejected, condemned, treated as black sheep for the past 20 years by Rome and by our bishops, if not for our fidelity to these "just requests." If we had not resisted, would they ever offer us these requests now?

May those conservative Catholics who rejoice at the promises of more Indult Masses after *Ecclesia Dei* meditate upon these words. The Vatican, through the intermediary of our bishops, is trying to work out, not a reconciliation, but recuperation. Well, Monseigneur, we shall not be "recuperated," [because we are not ill], but just faithful!

His Excellency Archbishop Lefebvre is almost the only prelate who courageously stood up against the "auto-destruction of the Church." All his brothers in the episcopate have cowardly abandoned him. We have been with him for a long time, with admiration and veneration, in the same fidelity and in the same fight for the honor of God and His Church. Today, we share his trials, since, though the penalty imposed by Rome is of no value, it hits us in the heart, because it comes from those who ought to be our shepherds and who became our torturers. However, our soul is in deep peace because we are sure to do the will of God, and desirous to obey and please God rather than men. We shall continue to pray for all those who have the duty to lead the flock towards the true pastures and who are leading it astray in poisonous prairies.

It is not the first time, and perhaps not the last time, that Rome condemns innocence. We are sure that our determination is pleasing to God;

we shall hold to it, asking Him to protect us from bitterness and hatred against those who treat us so unjustly.

The glory of the Church is in the fidelity and resistance of Archbishop Lefebvre. May the Churchmen realize it before it is too late. We pray for this intention and, as you exhort us, we pray St. Dominic, our blessed Father, to slay the heretics.

Deign to receive, Monseigneur, our most profound and religious respect.

Mother Anne Marie Simoulin
Superior of the Dominican Sisters
Fanjeaux, France

JULY 9, 1988

THE ROMAN COMMISSION

L'Osservatore Romano, (July 11, 1988)

The Holy Father has named His Eminence Paul Augustin Cardinal Mayer,[114] previously Prefect of the Congregation for the Sacraments and of the Congregation for Divine Worship, President of the Commission instituted in accordance with the terms of the motu proprio, *Ecclesia Dei* (§ 7, a.b.) of July 7, 1988.

It is significant that the President of this Commission is not Cardinal Gagnon, who was better disposed toward the Society of Saint Pius X, but rather the former Prefect of the Roman Congregation who participated in the recent degradation in the liturgy in his capacity as former Prefect of the Congregation for the Sacraments and Divine Worship.

It is also significant that the three members who prepared the May 5th Protocol are in this Commission. Archbishop Lefebvre said, in his interview with *30 Days*,[115] that during the discussions preparing this Protocol there was no real collaboration but the only way to progress in the discussions were by threats of the consecration: "It was necessary to continually threaten in order to obtain something. No collaboration was any longer possible."

---

[114] A German Benedictine, Cardinal Mayer was born in Altötting, Germany on May 23, 1911. He studied Philosophy in Salzburg and Theology at Sant' Anselmo in Rome. He was ordained on August 25, 1935. In 1939 after earning his doctorate, he became a professor at Sant' Anselmo. He remained for 27 years, from 1940 to 1966 as Rector. Mayer's fame as a scholar led first Pope John XXIII, then Pope Paul VI to make him secretary of the Preparatory Commission for Vatican II. Named in 1965 Ecclesiastical Delegate for the Focolare Movement and in 1966 Abbot of Metten (Germany), he was recalled to Rome in 1971 to become Secretary of the Congregation for Religious and Secular Institutes. Later, Mayer became Prefect of the Congregation for Divine Worship and President of the Pontifical Commission "Ecclesia Dei." He was named a titular Archbishop on January 6, 1972 and was elevated to the cardinalate by John Paul II during the Consistroy of May 25, 1985. (*Inside the Vatican,* Jan. 1997, p.55.)

[115] July-August 1988, p.13.

His Holiness has named as permanent experts of the Commission the Reverend:

> Msgr. Peter Tena Garriaga, Undersecretary of the Congregation for Divine Worship;
> Msgr. Milan Simcic, Undersecretary of the Congregation for the Clergy;
> Msgr. Jesus Torres Llorente, C.M.F., Undersecretary for Religious of the Congregation for Religious and for Secular Institutes;
> Msgr. Frantisek Rypar, Head of the Office for Seminaries in the Congregation for Catholic Education;
> Tarcisio Bertone, S.D.B., Consultor of the Congregation for the Doctrine of the Faith;
> Fernando Ocariz, Consultor for the Congregation for the Doctrine of the Faith;
> Benoît Duroux, O.P., Professor in the Pontifical University of St. Thomas Aquinas.

The Holy Father has named Secretary of the said Commission Rev. Msgr. Camille Perl, official of the Congregation for Divine Worship.

Fr. Tarcisio Bertone, of the Commission applies the detailed prescription of the law without reference to the prescriptions of law, the consideration of which is necessary to resolve particular cases in exceptional circumstances. This is the true letter and spirit of the law which legalists fail to see.[116]

Such a canonist can never understand the canonical principle of the actions of Archbishop Lefebvre and of traditional priests in the past 25 years, that is, the rules of the Church in exceptional cases. He does not understand that the masterstroke of Satan is to have led souls into disobedience to Tradition in the name of obedience. The enemies of the Church have infiltrated and climbed to its highest places to destroy it from the top. The presence of a canonist like Fr. Bertone and confreres of similar ilk on the *Ecclesia Dei* Commission is not a good sign.

---

[116] See *Texas Catholic Herald*, July 22, 1988.

JULY 13, 1988

SOME LESSONS TO BE LEARNED
FROM THE LEFEBVRE SCHISM

**The following is the text of an address by Cardinal Ratzinger,
Prefect of the Sacred Congregation of the Doctrine of the Faith,
given on July 13, 1988, in Santiago, Chile, before that nation's
bishops. In the address, His Eminence comments on the "schism"
triggered by Archbishop Lefebvre's illicit ordination of four
bishops and reflects upon certain internal weaknesses in the
Church which have provided fertile ground for the development
of the Lefebvre phenomenon. The text of Cardinal Ratzinger's
significant address appeared in Italian in the July 30-Aug. 5
edition of Il Sabato. This English translation is reprinted from
The Wanderer.**

In recent months we have put a lot of work into the case of Lefebvre,
with the sincere intention of creating for his movement a space within the
Church that would be sufficient for it to live. The Holy See has been criticized for this. It is said that it has yielded to blackmail; that it has not defended the Second Vatican Council with sufficient energy; that, while it
has treated progressive movements with great severity, it has displayed an
exaggerated sympathy with the traditionalist rebellion. The development
of events is enough to disprove these assertions. The mythical harshness of
the Vatican in the face of the deviations of the progressives is shown to be
mere empty words.[117]

Up until now, in fact, only warnings have been published; in no case
have there been canonical penalties in the strict sense. And the fact that
when the chips were down Lefebvre denounced an agreement that had already been signed, shows that the Holy See, while it made truly generous

---

[117] What an admission. How then can he use canonical penalties against those who just
keep the Faith? By his own words, he is convinced of double standards. Let Cardinal
Ratzinger first fulfil his duties as Prefect of the Congregation in charge of keeping the
purity of the Faith, by applying the proper ecclesiastical laws and penalties against the
many wolves in the Church. Then there will be no need of any severity towards the
Traditional Catholics, since he would have corrected the situation. He would even find
in them his best allies! As long as he does not fulfil his duty, he is not entitled to apply
any penalties against those who defend the Faith.

concessions, did not grant him that complete license which he desired. Lefebvre has seen that, in the fundamental part of the agreement, he was being held to accept Vatican II and the affirmations of the post-conciliar magisterium, according to the proper authority of each document.

There is a glaring contradiction in the fact that it is just the people who have let no occasion slip to allow the world to know of their disobedience to the Pope, and to the magisterial declarations of the last 20 years, who think they have the right to judge that this attitude is too mild and who wish that an absolute obedience to Vatican II had been insisted upon. In a similar way they would claim that the Vatican has conceded a right to dissent to Lefebvre which has been obstinately denied to the promoters of a progressive tendency. In reality, the only point which is affirmed in the agreement, following *Lumen Gentium, §25*, is the plain fact that not all documents of the Council have the same authority. For the rest, it was explicitly laid down in the text that was signed that public polemics must be avoided, and that an attitude is required of positive respect for official decisions and declarations.

It was conceded, in addition, that the Society of Saint Pius X would be able to present to the Holy See—which reserves to itself the sole right of decision—their particular difficulties in regard to interpretations of juridical and liturgical reforms. All of this shows plainly that in this difficult dialogue Rome has united generosity, in all that was negotiable, with firmness in essentials. The explanation which Archbishop Lefebvre has given for the retraction of his agreement, is revealing. He declared that he has finally understood that the agreement he signed aimed only at integrating his foundation into the "Conciliar Church." The Catholic Church in union with the Pope is, according to him, the "Conciliar Church" which has broken with its own past. It seems indeed that he is no longer able to see that we are dealing with the Catholic Church in the totality of its Tradition, and that Vatican II also belongs to that.

Without any doubt, the problem that Lefebvre has posed has not been concluded by the rupture of June 30. It would be too simple to take refuge in a sort of triumphalism, and to think that this difficulty has ceased to exist from the moment in which the movement led by Lefebvre has separated itself by a clean break with the Church. A Christian never can, nor should, take pleasure in a rupture. Even though it is absolutely certain the fault cannot be attributed to the Holy See,[118] it is a duty for us to examine

---

[118] Who is, by their own admission, letting the wolves go unpunished in the flock of Christ? Who has tried to "assimilate values which originated outside the Church" in 200 years of Liberal culture, *i.e.,* of humanism? Who is responsible for Assisi? Who is responsible for the new catechisms, new sacraments, new canon law, *etc.*? Take these away and there would be no "rupture." Therefore, whose fault?

ourselves, as to what errors we have made, and which ones we are making even now. The criteria with which we judge the past in the Vatican II decree on ecumenism, must be used—as is logical—to judge the present as well.

One of the basic discoveries of the theology of ecumenism is that schisms can take place only when certain truths and certain values of the Christian Faith are no longer lived and loved within the Church. The truth which is marginalized[119] becomes autonomous, remains detached from the whole of the ecclesiastical structure, and a new movement then forms itself around it. We must reflect on this fact: that a large number of Catholics, far beyond the narrow circle of the Fraternity of Lefebvre, see this man as a guide, in some sense, or at least as a useful ally. It will not do to attribute everything to political motives, to nostalgia, or to other cultural factors of minor importance. These causes are not capable of explaining the attraction which is felt even by the young—and especially by the young—who come from many quite different nations, and who are surrounded by completely distinct political and cultural realities. Indeed they show what is from any point of view a restricted and one-sided outlook; but there is no doubt whatever that a phenomenon of this sort would be inconceivable unless there were good elements at work here, which in general do not find sufficient opportunity to live within the Church of today.

For all these reasons, we ought to see this matter primarily as the occasion for an examination of conscience. We should allow ourselves to ask fundamental questions, about the defects in the pastoral life of the Church, which are exposed by these events. Thus we will be able to offer a place within the Church to those who are seeking and demanding it, and succeed in destroying all reason for schism. We can make such schism pointless by renewing the interior realities of the Church. There are three points, I think, that it is important to think about.

While there are many motives that might have led a great number of people to seek a refuge in the traditional liturgy, the chief one is that they find the dignity of the sacred preserved there. After the Council there were many priests who deliberately raised "desacralization" to the level of a program, on the plea that the New Testament abolished the cult of the Temple: the veil of the Temple which was torn from top to bottom at the moment of Christ's death on the cross is, according to certain people, the sign of the end of the sacred. The death of Jesus, outside the city walls, that is to

---

[119] What a scandalous view of schisms, which despises the history of the Church. Was Luther defending "a truth which was marginalized?" Were Photius, or Döllinger, or the Communist National Chinese bishops defending "a truth which was marginalized"? Those who had been defending the truth, and who were marginalised for a while by a bad shepherd have, rather, been the saints such as St. Athanasius, St. Joan of Arc, *etc.*

say, in the public world, is now the true religion. Religion, if it has any being at all, must have it in the non-sacredness of daily life, in love that is lived. Inspired by such reasoning, they put aside the sacred vestments; they have despoiled the churches as much as they could of that splendor which brings to mind the sacred; and they reduced the liturgy to the language and the gestures of ordinary life, by means of greetings, common signs of friendship, and such things.

There is no doubt that with these theories and practices they have entirely disregarded the true connection between the Old and the New Testament: It is forgotten that this world is not the Kingdom of God, and that the "Holy One of God" (Jn. 6:69) continues to exist in contradiction to this world; that we have need of purification before we draw near to Him; that the profane, even after the death and the Resurrection of Jesus, has not succeeded in becoming "the holy." The Risen One has appeared, but to those whose heart has been opened to Him, to the Holy; He did not manifest Himself to everyone. It is in this way that a new space has been opened for the religion to which all of us should now submit; this religion which consists in drawing near to the community of the Risen One, at whose feet the women prostrated themselves and adored Him. I do not want to develop this point any further now; I confine myself to coming straight to this conclusion: we ought to get back the dimension of the sacred in the liturgy. The liturgy is not a festivity; it is not a meeting for the purpose of having a good time. It is of no importance that the parish priest has cudgeled his brains to come up with suggestive ideas or imaginative novelties. The liturgy is what makes the Thrice-Holy God present amongst us; it is the burning bush; it is the Alliance of God with man in Jesus Christ, who has died and risen again. The grandeur of the liturgy does not rest upon the fact that it offers an interesting entertainment, but in rendering tangible the Totally Other, whom we are not capable of summoning. He comes because He wills. In other words, the essential in the liturgy is the mystery, which is realized in the common ritual of the Church; all the rest diminishes it. Men experiment with it in lively fashion, and find themselves deceived, when the mystery is transformed into distraction, when the chief actor in the liturgy is not the Living God but the priest or the liturgical director.

Aside from the liturgical question, the central points of conflict at present are Lefebvre's attacks on the decree which deals with Religious Liberty, and on the so-called spirit of Assisi. Here is where Lefebvre fixes the boundaries between his position and that of the Catholic Church today.

I need hardly say in so many words that what he is saying on these points is unacceptable. Here we do not wish to consider his errors, rather we want to ask where there is a lack of clarity in ourselves. For Lefebvre, what is at stake is the warfare against ideological liberalism, against the relativization of truth. Obviously we are not in agreement with him that—understood according to the Pope's intentions—the text of the Council or the prayer of Assisi were relativizing.

It is a necessary task to defend the Second Vatican Council against Archbishop Lefebvre, as valid, and as binding upon the Church. Certainly there is a mentality of narrow views that isolates Vatican II and which has provoked this opposition. There are many accounts of it which give the impression that, from Vatican II onward, everything has been changed, and that what preceded it has no value or, at best, has value only in the light of Vatican II.

The Second Vatican Council has not been treated as a part of the entire living Tradition of the Church, but as an end of Tradition, a new start from zero. The truth is that this particular Council defined no dogma at all, and deliberately chose to remain on a modest level, as a merely pastoral council; and yet many treat it as though it had made itself into a sort of super-dogma which takes away the importance of all the rest.

This idea is made stronger by things that are now beginning. That which previously was considered most holy—the form in which the liturgy was handed down—suddenly appears as the most forbidden of all things, the one thing that can safely be prohibited. It is intolerable to criticize decisions which have been taken since the Council; on the other hand, if men make question of ancient rules, or even of the great truths of the Faith—for instance, the corporal virginity of Mary, the bodily Resurrection of Jesus, the immortality of the soul—nobody complains or only does so with the greatest moderation.[120]

I, myself, when I was a professor, have seen how the very same bishop who, before the Council, had fired a teacher, who was really irreproachable, for a certain crudeness of speech, was not prepared, after the Council, to dismiss a professor who openly denied certain fundamental truths of the Faith.

All this leads a great number of people to ask themselves if the Church of today is really the same as that of yesterday, or if they have changed it for something else without telling people. The one way in which Vatican II

---

[120] At the beginning of his talk he himself admits that he falls under his own criticism.

can be made plausible is to present it as it is: one part of the unbroken, the unique Tradition of the Church and of her Faith.

In the spiritual movements of the post-conciliar era, there is not the slightest doubt that frequently there has been an obliviousness, or even a suppression, of the issue of truth: here perhaps we confront the crucial problem for theology and for pastoral work today.

The "truth" is thought to be a claim that is too exalted, a "triumphal-ism" that cannot be permitted any longer. You see this attitude plainly in the crisis that troubles the missionary ideal and missionary practice. If we do not point to the truth in announcing our faith, and if this truth is no longer essential for the salvation of Man, then the missions lose their meaning. In effect the conclusion has been drawn, and it is being drawn today, that in the future we need only seek that Christians should be good Christians, Moslems good Moslems, Hindus good Hindus, and so forth. If it comes to that, how are we to know when one is a "good" Christian or a "good" Moslem?

The idea that all religions are—if you talk seriously—only symbols of what ultimately is the Incomprehensible, is rapidly gaining ground in the-ology, and has already deeply penetrated into liturgical practice. When things get to this point, faith as such is left behind, because faith really consists in the fact that I am committing myself to the truth so far as it is known. So in this matter also there is every motive to return to the right path.

If once again we succeed in pointing out and living the fullness of the Catholic religion with regard to these points, we may hope that the schism of Lefebvre will not be of long duration.

In this long conference of Cardinal Ratzinger we can distinguish few accusations and many admissions.

He accuses Archbishop Lefebvre of two things. First, he says: "It seems indeed that he is no longer able to see that we are dealing with the Catholic Church in the totality of its Tradition, and that Vatican II also belongs to that."

Archbishop Lefebvre has always recognized the Pope as Pope, and wished to be able to have normal relations with him. The obstacles were not placed by Archbishop Lefebvre; he did his best to avoid them, fighting the introduction of new doctrines at the Council while the then Rev. Fr. Ratzinger was pushing for their introduction as a *peritus*. He did his best to prevent the Pope from calling the meeting at Assisi. [See his "Open Letter to the Pope," jointly signed with Bishop de Castro Mayer–*The Angelus*, Jan. 1984.] In spite of these new doctrines which entered the Church as a virus, he did his best to keep a relationship with the Pope. It makes no sense to admit that within the Church new values which "originated outside the Church," among the enemies of the Church, as Cardinal

Ratzinger admits in *The Ratzinger Report*,[121] and then pretend that the whole of Vatican II still belongs to the totality of Tradition: "The central points of conflict at present are Lefebvre's attacks on the decree which deals with Religious Liberty, and on the so-called spirit of Assisi....[W]hat he is saying on these points is unacceptable."

We take note that Cardinal Ratzinger accepts the spirit of Assisi and *Dignitatis Humanæ* as perfectly acceptable. But he himself says that "this particular Council defined no dogma at all." That being so we are not obliged to accept it.

Cardinal Ratzinger makes three admissions: the complete lack of sacredness in the modern liturgy, the raising of the Council as a super-dogma erasing all the past, and an obliviousness or even a suppression of the issue of truth. We are pleased to see these admissions, but what is he going to do to correct the situation? The Popes Paul VI and John Paul II have oftentimes spoken conservative words but their actions opened the doors to all kinds of abuses. For instance, on Wednesday, September 14, 1988, the Sacred Congregation for Divine Worship published a document allowing priests and faithful in Zaire to dance during the Mass: the priest will be able to accompany his prayers "with corporal movements according to the traditional rhythms of his people"; the faithful are authorized to accompany the priest "while remaining at their place."[122]

How can Cardinal Ratzinger then complain about loss of sacredness in the liturgy? Who is responsible?

Cardinal Ratzinger several times makes another kind of admission: that the reason why the Protocol failed was that Rome "defended the Second Vatican Council against Archbishop Lefebvre as valid and as binding upon the Church." He is not ready to abandon the principles which have borne so many bitter fruits in the past 30 years. He wants to cure the external symptoms of the crisis in the Church but wants to protect the virus inside!

However, we agree with his conclusion, that once he (and all the bishops to whom he was speaking) returns to "the fullness of the Catholic religion," then there will be no more problems with the bishops, priests and faithful attached to Tradition with Archbishop Lefebvre! Let us pray that Our Divine Savior may help the Pope, the Cardinal and all these bishops to return to this "fullness of the Catholic religion."

---

[121] See above, p.152*ff.*
[122] See *Notre Vie*, Sept. 15, 1988.

JULY 18, 1988

DECLARATION OF THE GERMAN-SPEAKING SUPERIORS OF THE SOCIETY OF SAINT PIUS X REGARDING THE TREATMENT OF ARCHBISHOP LEFEBVRE

On July 1, 1988, the Roman Congregation for Bishops declared Archbishop Lefebvre, Bishop de Castro Mayer and the bishops consecrated by them on June 30, excommunicated for lack of the required pontifical mandate. Many people, Catholic or not, are speaking of schism. The Society of Saint Pius X rejects this inexact presentation of the facts. It recalls the canon law which presupposes, for the validity of an ecclesiastical penalty such as excommunication, a grievous fault (*delictum*) which does not exist when, among other circumstances, the person considers himself bound in conscience not to follow the letter of the law in order to safeguard a greater good. (Case of necessity: see Canon 2205, §2, §3 of the *1917 Code of Canon Law*; Canon 1323, §4 and Canon 1324, §1, 5 of the *1983 Code of Canon Law*.)

Now the Universal Church finds herself today—to our greater sorrow—in a case of necessity that far surpasses all the precedent vicissitudes of her history, because of the falsehood of the official fundamental orientation of the pontificate of John Paul II. His guiding light is the doctrine of Assisi—which dissolves the First Commandment of God—a mixture of all religions, in its ideological conception as well as its socio-political realization. This doctrine fulfils in this end of the century the Modernist program condemned by St. Pius X under the name of "Organized Apostasy" in his Apostolic Letter *Notre charge apostolique* of August 25, 1910.

A good example of this extreme situation among the bishops is the "final report of the mixed ecumenical commission for the revision of the anathema of the 16th century" in which the German Episcopal Conference falls eleven times into heresy and thereby *ipso facto* into excommunication (*1917 Code of Canon Law*, Canon 2314). Indeed, contrary to the dogmatic condemnation by the Council of Trent of eleven heresies in the Protestant doctrine on the Last Supper, they declare that "it must not be automatically considered as heretical." The German Episcopal Conference has thereby separated itself from the Church because the integral Catholic Faith is the first and decisive condition of belonging to the Church. Given similar situations in all the episcopal conferences of the West, the future Cardinal Gagnon acknowledged on August 27, 1983, the existence of "a schism in the United States and European countries."

Numerous statistics and polls show that due to twenty-five years of Modernist domination over theology and in the hierarchy, between 90-95% of the Catholic population is now separated from the Church by heresy or apostasy; 93% of German Catholics no longer go to confession, according to Cardinal Höffner; 86% of religion teachers (priests or laymen) in the Diocese of Trèves challenges the duty to accept the totality of the Deposit of Faith according to a 1977 poll; 94% of the population in the strongly Catholic area of Tyrol have, in 45 years, rejected the Catholic teaching on the prohibition of contraception (Loewit-Studie, *Herderkorrespondenz,* Mar. 1984).

This data and these official facts illustrate the rapid and almost total destruction of the authentic life of faith, reduced to a small number of priests and laymen attached to the Faith who address themselves to Archbishop Lefebvre. In the face of the present situation they find in the Society of Saint Pius X and its environment the only means of serving the Church and the Pope according to the Catholic Faith. They are strengthened in this conviction by "the very positive report" of the Apostolic Visit of November-December 1987, re-affirming that "the Church must be re-built on this basis."

The present extreme necessity imposes upon Archbishop Lefebvre (and upon Bishop de Castro Mayer), the only bishop recognizable as fully Catholic, some special duties. Indeed, he is, "as successor of the Apostles, jointly responsible for the common good of the Church" (Pius XII, Encyclical *Fidei Donum*, Apr. 21, 1957). This joint responsibility in regard to the whole Church was fulfilled by Archbishop Lefebvre by the episcopal consecrations of June 30, performed in closest union with the Church and her law. Indeed, "the ultimate end, the supreme principal and the superior unity of the juridical life and of all juridical function in the Church is the solicitude for souls" (Pius XII, Oct. 2, 1944, Allocution to the Roman Rota).

Lastly, the immediate reason for the by-passing of the rule of the apostolic mandate on the consecrations of June 30 consists in the fact that the negotiations with Rome throughout the first half of 1988, in spite of a few concessions, demonstrated more and more strongly the following: Rome, because of its false modernist orientation, is not ready to guarantee in the long term, the freedom and vitality of Catholic Tradition.

Given all this, Archbishop Lefebvre has never wanted a schism, *i.e.*, a fundamental rupture with the papacy, but he acted according to the guidelines of Catholic theology, according to which "it is legitimate not to obey the orders of a pope and even to prevent the execution of his will if he puts souls in danger, especially if he strove to destroy the Church" (St. Robert Bellarmine, *de Romano Pontifice,* 2, 29). Archbishop Lefebvre, since June 30, follows the same path as the holy bishop and confessor Athanasius, who, in times of similar general blindness in heresy (Arianism), was one of the few bishops to refuse with vigor to take any part in the politics of Pope Liberius, who was favoring heresy: for this motive he was excommunicated by this Pope in 357 AD, a penalty as invalid as the excommunication of July 1, 1988.

† Bishop Bernard Fellay
Fr. Franz Joseph Maessen
Fr. Paul Natterer
Fr. Georg Pflüger

Stuttgart, Germany
July 18, 1988

JULY 25, 1988

LETTER OF CARDINALS RATZINGER AND MAYER TO DOM GÉRARD CALVET

Cardinals Ratzinger and Mayer wrote this letter in response to one written to Cardinal Ratzinger by Dom Gérard Calvet, superior of the Benedictine Monastery of St. Madeline at Le Barroux, France. To our knowledge, Dom Gérard's original letter was never released to the public, yet Cardinal Mayer disclosed parts of it in his interview with *30 Days* magazine. (See following chapter, p.204.)

The apostolate of Dom Gérard's Monastery of St. Madeleine was affiliated with that of the Society of Saint Pius X until shortly after Archbishop Lefebvre's consecration of bishops. Dom Gérard himself assisted at the episcopal consecrations, but then broke his association with the Society. He himself has since concelebrated the New Mass with Pope John Paul II, thus consumating his compromise and that of his monastery. His community now publicly defends the Second Vatican Council's idea of Religious Liberty (*Dignitatis Humanae*) as being in accord with Catholic Tradition which it manifestly is not.

Reverend Father,

In response to the letter which you addressed to the Prefect of the Congregation for the Doctrine of the Faith on July 8, last, and to the petition addressed to the Pope on the same date, the Cardinal Prefect of that Congregation and the Cardinal Prefect of the special Commission instituted by the motu proprio *Ecclesia Dei,* are happy to communicate together the following.

During an audience granted to Cardinal Joseph Ratzinger on July 23, 1988, the Sovereign Pontiff deigned with goodness:

1) To lift all censures and irregularities incurred due to the fact of the reception of sacred Orders from the hands of His Excellency Archbishop Lefebvre, then suspended *a divinis*, all the members of the communities of St. Madeleine of Le Barroux, and Santa Cruz de Nova Friburgo, who are in this case.

2) Grant to these same communities the full reconciliation to the Holy See under the conditions already offered by Cardinal Paul

Augustin Mayer during his visit to the Monastery of Le Barroux on June 21, 1988, and according to paragraph 6 (a) of the motu proprio *Ecclesia Dei*, that is:

3)

- the use in private and in public of the liturgical books in force in 1962, for the members of the communities, and those who frequent their houses.
- the possibility of asking a bishop, according to the existing canonical rules, for conferring the Orders according to the Pontifical cited above, the superior of each autonomous house granting the necessary dimissorial letters.
- the right of the faithful to receive the sacraments according to the books cited above in the houses of the communities, taking into account the Canons 878, 896 and 1122 of the *1983 Code of Canon Law.*
- the possibility to develop a pastoral influence through apostolic works and to keep the present ministries assumed by the communities, according to Canons 679-683.[123]

These measures shall take effect with the reception of the present letter. Other possible juridical problems will have to be submitted to the competence of the special Commission in charge of the application of the motu proprio *Ecclesia Dei.*

Concerning the insertion of these two communities in the Benedictine Confederation, the Cardinal President of the special Commission asks the Most Reverend Abbot Primate to take, in union with him, the necessary dispositions, given the wishes expressed in your letter of June 8, 1988, on this subject.

We must add that the Holy Father, touched by the expression of your sentiments of fidelity and attachment to him, does not doubt your sincere desire to contribute to the good of souls through your apostolate in communion with him and with all the Shepherds of the Church and relies especially upon your prayers and of your brethren.

Deign to accept, Reverend Father, our religious and devoted feelings in the Lord.

Joseph Cardinal Ratzinger
Paul Augustin Cardinal Mayer

---

[123] These canons all stress that this pastoral work is to be "under the authority and direction of the local bishop."

JULY 28, 1988

CREATION OF THE SOCIETY OF SAINT PETER

Despite the hopeful tone of this communique, by the end of October (1988), three months after its foundation, the new Society of Saint Peter was facing the difficulties and dangers which continue to haunt it. The Society of Saint Peter falls entirely at the mercy of the local modernist bishops.

For Archbishop Lefebvre, the essential problem with the May 5 Protocol was its failure to promise a bishop for the Society of Saint Pius X with unobstructed power to protect the faithful from modernist influences. On the contrary, the Protocol offered, for mere psychological reasons, a single bishop purposely lacking this power. In over a decade since its foundation the Society of Saint Peter still does not even have one traditional bishop, powerless or otherwise.

Communiqué of the Founding Members
from *la Documentation Catholique*, No. 1969.

In the aftermath of the rupture consummated by Archbishop Lefebvre on June 30 at the Seminary of Ecône, Switzerland, eight traditional priests from different movements went to Rome on July 5 and 6. They met with the Sovereign Pontiff as well as with Cardinal Ratzinger, Prefect of the Congregation for the Faith, and Cardinal Mayer, new president of the Roman Commission instituted by the Pope to solve the questions concerning Catholic Tradition.

They were strongly encouraged in their project to found a priestly society allowing them to keep "the traditions of spirituality and apostolate" (motu proprio *Ecclesia Dei*, July 2, §5a) to which they, as well as a great number of faithful, are attached. Such a society concretely fulfils the hopes raised by the Protocol signed on May 5 last between Cardinal Ratzinger and Archbishop Lefebvre.

This Society was founded on July 18 at the Cistercian Abbey of Hauterive (Canton of Fribourg, Switzerland), under the name of "The Society of St. Peter." The founding members, priests and deacons, have canonically elected as their Superior General Fr. Joseph Bisig (Swiss), and as his two assistants Fr. Denis Coiffet (French) and Fr. Gabriel Baumann (Swiss). All three are former members of the Society of Saint Pius X. Fr. Joseph Bisig, 36, had been First Assistant of the Superior General of this Society for six years (1982-1988), and had been Rector of the Seminary of Zaitzkofen, Germany, for seven years (1979-1986). Fr. Gabriel Baumann, 35, had been its Vice-Rector for four years.

The Society of St. Peter wishes to welcome into its bosom any priest desirous of serving the Church in a traditional spirit (motu proprio *Ecclesia Dei*, §5a, b; §6a). It takes as its first goal the urgent creation of an international seminary in Europe to welcome seminarians desiring a solid theological formation, based on St. Thomas, a traditional spirituality and liturgy, and wishing not to cut themselves off from the Church.

Msgr. Camille Perl came to support the founders of the Society of St. Peter gathered at Hauterive, with the encouragement of the Roman Commission of which he is the secretary.

In virtue of the agreement of May 5, and the motu proprio of July 2 (§5), the priests of the Society of St. Peter shall willingly offer their apostolic services to the dioceses and bishops.

Some modernist bishops have been very clear regarding their intentions to stifle the Society of Saint Peter. The now-deceased Cardinal Albert Decourtray, Archbishop of Lyon, France (in whose diocese one of the priests of the Society of Saint Peter is located), added his own condition for the Society of Saint Peter to minister in his diocese. He required acceptance not only of the validity of the Latin *Editio Typica*,[124] but also of its vernacular translations, suppressing the mention of "certain points taught by Vatican Council II, or concerning later reforms of the liturgy and the law which do not appear to us easily reconcilable with Tradition." He and Bishop Raymond Bouchex, Bishop of Avignon (in which diocese Le Barroux is situated), insist on "a strong attachment to the Second Vatican Council, to the whole Council."[125]

Moreover, Church authorities have said to Fr. Bisig, "Oh, we have no objection to the opening of a seminary–provided you have professors with the proper degrees." Now, the "proper degrees" can only be obtained in modernist universities. This is the reason why the professors in the seminaries of the Society of Saint Pius X refuse to pursue "proper degrees." This requirement obliged Fr. Baumann and Fr. Prösinger to go and study in a modernist university to obtain a "proper degree," and obliged Fr. Bisig to accept on the faculty of his seminary some other teachers who celebrate the New Mass.

---

[124] Official Latin text.
[125] *Documentation Catholique*, No. 1969.

Who can guarantee to ordain these seminarians? Local modernist bishops? How much leverage does the Society of Saint Peter have to insist in which rite they will be ordained? For the first ordinations, Cardinal Mayer agreed to ordain some of them with the traditional Mass. But this raises another question. Some conservative monasteries who accepted the *Novus Ordo* out of "obedience" have been begging for the traditional Mass and ordinations for many years. They are still denied their requests. The new rites of ordination were imposed on Dom Augustin when he made his own accord with the Vatican in 1985. [Dom Augustin was superior of a Benedictine monastery in Flavigny, France, founded in cooperation with Archbishop Lefebvre. Since Dom Augustine's compromise in 1985, his community is obliged to celebrate the New Mass.] It seems that Rome characteristically grants requests for the traditional Mass and rites, not to promote Catholic Tradition, but only to divide traditional Catholics.

Moreover, this first ceremony of ordination by Cardinal Mayer was not without difficulty. Strong protests from the German bishops prevented him from performing it in Germany. At the last minute, after invitations were sent, the place of ordination had to be changed to Rome. Stronger protests from the French bishops have prevented him from ordaining some monks of the Society of St. Vincent Ferrer[126] in Fontgombault. The ceremony was performed by a visiting bishop. If Rome gives in to such pressures of diocesan bishops now, how much more later!

---

[126] Fr. de Blignières left the Society of Saint Pius X as a seminarian and was ordained by Archbishop Lefebvre in 1977 under the condition of remaining under obedience to Dom Gèrard (of Le Barroux), who at the time was both fully traditional and supportive of the Society of Saint Pius X. But he later violated this condition, and in 1979 started a religious community on his own, modeled after the Dominican life. This community was openly sedevacantist from the beginning. For that reason, Archbishop Lefebvre always refused to ordain the members of that community, even though it celebrated the Latin Mass.

Fr. de Blignières pretended to "prove" that the Pope was not Pope because of the "contradiction" between the teachings of Vatican II (especially on the issue of religious liberty) and the encyclical *Quanta Cura* of Pope Pius IX. In 1987, Fr. de Blignières made a flip-flop, and announced that there was no direct contradiction between the two and therefore the Pope was Pope, that one was not entitled to resist him, and Archbishop Lefebvre should not perform the consecrations of bishops (1988).

After the issuance of the motu proprio *Ecclesia Dei* following upon those consecrations, Fr. de Blignières sought to put himself under the *Ecclesia Dei* commission. His community was officially recognized under the name of the Society of St. Vincent Ferrer. Numbering about a dozen members (1979) when Fr. de Blignières started his group, they have not grown either before or after his flip-flop. Fr. de Blignières has published an essay defending the Religious Liberty of Vatican II.

AUGUST 18, 1988

DECLARATION OF DOM GÉRARD

Reprinted from *Présent,* no.1638

By this declaration which follows, Dom Gérard, superior of the Benedictine Monastery of St. Madeleine of Le Barroux, France, publicly explained the reasons why he signed the Protocol which Archbishop Lefebvre rejected and the conditions he included with his signature.

I deny, first of all, as absolutely unfounded, the rumor that was spread that I would have been chosen to be consecrated bishop.[127]

Why have I accepted the Protocol which Archbishop Lefebvre rejected just after he signed it? This is a long story, for which I ask a few minutes of attention. For the past 15 years we asked to be relieved from our suspension, and to be re-integrated into the Confederation of the Benedictine Monasteries; but since the conditions were unacceptable (renouncement of the traditional Rite) we refused, resigned to remain in the illegality rather than to lack the Truth. Then, a long time after these efforts, on Friday, June 17 of this year, a phone call from the Vatican asked for the Prior. Cardinal Mayer asked to pay us a visit. He would arrive on Monday, June 20, at 6:30pm with Msgr. Perl in order to propose on behalf of the Holy Father, the Protocol signed [by Archbishop Lefebvre] on May 5, and rejected [by His Grace] on the night of May 5-6.

The next day, we gathered ten fathers around the Cardinal to study the proposal of the Pope; thus there were morning and afternoon meetings of intense discussion where no aspect of the question was ignored. The adaptation of the Protocol that was offered to us represented the total of our requests submitted to the Holy See since 1983. What we asked from the beginning (Mass of St. Pius V, catechism, sacraments, all in conformity

---

[127] On the question of bishops, it must be noted that a very important point of the May 5 Protocol was the granting of a bishop from those attached to Tradition. Cardinal Mayer, President of the new Commission, himself admits that. "The question of a specific bishop is no longer being posed"—much less solved! (See *30 Days,* October 1988).

to the centuries-old Tradition of the Church), were granted to us, without doctrinal counter-part, without concession, without denial.[128]

The Holy Father was thus offering us to be integrated into the Benedictine Confederation as we are.

Our Reasons

After having weighed everything, after several meetings of the council of the fathers, I have thus accepted the proposal and explained to our faithful at the Sunday Mass the reasons which, in our case, support our acceptance:

a) That the tradition of the Church be pushed out of her official, visible perimeter brings prejudice to it. This is contrary to the honor of the Spouse of Christ. The visibility of the Church is one of its essential marks.

b) It is sad that the only Benedictines who are put aside from the great Benedictine family are precisely those who keep its liturgical tradition. Isn't this a proper mark of the Benedictine Order?

c) All things being equal, *i.e.,* the Faith and the Sacraments being intact, it is better to be in agreement with the laws of the Church rather than contravene them.

Lastly the reason, perhaps the determining one, which inclined us to accept that the *suspens a divinis* be lifted from our priests, is a missionary reason: should not the maximum number of faithful be enabled to assist at our Masses and liturgical celebrations without being hindered by their local priests or bishop? I think, especially, of some young college students, scouts and seminarians who have *never* seen a traditional Mass.

It seems that we would be guilty if, because of our refusal to take the occasion, thousands of young people would be forever deprived of the Latin Gregorian Mass, of the Mass facing God, where the Canon is surrounded by silence, where the Holy Host, Center of adoration for the faithful, is received on the tongue, kneeling.

The stakes are not small, as one can see.

Our Conditions

We have placed two conditions on the signing of this agreement.

1) That this event be not considered as a discredit on the person of

---

[128] Note Cardinal Mayer's comment on Dom Gérard's statement at the end of this chapter (see p.204)!

Archbishop Lefebvre: this was brought up several times in the course of our discussion with Cardinal Mayer, who agreed to it. Indeed, isn't it thanks to the tenacity of Archbishop Lefebvre that such a status is being granted to us?

2) That no doctrinal or liturgical counterpart be requested from us and that no silence be imposed on our anti-Modernist preaching.

The Reactions

Many of our uninformed correspondents had fears and suspicions. We hoped to have appeased their worries. We regret, here or there, certain bitter reactions, which come more from a partisan spirit than from the sense of the Church. They summoned the faithful to choose their camp, disregarding the respect due to the souls, which is the first condition of any apostolate. It would be a grave error to constitute within the Church a sort of great unified party, choosing at its head a leader who maneuvers his troops at will. Forced by the events, the faithful attached to Tradition were placed in a posture of resistance. We, ourselves, remain strongly attached to the requirements of an integral Faith and to the immutable Tradition of the Church, but our legitimate resistance should not become *resistentialism*, where suspicion and purges are the law: the holy liberty of the children of God would be the first victim of this, and many other precious virtues would suffer too—charity, in the first place.

Our Three Wishes

I would like to finish with three wishes which I hold dear to my heart.

1) That rash judgment on complex situations, without having all the elements in hand, be avoided. Precipitation and ill will work for the enemy. With a little patience one will be able to judge the tree by its fruits—Isn't this the evangelical criterion?

2) That we do not exhaust ourselves in quarrels among ourselves, rivalry of clan or jurisdiction. On the contrary, let all those who fight for Tradition, doctrine, preaching, Mass and Sacraments, remain attached in fraternal charity. Who can divide us if we all fight for Christ the King?

3) Lastly, I wish that we all profit from the passage in the Gospel where St. John says to Our Lord: "Master, we saw a certain man casting out devils in Thy Name and we forbade him because he followeth not with us. And Jesus said to him: Forbid him not for he that is not against you is for you" (Lk. 9:49).

Dom Gérard, O.S.B.

FR. SCHMIDBERGER'S REMARKS
ON DOM GÉRARD'S DECLARATION

Rev. Fr. Franz Schmidberger, Superior General of the Society of Saint Pius X from 1983-1994, responded to Dom Gérard's Declaration (of August 18, 1988) by rebutting individual citations. These citations from the Declaration (see pp.199ff.) appear in regular typeface while Fr. Schmidbergers remarks are boldfaced.

"*a)* That the tradition of the Church be pushed out of her official, visible perimeter brings prejudice to it. This is contrary to the honor of the Spouse of Christ. The visibility of the Church is one of its essential marks."

It seems rather contrary to the plan of Divine Providence that the Catholic Tradition of the Church be re-integrated into the pluralism of the Conciliar Church, as long as the latter dishonors the Catholic Church and scandalizes its unity and visibility. "Jesus...suffered without the gate" of Jerusalem, says St. Paul, "let us go forth therefore to Him without the camp, bearing His reproach" (Heb. 13:12-13).

"*b)* It is sad that the only Benedictines who are put aside from the great Benedictine family are precisely those who keep its liturgical tradition...."

On the contrary, it is an honor for Le Barroux to have been rejected by the other Benedictines for its integral fidelity to the Mass of All Times, and thus to have become a wonderful sign of contradiction.

"*c)* All things being equal, *i.e.,* the Faith and the Sacraments being intact, it is better to be in agreement with the laws of the Church rather than contravene them."

On the contrary, when the laws of the Church are abused everywhere, in such a way as to desiccate the living sources of Faith and grace, it is better not to succumb to this scheme.

"Lastly the reason, perhaps the determining one, which inclined us to accept that the *suspens a divinis* be lifted from our priests, is a missionary reason: should not the maximum number of faithful be enabled to assist at our Masses and liturgical celebrations without being hindered by their local priests or bishop?"

If the priests of Le Barroux considered that they were validly suspended, they have been living for 15 years in mortal sin. If they think that the so-called *suspens a divinis* merely damages their apostolic influence, they are wrong. The hard way of the Cross is more fruitful than the easy way. Moreover, they should have placed the missionary influence of the whole of Tradition in its necessary cohesion above the influence of their own monastery alone. The common good should be given pride of place over the individual good.

> "It would be a grave error to constitute within the Church a sort of great unified party, choosing at its head a leader who maneuvers his troops at will."

The truly Catholic faithful have acknowledged in Archbishop Lefebvre the good shepherd that the Good Lord provided to them when they were scattered by the modernists. Neither on May 6 nor on June 30 has the grace of his mission left this good shepherd. Much to the contrary! The fidelity of the sheep to the shepherd is a grace for the sheep. The infidelity is first of all an ingratitude and, in the end, a great tragedy.

> "We, ourselves, remain strongly attached to the requirements of an integral Faith and to the immutable Tradition of the Church, but our legitimate resistance should not become *resistentialism*, where suspicion and purges are the law: the holy liberty of the children of God would be the first victim of this,...."

It is not "suspicion," it is a fact. It is the height of the battle; friends are struck by the enemy. Is it the opportune moment to negotiate private peace with the enemy? There is only one name for such an attitude.

> "On the contrary, let all those who fight for Tradition, doctrine, preaching, Mass, and Sacraments, remain attached in fraternal charity. Who can divide us if we all fight for Christ the King?"

For 15 years [*i.e.*, since the early 1970's], there had been a wonderful covenant of charity between all the traditional communities. All that was needed was to continue it through June 30 in doctrinal and prudential unanimity. This was needed to continue the fight for Christ the King. The one who had broken this covenant now was calling for a new covenant!

Fr. Franz Schmidberger
Superior General,
The Society of Saint Pius X

OCTOBER, 1989

CARDINAL MAYER'S INTERVIEW
IN *30 DAYS* MAGAZINE

It is well to place here a excerpt from the interview given by Augustin Cardinal Mayer, inaugural President of the *Ecclesia Dei* Commission, to Stefano Maria Paci of *30 Days* magazine (Oct. 1988). It adds some interesting insight as to the perspective of Rome regarding Dom Gérard's Declaration, that is, the only perspective which counts.

Paci: When Dom Gérard announced that an agreement had been reached with Rome, he also said, "no doctrinal or liturgical concession was requested, and no ban was imposed on anti-Modernist preaching." The statement sparked considerable debate. What are the actual terms of the agreement?

Cardinal Mayer: Dom Gérard's statement was not exact.

[Then the Cardinal explains how Dom Gérard was not exact.]

They cannot just accept the concessions offered by the Protocol and forget the obligations! [It] required the acceptance of the doctrine contained in the dogmatic Constitution *Lumen Gentium* (§25); the adoption of a positive attitude, one open to dialogue, toward the Holy See regarding those points that could[129] cause difficulties; the recognition of the validity of the Sacrifice of the Mass and of the Sacraments celebrated according to the rites promulgated by Pope Paul VI and John Paul II; and obedience to the prescriptions contained in the *1983 Code of Canon Law*....In the same way, one cannot simply approve of the opening toward legitimate[130] spiritual and liturgical aspirations in the motu proprio *Ecclesia Dei* of last July 2, and neglect the criticism made there of a false notion of Tradition.

---

[129] Note the conditional tense.
[130] If these aspirations were legitimate, why did the priests and faithful have to wait so long for this opening? Why to give it only at the price of criticizing the true notion of Tradition?

The price of this compromise will be to criticize the notion of Tradition held by Archbishop Lefebvre in order to accept a new notion of living Tradition which allows all the changes we have witnessed over the past 30-35 years. I have already noted how this is not the true life of Tradition.

Please note also the requirement to accept all the prescriptions of the *1983 Code of Canon Law*, including Canon 844 of the *1983 Code of Canon Law* (see p.150*ff.*).

[Cardinal Mayer continues:]

Dom Gérard, in addition, stated in a letter to the Holy Father, sent on July 8, 1988, that he and his monks wanted "to lay at the feet of Your Holiness...the testimony of our attachment to the magisterium of the Church."

"Magisterium" can be understood in two ways: an objective way, *i.e.,* the teachings; or a subjective way, *i.e.,* the teachers. If Dom Gérard meant the objective 20-centuries-old magisterium of the Church, wasn't his attachment to this magisterium already very clear by his stand for Tradition? No need for a new testimony of it. If he meant the objective new teachings of Vatican II, then beware! If he meant an attachment to the teachers, *i.e.,* to the Pope as Successor of Peter, then I think it was sufficiently manifested by the very fact that he and the other priests and faithful attached to Tradition continued to recognize the Pope even though they were persecuted by him. If we recognize the Pope even though he uses all kinds of ecclesiastical pressures against us because we keep Tradition, can he doubt our attachment to him the day he returns to Tradition? If a loyal wife remains faithful to an errant husband even though he is physically abusive to her, is there any doubt that such a good woman will remain faithful when her husband comes to his senses and stops such abuse? "*Maledicimur et benedicimus*: we are cursed and we bless, we overcome evil by good," as St. Paul says; this is a sign of the Spirit of God.

The next question was about Dom Gérard's condition that "this event be not considered as a discredit on the person of Archbishop Lefebvre." The Cardinal "expressed his understanding for the feelings of affection and veneration towards Archbishop Lefebvre...but it was obvious...that they could not follow him in any way on the path towards schism." Therefore, the Cardinal was requesting that they now consider Archbishop Lefebvre as schismatic. How can such an agreement "not be considered as a discredit" with such a condition? Isn't there a contradiction?

If, on the contrary, Dom Gérard thought that the ceremony of June 30 was not schismatic–he had to, otherwise he committed a mortal sin by taking part in it–then why accept such a condition? And why did he write in his letter of July 8, according to the testimony of Cardinal Mayer: "We want to reassure Your Holiness that we reject any idea of separating ourselves from the

Church by approving an episcopal ordination conferred without an apostolic mandate"?

Let us pray for these monks that they not be led into further compromises, such as accepting the New Mass. The example of Père Augustin shows the need for such prayers. Let us support Dom Tomàs Aquino[131] who did not compromise.

---

[131] Prior of the Monastery of Santa Cruz in Brazil, South America.

AUGUST 24, 1988

DECLARATION OF DOM TOMÁS AQUINO

The original declaration is in Portuguese and was signed by Dom Tomás Aquino, Prior of the Monastery of Santa Cruz [Monastery of the Holy Cross], Nova Friburgo, Brazil. It was sent on August 25, 1988 to Dom Gérard Calvet, Prior of the Monastery of St. Madeleine, Le Barroux, France, and also to Cardinals Joseph Ratzinger and Paul Augustin Mayer, at the Roman Congregation for the Doctrine of the Faith at the Vatican.

As Prior of the Monastery of Santa Cruz at Nova Friburgo, and after serious reflection and prayer before Almighty God, considering my responsibilities to this monastery, and for my eternal salvation, I come in front of my superiors, in front of my brothers, and in front of Holy Church, to fulfil my duty to declare the following:

The Monastery of Santa Cruz refuses the agreement entered into between the Sacred Congregation for the Doctrine of the Faith in the person of Cardinals Ratzinger and Mayer and Dom Gérard Calvet, Prior of the Monastery of St. Madeleine du Barroux.

Without us having been consulted, even though we were present at Le Barroux during these negotiations and our disagreement was known, our monastery had been included in the terms of the agreement which we hereby reject.

Here are the reasons for our rejection:

1) This agreement signifies our insertion and our practical engagement into the "Conciliar Church." This is a direct conclusion from the canons quoted in the agreement, which put us in a close relationship with the diocesan bishop and under his control. According to Canon 679 of the *1983 Code of Canon Law*, which is a part of the agreement, the diocesan bishop, whose guiding spirit remains that of the new Church, has even the power to expel us from his diocese.

2) The agreement foresees our full reconciliation with the Apostolic See according to the terms of the motu proprio *Ecclesia Dei*, a document which has proclaimed the excommunication of Archbishop Lefebvre. Now, we have never been separated from the Holy See and we continue to profess a perfect communion with the Chair of Peter, but we separate ourselves from the modernist and liberal Rome which organized the meeting at Assisi and praises Luther. With *that* Rome, we want no reconciliation!

3)   The agreement is based upon the motu proprio *Ecclesia Dei* which excommunicates Archbishop Lefebvre. Therefore, taking part with this agreement we would have to acknowledge the injustice perpetrated against Archbishop Lefebvre, Dom Antônio de Castro Mayer, and the four new bishops, whose excommunications were null and void. We do not follow Bishop de Castro Mayer or Archbishop Lefebvre as party leaders. We follow the Catholic Church, but at the present time these two Confessors of the Faith have been the only two bishops to stand against the auto-demolition of the Church. It is not possible to separate ourselves from them. So, as in the fourth century at the time of Arianism, to be "in communion with Athanasius" (and not with Pope Liberius), was a sign of orthodoxy, so now to be united with Archbishop Lefebvre and Bishop de Castro Mayer is a sign of fidelity to the Church of all times. St. Paul the Hermit gives us an enlightening example by asking St. Anthony, Patriarch of the Coenobites, to bury him in St. Athanasius' coat. The reason, according to St. Jerome, was to clearly indicate that he wanted to die in the faith and communion of St. Athanasius, Defender of Orthodoxy against the Arian heresy.

4)   The desire manifested by all our Brazilian benefactors leads us also to refuse this agreement. In doing so, we respect Canon 1300 of the *1983 Code of Canon Law*.

We feel our duty, out of love for our Faith and vocation, to repeat to our superiors the words of St. Godfrey of Amiens and St. Hugh of Grenoble to Pope Pascal II: "...God forbid, since you would thus lead us away from your obedience."

And St. Bernard teaches us: "He who does evil because he has been commanded does not perform an act of obedience but rather of rebellion. He upsets the order: he neglects obedience to God in order to obey men."[132]

Dom Tomàs Aquino
On the Feast of St. Bartholomew the Apostle
In the Year of Our Lord 1988

---

[132] *Complete Works of St. Bernard*, Charpentier, Book I, Ep. VII.

On August 26, 1988, the Friends of the Monastery of Santa Cruz published a text entitled "Reasons to Refuse the Road Proposed by Dom Gérard Calvet." They expressed four points of concern:

1) By the agreement, Dom Gérard will be too much in contact with many modernist influences, from which it will be very difficult to protect himself and his monastery. These modernists do not have the Catholic spirit. Gustavo Corção expressed it beautifully by saying, "Give us back Catholicism."[133]

2) It was imprudent to disregard Archbishop Lefebvre's judgment, since the past has proved that he was the only bishop who had been capable of efficiently resisting the invasion of Modernism.

3) The sincerity of the Vatican in granting the requests of Dom Gérard may be put in question since it comes at the same time they condemn Archbishop Lefebvre. Are they not trying "to divide and conquer"?

4) Dom Gérard loses the support of Archbishop Lefebvre, the Society of Saint Pius X and many other traditional communities: it will be very difficult to resist modernist influences after having thus isolated himself.

To the third reason, one may add that many conservative monks (*e.g.*, Monastery of Fontgombault) or priests have asked for the traditional Mass and Sacraments. If the Vatican was sincerely desirous to grant Tradition, it seems rather logical that they should grant it first to those who have been "obedient," rather than to those who have been (apparently) "disobedient." Now, they have not followed this logical order: Fontgombault received its indult only much later. Therefore, one can really raise doubts on the sincerity of the Vatican's desire to grant Tradition. Their real desire seems more frankly expressed by Cardinal Gagnon: we have been "too swift"; therefore, let us give these poor slow-moving faithful more time to adopt the changes.

There is another possible explanation: those in authority in the Vatican consider loyalty to their own authority more important than loyalty to Tradition. Therefore they use Tradition in order to bring back these so-called "disobedient" religious orders to a certain loyalty to their own authority. They, themselves, are concerned for maintaining their authority over both sides (Progressives and Traditionalists) much more than they are concerned for maintaining the purity of Faith and morals.

We, on the contrary, consider that authority is a service: all authority in the Church is established by God in the service of the Deposit of Faith and of the salvation of souls! Our Lord Himself gave the example: "I am in the midst of you as He that serveth" (Lk. 22:27).

---

[133] *i.e.,* the true worship of the True God!

AUGUST 25, 1988

"SOME SIMPLE REFLECTIONS WHICH WE MAKE WITHOUT BITTERNESS"

Fr. Michel Simoulin, Rector of the Society of Saint Pius X's seminary in Ecône, Switzerland

Supporters of Dom Gérard began to insist that Archbishop Lefebvre approved Dom Gérard's decision to sign his accord with Rome and that Archbishop Lefebvre had agreed to say so publicly in the main magazine publication of the Society of Saint Pius X in Europe, *Fideliter*. When this didn't happen (since it was a total fabrication), Dom Gérard's supporters accused the Archbishop of not fulfilling his promises. To these falsehoods Fr. Michel Simoulin, then rector of the seminary in Ecône, Switzerland, felt obliged to answer.

On August 10, 1988, Reverend Fr. Jean-Baptiste (of Le Barroux) wrote to Mother Anne-Marie Simoulin of Fanjeaux:[134]

> We have done nothing without seeking the Archbishop's advice. He had even agreed to write in *Fideliter* that he agrees with us. Meanwhile, he has changed his mind. Once again at your house, he agreed to receive us in order to counsel us. Can you permit us the time to comprehend the Archbishop's attitude?

Charity and friendship oblige me to believe in good faith, but I have the right to think that it may have been abused. How? By whom or by what? I do not know. But what I do know is what I have been witness to, or what the Archbishop just told me, having been consulted on this subject.

- It is true that Dom Gérard came to consult Archbishop Lefebvre at Ecône before the consecrations and, then, on July 26, while he was travelling toward Fanjeaux.
- In the course of these conversations, the Archbishop advised Dom Gérard not to sign an agreement, while recognizing that the dan-

---

[134] The traditional Dominican convent which supports Archbishop Lefebvre and the Society of Saint Pius X.

gers—although certain—were less for a monastery, all of whose subjects are grouped together. Dom Gérard thus indeed took counsel but he did not follow the advice given.

- Dom Gérard asked the Archbishop to make a statement in *Fideliter* to express his approval but the Archbishop declined, since he did not approve of this agreement.
- In the course of their last interview on July 26, Dom Gérard said nothing to the Archbishop about his letters of July 8 to the Pope and to Cardinal Ratzinger. They have remained secret to this day.
- While at Fanjeaux, the Archbishop learned by telephone and through the press, of the recognition of Le Barroux. Dom Gérard offered to come to show him the documents but Archbishop Lefebvre refused to receive him by reason of the concealments of July 26.

Such are the facts. I do not want to accuse anyone of lying and there remains for me no other solution than a gigantic lack of understanding, but who will believe it? In any case, let people stop saying that Archbishop Lefebvre gave his approval to this agreement.

The Archbishop does not wish to engage in polemics; we certainly wish to imitate him. But is it forbidden for us to be hurt and wounded by certain passages of the declaration of Dom Gérard? That he chose a different route—that is his perfect right, and within limits, we would have nothing to say—but was it necessary to draw us into it, as if we were his only adversaries?

On two occasions and with no necessity whatever, the famous "denunciation" of May 6 of the Protocol on May 5 is mentioned. Beyond the fact that this appeal added nothing to the declaration, it does nothing but to revive the Vatican thesis, which is intended to put the Archbishop's intellectual faculties and the sureness of his judgment into doubt. Was it necessary to persist in this direction? Toward what purpose?

Let the letter of May 6 be read and re-read and let someone tell me where the terms are that indicate a refusal, a breaking of the accords of May 5. For myself, I see there only an insistence and a demand for precisions not determined by the agreement.

Moreover, Dom Gérard's declaration does not concede to Archbishop Lefebvre any merit other than his tenacity. It is perhaps a little short. As for his struggle and the work that he has founded, these are not treated anywhere; it seems of no importance that the Society or the other foundations be covered with disrepute.

The Society thus apparently has neither importance nor existence. Doubtless we are all imperfect but what Dom Gérard says he wants to do, owing to this agreement—is this not truly already being done elsewhere?

Has no school child, scout, seminarian, St. Cyrien,[135] ever had access to the true liturgy and to the true doctrine in our priories or elsewhere than at Le Barroux—without counting the families, the children, the sick, the elderly, the dying—does he not count all that? Has this not been possible even without an agreement for years now?

"Party spirit." "A great unified party electing for its head a superior who makes his troops maneuverer at his good pleasure." "Resistentialism, where suspicion reigns and where the purge makes the law." "Haste and ill will." "Internal quarrels, rivalries of clique or of jurisdiction."

May I ask who is referred to by these unsupported insinuations? Whom is he shooting at thus without designating the target?

While those who have been destroying Tradition for the past twenty-five years are carefully spared, is it not those who, during the same time, have had confidence in the Archbishop and worked with him, who are thus publicly abused? If the retorts come, who will have thrown the first one?

Curiously, the text of the second wish has been modified in the version that *Présent* published (See text as published in its modified version on p.201). The original text, which was sent to us, said, "...On the contrary, *we propose a pact of alliance* with all those who are fighting for Tradition...." Several questions came up: Why this modification in the published text? Has Dom Gérard been made to see and understand that it was a little strong?

This "pact of alliance" existed already with no confusion of institutions, in a generous collaboration of those who wanted it. Who has broken it? Is not this "proposition" a little daring and presumptuous? The Archbishop has always declined to be the "head" of a "great, unified party," and this is, moreover, why he allowed every liberty to Dom Gérard to attempt an accord that he had himself refused without, however, approving of it. (How could he have done so without being illogical?)

Visibly raised up by Providence, Archbishop Lefebvre has responded to requests (including those of Dom Gérard). He has founded an institution and fought with all those who were doing so already—either beside him or following him. He had over them all no other authority than that of his episcopate, of his experience, of his sense, and of his knowledge of the Church and of souls, and of his wisdom. No one ever "elected" him—except in the sense of choosing—and it is confidence which drives his "troops," not a narrow and elementary militarism, or a strict fanaticism or

---

[135] Fr. Michel Simoulin is a former captain in the French Army, and a graduate of St. Cyr, the French equivelent of Westpoint Military College in the US. He was formerly Rector of the Society of Saint Pius X's seminary in Ecône. In 1997 he was appointed the Society's District Superior in Italy.

an unhealthy adulation. It would be to insult many simple and noble souls to suggest that such could be the case. In all this, the Archbishop's attitude has always remained religious and humble, not intervening except where and when he has been asked to do so.

It is strange that Dom Gérard raises himself up as the center of a new alliance and offers himself thus to those whom the old alliance was uniting—the old one, not repealed—which he has just left. This is a completely different attitude.

I am saying all this without anger and with much sadness—not to stir any controversy, but to defend the Archbishop, my colleagues in the Society, and others upon whom very distressing suspicions have been cast.

I will add that I would have granted that Dom Gérard attempt the experiment of an agreement but not at this moment of our condemnation and not in the terms of his declaration.

In any case, whatever may be my esteem for Dom Gérard, I have—confirmed in this by the present experience—much more esteem for Archbishop Lefebvre, more trust in his judgment, his word, his disinterestedness and his wisdom. May Dom Gérard pardon me for this, but he is wrong in not having enough esteem for the Archbishop.

Rev. Fr. Michel Simoulin
Rector, St. Pius X International Seminary

AUGUST/SEPTEMBER 1988

TRAGEDY AT ECÔNE

Fr. Crane analyzes the status of Archbishop Lefebvre with Rome, concluding that the crisis in the Church requires not more experts, but courage. Archbishop Lefebvre had the courage "to stand firm in the face of neo-modernist attack, defending the Faith and confounding its enemies." Is this not an excellent justification for the consecration of bishops by Archbishop Lefebvre and against his unjust excommunication?

Christian Order, **edited by Paul Crane, S.J.,
vol.29, Aug./Sept., No.8/9, 1988.**

I found myself wondering as I read in *The Daily Telegraph* (Nov. 7, 1988):

> The battle for the hearts and minds of Archbishop Lefebvre's followers has opened in earnest with the Pope appointing a senior cardinal to seek ways to keep them within the mainstream Roman Catholic Church.
>
> Cardinal Paul Mayer, a 77-year-old West German, will lead a Vatican Commission of eight Church experts who have the task of persuading the traditionalists to remain loyal to Rome, while making allowance for their "spiritual and liturgical" needs.

There you have it. The lines apparently are drawn. With great respect, I would suggest that, in fact, they were drawn long ago; the gulf that now separates what we may call the New Church from the True[136] saw its first beginnings as no more than a somewhat turbulent stream, when the New Mass was thrust on the faithful, overnight as it were, in the immediate wake of the Second Vatican Council. The effect was traumatic where vast numbers of the faithful were concerned. At one stroke, you might say, the lynch-pin of their faith was destroyed. This they sensed; knew to be so. They knew it within themselves without being able clearly to express it. Which is not to be wondered at. The dearest things in life are loved beyond words. The whole of their faith was in the Old Mass. This the faith-

---

[136] This implicitly says that Archbishop Lefebvre represents the True Church.

ful knew. Now they see it as gone; not only from the New Mass, but every-where within the Church.[137]

The New Mass in their eyes, valid though it is, where they are con-cerned—and increasingly in practice—is little more than a community gathering, protestantized to the point where it is increasingly man-cen-tered; drifting away from God. And, with it, naturally enough, what prac-tice there remains of the Catholic Faith drifts away as well. Over the years, doctrine has tended to follow suit. There is no need to enlarge on this point. It has been covered again and again in the pages of *Christian Order.* Small wonder that the split which came with the overnight imposition of the New Mass has widened beyond words into the abyss which today di-vides the Old Church from the New, as it divided originally the Old Mass from the New.

Working on that original rupture, which was largely their own cre-ation, the neo-modernist establishment, from its position of power at all levels within the Church,[138] has worked away at its task of diverting the Church's doctrinal and evangelizing thrust to suit no more than man's mo-mentary needs, as distinct from holding out to him the eternal truths of God. Those in opposition to this trend, who stand by the faith of their fathers, have been, in so many cases I know of, rebuffed, marginalized, isolated. The marvel is that they now stand at all. The onslaught on all they hold dear has, in so many cases, been pitiless in its insensitivity. Does Rome know anything of this—the plight of its marooned faithful?—If it does, I have to say with respect that, in practice, it appears to so many, not only as having done nothing about it; but as incapable now of doing any-thing in the future to save what is an increasingly desperate situation. The hungry sheep are not merely not being fed; they are being left to die; and, with them, the Faith they have refused to surrender to the predators within the Church they love, who are busier now than ever shredding that Faith to pieces.

I am not a Lefebvrist. I never have been, But I can understand com-pletely why so many have turned to him. It is simply because they find once more within Archbishop Lefebvre's Society of Saint Pius X and its ministrations—above all, the Old Mass—everything that has been taken

---

[137] The modernists changed the rites of every one of the seven Sacraments, the Catechism, Canon Law, the rules of all the religious orders. They introduced a new curricula in seminaries, and a new morality where personal conscience is the rule of conduct rather than that of the Ten Commandments.

[138] Cardinal Ratzinger himself acknowledges that all the bishops appointed in the wake of the Council were chosen from the most liberal candidates: "In the first years after Vat-ican II, the candidate for the episcopate seemed to be a priest who above all was 'open to the world'. At any rate this criterion came entirely into the foreground" (*The Ratz-inger Report*, p.65).

from them in the wake of the Council and in the name of that which was claimed so fraudulently to be within its spirit. Now, most tragically, the break has come. I regret it more deeply than I can say; but, without excusing it, I do understand it. In what way? Simply this. For more than twenty years now, as it appears, High authority in the Church has received complaint after complaint from faithful Catholics shocked at what is going on in the Church they love. And what has come of their complaints? So far as they can see, nothing; absolutely nothing at all. In the eyes of so many, Church authority has stripped itself of credibility in their eyes. There have been words. There have been no deeds. They have found and still find themselves with nowhere to go. I am in no way surprised that, under these sad circumstances, so many have taken the road to Ecône. I do not commend them for doing it; but I do understand why they have done it. Sheep without a shepherd; "Lord to whom shall we go?" As has appeared so tragically to so many, there was only one road left and they took it. Now Rome, as it seems to them, has blocked that road. They stand up-ended. One might ask the question: Who, in the last analysis, is responsible not only for the tragedy that has brought schism to the Catholic Church, but for the countless thousands of broken-hearted Catholics who have never taken the road to Ecône, but whose lives have been shattered by the neo-modernist wave that has engulfed the Church and deprived them of the Mass they prized and loved beyond anything they had on this earth?

Let us realize straightforwardly, but with no rancor of bitterness, the reason why the Church is beset with the disintegration that has brought sadness and sorrow to so many. It is so beset because it is beset with neo-modernism and the reason for this can only be the failure, in practice, of the Church's bishops, priests and religious to stand firm in the face of neo-modernist attack; defending the Faith and confounding its enemies. This they have not done. This is a fact. Those who have watched, with mounting sorrow and frustration, the progressive ruination of the Catholic Church at the hands of its neo-modernist enemies know that this is so. The faithful have been betrayed by their pastors. If the faithful are to be brought back, whether they are in the family of Ecône or outside it, and peace restored to the Church once more, there is one thing that has to be done by way of a beginning. The Old Mass must be restored to the whole Church now, unconditionally and, at least, on a basis of parity of esteem with the New. The Holy Father must do this and bishops and religious superiors be placed under the most severe injunction to see that this is done. There is no other way. With all respect, at this twenty-fourth hour it is not experts who are needed to rescue the Church from disaster. What is needed is courage. Under God, no more and no less than that.

OCTOBER 1988

THE STRATEGY OF "REHABILITATION" UNVEILED BY CARDINAL DECOURTRAY

In this text on of the four bishops consecrated by Archbishop Lefebvre, Bishop Tissier de Mallerais analyzed the Declaration of Cardinal Decourtray, President of the French Bishops' Conference, published in *Documentation Catholique,* No.1969, Oct. 1988. Bishop Tissier de Mallerais cites from Cardinal Decourtray and follows with his commentary. The Cardinal's Declaration exposes a strategy by which a traditional priest is to be marginalized and made of no effect in a diocese.

In a communiqué to the priestly council and to the diocesan pastoral council which met in an extraordinary session, the Cardinal Archbishop of Lyon did not hide the fact that the reception of the priests who leave Archbishop Lefebvre will be made with no gift attached; it will be, in fact, their rehabilitation into the Conciliar Church.

Let us take up the interesting passage of the Cardinal's document. We emphasize [in italics] what should be emphasized:

Dear Friends, From now on you will know a little better the conditions under which I was brought to welcome Fr._____, lately ordained by Archbishop Lefebvre and put in charge of the St. Pius X priory on the Rue de Marseille, and to entrust him, *in urgency and in a provisional way,* with the agreement of the Sisters of the Good Shepherd, with the Chapel of Notre-Dame-des-Martyrs at the Place Saint-Irénée. *Obviously it is not a question of a parish* but of a shrine open to the faithful who desire to follow the Tridentine Tradition of the Mass (according to the typical edition of the Roman Missal of 1962)....I have given a *place of worship for the Tridentine celebration of the Mass.*

Thus no parish apostolate, only the celebration of Mass. One is far from the activity of the priory: catechism classes, youth movements, conferences, *etc.*

...This priest is therefore right now in order with the Church and has received the necessary jurisdiction for the valid exercise of the ministry of Penance or Reconciliation. The questions relative to the other sacraments, notably to marriage, remain pending. It will be necessary to take one's time. While waiting, Father…will see with the pastor of Saint-Irénée how to respond, in a way that is pastoral and consistent with the present day law of the Church, to certain prompt and exceptional requests.

Thus we have dependence with respect to an official parish and its pastor. The only autonomy is to be in the administration of the Sacrament of Penance.

> For the future, here is the text of the declaration that I will ask from the priests who, having recently manifested more or less explicitly, in word or in act, their approval of the actions and of the remarks of Archbishop Lefebvre, desire to exercise the priestly ministry in the Diocese of Lyon (jurisdiction for Confession and the *cura animarum*) and to obtain *contingently* the Indult permitting the use of the Roman Missal according to the typical edition of 1962.

Thus it is not only the ex-members of the Priestly Society of Saint Pius X who will be compelled to sign a declaration but all "suspect" priests, those who would hardly have manifested explicitly, even if only in words, their approval, even though only the utterances of Archbishop Lefebvre. And what is more, it is not certain that these suspect priests will be allowed to celebrate the Mass of all times.

> The diverse points of this declaration are *nearly* those of the protocol refused on May 6 by Archbishop Lefebvre.

> I promise always to be faithful to the Catholic Church and to the Roman Pontiff, its supreme Pastor, Vicar of Christ, successor of the blessed Peter in his primacy, and head of the body of bishops, in accordance with the First Council of the Vatican (Denzinger-Schönmetzer, 3059-3064), and with Vatican II (*Lumen Gentium*, §22), as well as *to the bishop of Lyon, to whom I promise respect and obedience.*

To the text of the Protocol are thus added new requirements. First of all, obedience to the bishop of the place. Will it therefore be necessary to obey his "pastoral of the Community,"[139] and adopt the catechism, *Pierres Vivantes?*[140]

> I declare that I adhere to the teachings of the magisterium of the Pope and the bishops, in conformity with the doctrine of the First Vatican Council (Denzinger-Schönmetzer, 3065-3074) and of the Second Vatican Council (*Lumen Gentium,* §25).

A demand that is new and without limits! This is not to adhere to the magisterium when it is truly a magisterium, that is to say, when it faithfully transmits the revealed deposit; but there is demanded the adherence *to*

---

[139] *i.e.,* the Cardinal's pastoral policy to develop base communities.
[140] A heretical French catechism.

the teachings [of the magisterium] *of the pope and the bishops* of this time: therefore, to ecumenism, to religious liberty, to the rights of man, *etc.*

> I pledge myself to have a positive attitude, of studying the decrees of the Second Vatican Council, of the liturgical books, and of the Code of Canon Law promulgated following the Council by the Sovereign Pontiff.

It is self-evident that Cardinal Decourtray erased from his text what Cardinal Ratzinger was conceding to Archbishop Lefebvre, namely, the right to consider that "certain texts" of the Council are "difficult to reconcile with Tradition." It is on these texts that Archbishop Lefebvre promised to have a positive attitude of study, *etc.* Visibly, at Lyon and in the dioceses, no dispute of the conciliar documents will be permitted, not even a question mark. No, one must stick to everything and "study" everything, as if he were culpably ignorant of these texts, as well as of those of the Mass of Paul VI and of the new Canon Law.

> I declare that I recognize the validity of the Sacrifice of the Mass and the Sacraments celebrated with the intention of doing what the Church does *in communion with the Pope* and according to the rites indicated in the typical editions *and the translations* of the missal and of the rituals, promulgated and approved by Popes Paul VI and John Paul II.

You will notice the two added points that we have emphasized. Non-communion with the Pope does not affect, in any case, the validity of the Mass. On the other hand, the bad translations (such as *"pour la multitude"* and, still more serious, the "for all" of the English and German [and Italian] translation—betrayals) *do indeed affect the validity*, or, at the least, place a doubt in their regard. Approved of or not by the present-day Roman bureaus, a translation that changes even only partially the meaning of the sacramental words can render the sacrament invalid. The *creativity* of the national centers of pastoral liturgical study and the frivolity of the Roman commissions are the cause of numerous erroneous vernacular versions, which are indeed bluntly whimsical ones that can bring about the invalidity of the sacrament.

Even in *Latin* certain new sacramentary texts yield, by their ambiguity, to an interpretation that is Protestant in a sense, and that can exert influence on the celebrant by giving him a *counter-intention* which invalidates the sacrament.

> I promise to observe the common discipline of the Church and the ecclesiastical laws, particularly those contained in the Code of Canon Law promulgated by Pope John Paul II.

Here there is no change in the text that Archbishop Lefebvre had judged on May 5 as being at the extreme limit of acceptability, with the restriction placed on No. 3, concerning the "texts difficult to reconcile with Tradition." Deprived of this restriction, the declaration demanded by Cardinal Decourtray asks for the acceptance of the entirely questionable passages from the new Canon Law. For example: the "double subject of the supreme power in the Church"; the reversal of the two ends of marriage (the perfecting of the spouses put before the procreation and education of the children!); the suppression of the promises of the non-Catholic spouse in a mixed marriage, concerning the baptism and the Catholic education of all the children; and finally, intercommunion foreseen in certain cases.

> Thought must also be given to the pastoral accompaniment of the faithful attached to the Tridentine Mass but faithful to the pope and to the bishops...to receive the confidence of the faithful attached to the liturgy and to the catechesis such as they knew them before the reforms, but also to help them *progress in the living communion* of the Catholic Church. For this I count very much on the movements of Catholic Action, in the strict or the broad sense.

In this excerpt you have the purpose of the intended rehabilitation: "...to help them to progress in the Living Communion of the Catholic Church..." How are we to interpret this except to mean that we must "get into line," to be "re-integrated" into the system, to accept the new ideology of the conciliar Church?..."Let us not set foot in the opposing camp, because we would thus be giving the enemy a proof of our weakness, which the enemy would try to interpret as a sign of weakness and a mark of complicity." —St. Pius X

† Tissier de Mallerais

NOVEMBER-DECEMBER 1988

INTERVIEW OF ARCHBISHOP LEFEBVRE GIVEN TO *FIDELITER* MAGAZINE

Bishop Bernard Tissier de Mallerais ordained seven priests at Ecône, Switzerland, on September 25, 1988, and Bishop Bernard Fellay, another of the four bishops consecrated by Archbishop Lefebvre, ordained three at Zaitzkofen, Germany, on October 1, 1988. These constitute the most important actions after the consecrations. After the ordinations, His Excellency Archbishop Lefebvre granted an interview to *Fideliter*.

Interviewer: After these ordinations, what are your feelings?

Archbishop Lefebvre: I can feel nothing but joy. It was, indeed, this desire to insure the continuity of the transmission of the Catholic priesthood that led me to consecrate four bishops.

This was my wish—to see the work continue. It was a feeling that I had already experienced when I passed on the charge of Superior General of the Society to Fr. Schmidberger. I acknowledge that I will be happy if the Good Lord grants me a few more years to live and see the continuation of the Society. Now there are signs that it will last, that it will endure, and that it will be strengthened. I am happy to see that my episcopacy shall not be the last one faithful to Tradition, and that Tradition will continue even should I die now. The fact of having bishops is of paramount importance.

It was certainly a decision not easily made. On Jan. 2, 1988, I wrote to Fr. Aulagnier, "Behold, a new year is beginning; it will be a year for great decisions, whether the proposals from Rome are good or not. I am almost certain that they will be inadmissible, and that we shall have to continue the work of the Church without the support of the Vatican. It shall be the year of the bishops of the Society, God willing—Let us hope that it shall be a source of blessings. He who says blessings, says trials too..."

It is with that spirit that I went to the negotiations which I feared would not succeed.

Interviewer: At the end of July, in the conference to the Chilean bishops, Cardinal Ratzinger had severe words regarding the disastrous effects of

Vatican II, without identifying their causes.

Archbishop Lefebvre: Yes, indeed. He called for an examination of conscience for "the post-schism." He proposed three areas of reflection.

1)   The question of the liturgy too much desacralized;
2)   Whether it was an error to present Vatican II as a super-dogma, blotting out the whole of the Tradition of the Church;
3)   That the documents of the Council do not all have the same importance.

The Cardinal said that many see, in Archbishop Lefebvre, a guide and a useful master....One must take into account the positive elements which do not find a vital place in the Church today. He expressed the opinion that if the areas are corrected "the schism" of Archbishop Lefebvre will not last long. What can be the deep feelings of the Cardinal? One is forced to acknowledge that, for the Cardinal, one must return to the Council.

We indeed had a little hope that something had changed in the Vatican; especially after the Visit of Cardinal Gagnon and Msgr. Perl and their declarations, I had hoped that things would develop in Rome.

But, then, when we found out their deeper intentions in the meetings, the discussions on the Protocol, and the Protocol itself, I realized that nothing had changed. We were faced with a brick wall. They had hoped to put an end to Tradition. This is, indeed, the position of Rome, of the Pope, of Cardinal Ratzinger, of Cardinal Mayer, of Cardinal Casaroli....All these people hold desperately to the Council, to this "new Pentecost," to the reform of the Church. They do not want to depart from it.

Cardinal Ratzinger said it openly in an interview to the great Frankfurt newspaper, *Die Welt,* about the consecrations: "It is inadmissible, one cannot accept that there be in the Church groups of Catholics who do not follow the general way of thinking of the bishops in the world."

Here you have it; it is clear!

For a while I thought something had changed in him, but I have to acknowledge that all he did was with the intention to suppress the group that we were forming and to bring us back to the Council. It would be a mistake to impute only to Cardinal Decourtray and to the French Bishops this will; it is the position of Rome. The only difference is that the Vatican has more facilities to grant things to attract the traditionalists and, then, later, destroy them and bring them back to the Council. It is just a question of Roman diplomacy.

The French, German and Swiss bishops are not happy with the groups to which Rome has now granted some privileges. So they have said to the

Vatican, "Don't give us such groups. We don't know what to do with them! They are going to cause trouble. We had condemned them; we had rejected them, and now you say they have the right to do what they want. It cannot go like that."

I would not be surprised that there be confrontations between the bishops and Rome. Some have already started. Recently, in the name of the Swiss bishops, Msgr. Henri Schwery made a violent declaration against Rome, saying that it was inadmissible to have given such admissions to the traditionalists without consulting them. They have not been consulted and Rome has caused disorder in their dioceses.[141]

I will, therefore, not be surprised if during the next bishops' meeting of France, Germany and Switzerland there be violent reactions against Rome. The Vatican shall be brought to say to those who have left us, "You must accept the Council; you must accept the New Mass. You must not be so intransigent."

The Vatican "will get them!" It's impossible that it should be otherwise.

Interviewer: Cardinal Oddi recently declared, "I'm convinced that the division shall not last long, and that Archbishop Lefebvre shall soon be back in the Church of Rome." Others say that the Pope and Cardinal Ratzinger feel that the "Lefebvre affair" is not closed. In your last letter to the Holy Father[142] you declared that you were waiting for a more propitious time for the return of Rome to Tradition. What do you think of a possible re-opening of the dialogue with Rome?

Archbishop Lefebvre: We do not have the same outlook on a reconciliation. Cardinal Ratzinger sees it as reducing us, bringing us back to Vatican II. We see it as a return of Rome to Tradition. We don't agree; it is a dialogue of death. I can't speak much of the future, mine is behind me, but if I live a little while, supposing that Rome calls for a renewed dialogue, then, I will put conditions. I shall not accept being in the position where I was put during the dialogue. No more.

I will place the discussion at the doctrinal level: "Do you agree with the great encyclicals of all the popes who preceded you? Do you agree with

---

[141] "Msgr. Henri Schwery, President of the Swiss Episcopal Conference, has publicly lamented 'the lack of openness of the Vatican regarding the re-integration of some traditionalist communities.' According to Schwery, open relations and negotiations do not exist between 'the Holy See and the local bishops,' and in his view the Commission should continue to operate only 'on the condition that the bishop of the place concerned be informed and consulted'" (*30 Days,* No.6, Oct. 1988).

[142] June 2, 1988.

Quanta Cura of Pius IX, *Immortale Dei* and *Libertas* of Leo XIII, *Pascendi Gregis* of Pius X, *Quas Primas* of Pius XI, *Humani Generis* of Pius XII? Are you in full communion with these Popes and their teachings? Do you still accept the entire Anti-Modernist Oath? Are you in favor of the social reign of Our Lord Jesus Christ? If you do not accept the doctrine of your predecessors, it is useless to talk! As long as you do not accept the correction of the Council, in consideration of the doctrine of these Popes, your predecessors, no dialogue is possible. It is useless."

Thus, the positions will be clear.

The stakes are not small. We are not content when they say to us, "You may say the traditional Mass, but you must accept the Council." What opposes us is doctrine; it is clear.

This is what Dom Gérard did not see, and what confused him. Dom Gérard has always seen the liturgy and the monastic life, but he does not clearly see the theological problems of the Council, especially Religious Liberty. He does not see the malice of these errors. He was never too much worried about this. What touched him was the liturgical reform and the reform of the Benedictine monasteries. He left Tournay, saying, "I cannot accept this."

Then, he founded a community of monks with the liturgy and with a Benedictine spirit. Very well, wonderful. But he did not appreciate enough that these reforms which led him to leave his monastery were the consequences of errors in the Council itself.

As long as they grant him what he wanted—this monastic spirit and the traditional liturgy—he has what he wants and is indifferent to the rest. But he has fallen into a snare: the others have given up nothing of their false principles.

It is sad because there are around sixty monks, twenty priests, and thirty nuns. There are nearly one hundred youth there, bewildered, whose families are worried or even divided. It is a disaster.

Interviewer: The nuns of the monastery Notre Dame de l'Annonciation remain very much attached to you.

Archbishop Lefebvre: Yes, indeed. They came to manifest their affections....However, I do not seek this affection, but rather that they remain attached to Tradition. Are they willing to submit to a modernist authority? Here, indeed, is the question. If needed they must separate themselves from Dom Gérard to keep the Faith and Tradition.

At least the monastery in Brazil [Dom Tomás Aquino's Monastery of Santa Cruz] refused to follow Dom Gérard and that is an important point.

I believe that what has contributed to the loss of Dom Gérard was his desire to open to those who are not with us and who would profit from following Tradition. This was the theme of what he wrote in his letter to the Friends of the Monastery two years after his arrival at Le Barroux. He was saying, "We will strive not to have this critical, sterile, negative attitude. We will strive to open our doors to all those who, though they might not have our ideas, would love the liturgy, so that they too may benefit from the monastic life."

From that period, I was worried, considering this as a dangerous operation. It was the opening of the Church to the world, and one must acknowledge that it was the world that converted the Church. Dom Gérard let himself be contaminated by the milieu which he welcomed in his monastery. Rome may be proud to have won a big battle and to have hit in the right place. It is sad....

Interviewer: Do you believe in the future of the Society of St. Peter?

Archbishop Lefebvre: It is a phantom society. They have copied our statutes and all that we have done.

Interviewer: Even Cardinal Oddi was skeptical of its future, referring himself to the previous attempts of Rome to rehabilitate seminarians from the Society of Saint Pius X.

Archbishop Lefebvre:....In one year, one and a half, they may be asked to return to their dioceses....They will have to choose priests from the dioceses to take care of their seminarians. They will have to wait for a year and to undergo an examination before being accredited. How can they see that they are being played with? They came to Rome to deliver themselves into their hands with the hope of keeping Tradition and they are already rejected. "You are not allowed to teach in your seminary. You must pass an exam first, because we do not trust you." It is unbelievable. It manifests that there is, in Rome, the will to put an end to Tradition.

This is also the reason that they did not want to give us bishops. Rome did not want traditional bishops. This is why the consecrations annoyed them and caused such a terrible shock. It is like the stone which hit Goliath.

To excommunicate us after having lifted all other excommunications, is the end of their ecumenism. How can they imagine that those with whom they wish to shake hands trust them when they excommunicate those who uphold Tradition?

The most recent issue of *Fideliter* was entitled, "Rome Is Perplexed." This is true; they don't know what to do: attacking us they attack the Church of all times and the Good Lord cannot allow that.

SEPTEMBER 2, 1992

LETTER OF FR. JOSEPH BISIG TO AN AUSTRALIAN FAITHFUL

Less than five years after their foundation, the Superior General of the Society of Saint Peter positively encouraged people to attend the *Novus Ordo*, even though it may be partially scandalous to their Faith. As of 1999, Fr. Bisig still remained the Society of Saint Peter's first and only Superior General.

Dear Mr. _____,

The following replies are in response to the questions in your recent letter dated on August 4, 1992.

Q.1: Is it permissible to attend a Society of Saint Pius X Mass when there is no Latin Mass in the district?

A.1: You should try your best to attend a *Novus Ordo* Mass which is piously celebrated or not totally scandalous to the Roman Catholic Faith.

Rev. Josef Bisig, Superior General

PART III

EPILOGUE

FEBRUARY 2, 1634

THE APPARITION OF
OUR LADY OF GOOD FORTUNE,
QUITO, ECUADOR (1634)

Among the numerous manifestations of Our Lady's predilection for the land of Ecuador (South America), we find her apparitions to Mother Mary Anne of Jesus in 1634. Her image is still venerated today in the convent of her Immaculate Conception at Quito. This apparition is approved by the Church. The prophecy is striking. Archbishop Lefebvre himself cited this apparition in his sermon delivered the day of the episcopal consecrations (June 30, 1988). That sermon appears starting on p.116 of this book.

On February 2, 1634, Mother Mary Anne of Jesus Torres was praying in front of the Blessed Sacrament when suddenly the sanctuary lamp burning in front of the altar went out. While she was trying to re-light it, a supernatural light filled the church. In the light, the Mother of God appeared to her and said:

> Beloved daughter of my heart, I am Our Lady of Good Fortune, your Mother and Protectress, carrying my Most Holy Son on my left arm and holding the scepter in my right hand. I have come to tell you some good news: in ten months and ten days you will close your eyes to the earthly light of this world in order to open them to the brightness of light everlasting.

> Oh, if only human beings and religious knew what heaven is and what it is to possess God, how differently they would live, sparing no sacrifice in order to enter more fully into possession of it! But some let themselves be dazzled by the false glamour of honors and human greatness while others are blinded by self-love, not realizing that they are falling into lukewarmness, that immense evil which in religious houses destroys their fervor, humility, self-renunciation and the ceaseless practice of religious virtues and fraternal charity, and that child-like simplicity which makes souls so dear to my Divine Son and to me, their Mother.

Then Our Lady of Good Fortune began to speak of the Order of the Immaculate Conception and, in particular, of the convent of the Conception in Quito:

This house will be attacked with a fury out of hell to destroy and annihilate it; but Divine Providence and I will be watching over it to preserve it, by favoring the virtues practiced by the nuns in this house....Know also, my beloved daughter, that my motherly love will watch over the convents of the Order of my Immaculate Conception, because this Order will give me great glory through all the daughters I shall have here. I shall take special care of the convents formed in this land by the members of this house. Often they will be on the brink of annihilation, but miraculously they will come to life again. Only one will close, in conformity with God's will: you will know which, when you are in heaven.

The sanctuary lamp burning in front of the Prisoner of Love, which you saw go out, has many meanings...

First meaning: at the end of the 19th and for a large part of the 20th, various heresies will flourish on this earth which will have become a free republic. The precious light of the Faith will go out in souls because of the almost total moral corruption: in those times there will be great physical and moral calamities, in private and in public. The little number of souls keeping the Faith and practicing the virtues will undergo cruel and unspeakable suffering; through their long, drawn out martyrdom many of them will go to their death because of the violence of their sufferings, and those will count as martyrs who gave their lives for Church or for country. To escape from being enslaved by these heresies will call for great strength of will, constancy, courage and great trust in God, all of which are gifts from the merciful love of my Divine Son to those He will have chosen for the work of restoration. To put to the trial the faith and trust of these just souls, there will come moments when everything seems lost and paralyzed, and just then comes the happy beginning of the complete restoration.

Second meaning: My communities will be abandoned; they will be swamped in a fathomless sea of bitterness, and will seem drowned in tribulations. How many true vocations will be lost for lack of skilful and prudent direction to form them! Each mistress of novices will need to be a soul of prayer, knowing how to discern spirits.

The third meaning of the lamp's going out is that in those times, the air will be filled with the spirit of impurity which, like a deluge of filth, will flood the streets, squares and public places. The licentiousness will be such that there will be no more virgin souls in the world.

A fourth meaning is that by having control of all the social classes, the sects will tend to penetrate with great skill into the heart of families to destroy even the children. The devil will take glory in feeding perfidiously on the heart of children. The innocence of childhood will almost disappear. Thus priestly vocations will be lost, it will be a real disaster. Priests will abandon their sacred duties and will depart from the path marked out for them by God. Then the Church will go through a dark night for lack of a prelate and father to watch over it with love, gentleness, strength and prudence, and numbers of priests will lose the spirit of God, thus placing their souls in great danger.

Pray constantly, cry out unwearyingly and weep unceasingly with bitter tears in the depths of your heart, asking Our Father in heaven, for love of the Eucharistic Heart of my most holy Son, for His Precious Blood so generously shed and for the profound bitterness and sufferings of His Passion and death, that He have pity on His ministers and that He put an end to such fatal times, by sending to His Church the prelate who will restore the spirit of His priests.

Upon this my beloved son, whom my divine Son and I love with a love of predilection, we shall heap many gifts—of humility of heart, of docility to varying inspirations, of strength to defend the rights of the Church and of a heart with which he will, like a new Christ, take possession of the mightiest of men as of the lowliest, without scorning the least fortunate amongst them. With a wholly divine gentleness he will lead consecrated souls to the service of God in religious houses without making the Lord's yoke weigh heavy upon them. He will hold in his hand the scales of the sanctuary for everything to be done in orderly fashion for God to be glorified. This prelate and father will act as a counterweight to the lukewarmness of souls consecrated in the priesthood and in religion.

Satan will gain control of this earth through the fault of faithless men who, like a black cloud, will darken the clear sky of the republic consecrated to the Most Sacred Heart of my Divine Son. This republic, having allowed entry to all the vices, will have to undergo all sorts of chastisements: plague, famine, war, apostasy, and the loss of souls without number.

And to scatter these black clouds blocking the brilliant dawning of the freedom of the church, there will be a terrible war in which the blood of priests and of religious will flow....That night will be so horrible that wickedness will seem triumphant. Then will come my time: in astounding fashion I shall destroy Satan's pride, casting him beneath my feet, chaining him up in the depths of hell, leaving Church and country freed at last from his cruel tyranny.

The fifth meaning of the lamp's going out is that men possessing great wealth will look on with indifference while the Church is oppressed, virtue is persecuted, and evil triumphs. They will not use their wealth to fight evil and re-construct the Faith. The people will come to care nothing for the things of God, will absorb the spirit of evil and will let themselves be swept away by all the vices and passions. Ah, my beloved daughter, were it given you to live in those fatal times, you would die of grief at seeing everything I have told you come about. My most holy Son and I have such a great love for this earth, our property, that it is our wish as of now to apply your sacrifices and good works to the lessening of the duration of such a terrible catastrophe.

FEBRUARY 2, 1988

SERMON OF ARCHBISHOP LEFEBVRE

As envisioned by Archbishop Lefebvre in its statutes, the apostolate of the Society of Saint Pius X is the restoration of the Catholic Priesthood and the preservation of the Holy Sacrifice of the Mass. These ends were clearly on His Grace's mind when he gave this sermon at the Society's International Seminary of the Holy Curé of Ars (Flavigny, France) on February 2, 1988. The occasion was the Feast of the Purification of Our Lady on which date seminarians were tonsured and received the clerical habit known as the "cassock." The Order of Tonsure is the official public act of the Catholic Church making a man a cleric. In reading this sermon, who can deny that Archbishop Lefebvre was a prelate sent to the Catholic Church to restore the spirit of God's priests?

My dear Brethren,

I am glad to give the cassock, the clerical habit, and particularly to give the tonsure to those who entered last year, thereby marking the official entry into the clergy and preparing them to receive the Orders, steps toward the Priesthood. It is always a very moving celebration.

The Purification itself is a moving Feast. We can imagine the Virgin Mary coming to the temple with the Child Jesus and St. Joseph, bringing the offering—doves—and meeting on their way the old man, Simeon, who acknowledged his God in this little Child carried by the Virgin Mary; and as it had been promised to him that he would not leave, would not die, without seeing his Savior, he took Him in his arms and sang this magnificent hymn, *Nunc dimittis servum tuum Domine*—Now thou dost dismiss thy servant, O Lord, according to thy word in peace. Our Lord, Who is the King of all things, entered into the temple carried by the Virgin Mary. It was His temple because it was the temple of God. He did not come there as other creatures, to give themselves to God. He *was* God. He came to take possession of His temple, which belonged to Him, and He had a right to all the honors which were given in this temple to God Himself.

And you, my very dear friends, who are going to be tonsured in a very few moments, you shall also enter in the temple of God. You shall enter by the tonsure; you are indeed going to receive the cassock and the tonsure but these two things are very distinct; indeed, one can receive the religious habit, yet without receiving the tonsure. There are in holy Church diverse families: the two principle families are the family of the simple faithful and the family of the clergy—the laity and the clergy. Among the laity there are also two families: there is the family of those who destine themselves to remain in the world, to found families, Christian families, and there are those who give themselves to the Good Lord, who consecrate themselves to God as religious, monks or nuns, though they do not participate in the sacred Orders. They receive the religious habit, they pronounce the vows of religion, totally consecrate themselves to God, and dedicate themselves in a very particular way to their neighbor, yet, they do not belong to the clergy. Only those who are tonsured belong to the clergy. One enters into the clergy by the tonsure. This is the Tradition of the Church. Once one is tonsured, then, one can accede to the Minor Orders and, later, to the Major Orders. Certainly, the decisive step shall be taken at the moment of the subdiaconate, but to receive the tonsure is already a promise to go to the altar—to ascend to the altar.

It is, therefore, a very important thing for you, my very dear friends. You know that from the moment you receive the tonsure—the Pontiff shall say this during his last instruction—you are accountable to the Church, you belong to the clergy of the Church. You are no longer subject to certain laws that are for the lay Catholic. You can say, my very dear friends—and, I think, this is the main thought that you should have today: "I do not have the intention to remain among the faithful to found a family. I want to give myself to God for my whole life; I want to serve Him and I hope, one day, to become a priest." Moreover, you are not like the monks, at least not as many of them who enter the different orders and have made their religious profession but have not become clerics; no, this is not your intention. You wish to ascend the degrees of the altar.

Now, what is your responsibility? What responsibility do you take in front of the Church, in front of God, in front of the faithful, in front of the religious who are not clerics? What is your obligation to holiness, to go in the way of perfection that you are entering? Are you more or less engaged in the way of perfection than those that found Catholic families, than the religious who enter diverse orders without becoming priests? Tell me!

I think that this obligation to holiness is greater, is more incumbent upon you by the very fact that you enter the clergy, and that you want to become priests. Greater even than for those who pronounce the vows of religion and who are not clerics, than the faithful who remain in the world to found a Catholic family. You obligation to holiness is greater. Why? Because your condition is different.

The Catholic who does not enter into a religious society, who does not enter the clergy, this Catholic has an obligation to pursue holiness because of his Baptism, because of his Confirmation; he must fulfil the promises of his Baptism: I attach myself to Jesus Christ for always, I renounce Satan, his scandals, his sins, and I attach myself to Jesus Christ for always. This is not a promise in vain. It is important; the priest says this when he puts the white veil on the head of the child and then when he gives him the candle through the intermediary of his godfather or godmother; he says to them, "*serva Dei mandata*—keep the commandments of God," "Receive this white robe and carry it unstained to the judgment seat of Our Lord Jesus Christ, so that you may have everlasting life." Here you have the obligation that the Catholic makes for his whole life. Therefore, even if he remains in what is called the "world," he is *in* the world but he is not *of* the world, he has an obligation to come and offer himself at the Holy Sacrifice of the Mass, but to offer himself through the intermediary of the ministry of the priest. He cannot himself go up to the altar and offer the Sacrifice of his family, of his goods, of what he has; no, God has willed that there be priests who participate in the Priesthood of Jesus Christ and who be intermediaries between Him and the faithful people.

The religious who pronounce the vows of religion engage themselves even in a more solemn way than the faithful, in front of the Church and in front of God. Pronouncing the vows of religion, they engage themselves in a public and official way, acknowledged by the Church to practice the holiness of the three vows of poverty, chastity and obedience. This is what constitutes a religious: he has made as profession of holiness. This is true. In spite of the fact that the obligation undertaken by the religious by pronouncing his vows is grievous and great in front of the Church and in front of God, however, he is still not allowed to go up to the altar and offer the Sacrifice, because he is not a cleric, because he is not a priest. He does not participate in the Priesthood of Our Lord Jesus Christ.

Now, the cleric, that is, he who intends to participate in the Priesthood of Our Lord Jesus Christ, engages himself to holiness by his very function. It is no more the matter of a promise made in front of God, in front of Heaven, in front of the Elect of Heaven, in front of the Church, to profess holiness, but his very function is one of holiness because he participates in the Priesthood of Our Lord Jesus Christ. To be a priest and not to search for holiness is a contradiction in terms. The priest must essentially be holy because of his function, because of the Order that he receives. Every admonition the bishop gives on the occasion of each ordination recalls this exigency. You, my very dear friends, who received the Orders of Lector and Porter yesterday, you remember well that the bishop told you: you must give the example by your life; you must sanctify the faithful by the example of your life, not only by your words, not only by your functions, but by the example of your life. And the same is true of every ordination, and much more by the priestly ordination. This is very important; it is a very profound commitment.

It is inadmissible that a priest does not search for holiness, and thus does not seek to be separated from the world, as Our Lord Jesus Christ, does not seek to be detached from the goods of this world, does not seek poverty, chastity and obedience. Even if he does not make a solemn profession in front of the Church to search for these virtues essential to holiness, nevertheless he engages himself to follow Our Lord Jesus Christ to perform the most important act which Our Lord Jesus Christ performed here below: his Sacrifice.

We have said that the religious pronounce vows of religion, that is, vows that bind them to God, that elevate them towards God, that place them, in a certain way, in eternity, already blessed, united with God by the vows of religion. However, I say it once more, they cannot perform the principle act of religion, the essential act of religion, which is the Sacrifice.

In this Sacrifice, all the acts of religion are summed up: devotion, contemplation, adoration; but all these acts of religion which are a part of the virtue of religion are nothing compared with the Sacrifice. As St. Thomas says, the Sacrifice can be offered only to God, because we can make a total gift of ourselves, of what we are, make the sacrifice of what we are only to the One who has given us these things and not to a creature. We may have a certain devotion to some creatures, in a certain measure, a kind of adoration, but we may not perform the act of Sacrifice in front of a creature. This is inconceivable. The Sacrifice is reserved to God.

This is the reason why the Sacrifice of Our Lord Jesus Christ is the supreme act, the central act, of all His life. All His life was directed towards His Cross, and then, it is from His Cross, that all goods flow upon mankind unto eternity. And this is what you are going to perform, my dear friends, the act of Our Lord Jesus Christ. It is not another act, another sacrifice, you shall be *alter Christus*. Offering the Sacrifice of the Mass you are no longer yourself; you act in the Person of Christ, you shall open heaven in a certain way and make the most marvelous, the most extraordinary, gifts come down: God Himself in your hands! You hold the Holy Trinity in your hands, and it is you who, by your words, open heaven so that the gifts of heaven come down and be given to the faithful. And you alone are able to do this. Even if one of the faithful tries to pronounce the words of consecration, nothing particular would happen on the altar; even if a monk who is not a cleric pronounced the words of consecration, there would be nothing on the altar more than bread and wine. When you become priests and you pronounce the words of consecration, God comes down, the Holy God comes and takes the place of the substance of bread and wine, and thus you can give God to the faithful. This is what a priest is.

And now, how can you tell me that you do not have the obligation to be holy, as Jesus Christ Himself was holy? Is He not on the Cross the Model of Poverty? Could He give a greater example of poverty than the one He gave on His Cross? Could He give a greater example of obedience than the one He gave on the Cross, "obedient unto death"? Could He give a greater example of chastity than by his virgin Body lacerated by the flagellation for all the sins of the world against chastity? This is the example that Our Lord Jesus Christ has given to us. We would not follow Him, we would not imitate Him, and we would like to offer His Sacrifice? No, my dear friends!

Today, receiving for the first time this sign of detachment that the tonsure is, sign of abandonment of the things of this world in order to attach yourself to Our Lord Jesus Christ anew, take with your whole heart, with your whole soul, with your whole strength, the resolution to pursue holiness. Holiness is not a little thing, it is not a mere word; it is a reality. This holiness will have to be practiced in your life, in the life of your seminary and after the seminary.

I take the occasion of the presence here of many of our dear confrères, who are already in the ministry and who have a little experience, some two years, some five years, some ten years, some already fifteen years of ministry....May they also on the occasion of this ceremony, think about what they promised at the moment of their ordination, about what they longed for during their seminary years, and ask themselves if they realize every day what they have promised. There may be need on certain points to see whether some efforts should not be made to practice better poverty, to practice better chastity, to practice better obedience. We must get away from the world, we must separate ourselves from the world. Tepidity is what has lost so many priests. One wants to be a priest and still wants to be of the world. One wants to enjoy what those who have remained in the world may enjoy, those who are not clerics, who have not made a profession of religion. These priests want to be both priests and men of the world at the same time. This is not possible. This is against the very essence of the priesthood. The priest is a man detached, the priest is a man poor, a man chaste, a man obedient.

Let us strive in this period of the Church when priests have precisely lost all these priestly virtues, these religious virtues, these virtues that make real holiness; they have abandoned them and have called themselves common men. We want to reform the priesthood and this was the reason why the seminaries have been founded. It is useless to found seminaries if we follow in the ways that have lost these priests. It is useless, we are losing our time.

Why have these priests been lost? It was not big actions; it was the slow abandonment of priestly virtues. You know it, no need to give details, to enter into the particulars. The life these priests were living in general, unfortunately, before the Council, prepared them for the failures and the faults that have happened since the Council. And, if ourselves, after having justly desired to fight against these abandonments, against this decadence, we follow in the same ways, we shall reach the same results; it is evident. It is useless to think that we are stronger than our predecessors. If we take the worldly ways, in the middle of the world, we shall fall—there is no other outcome possible, and we shall do no good around us.

On the contrary, we must be an army, an armada, which pleases Our Lord Jesus Christ, which follows Our Lord Jesus Christ, who fights this crusade that Our Lord wishes to wage today, and through which we must convert the world, through which we must be a light in the world. With the grace of God we are already a little of this through your apostolate, my dear friends. Through your dedication, through your zeal, through the example of your holiness, you have brought back many souls. How many testimonies of persons lost, disoriented, abandoned, tell us their gratitude, give us their thanks for you, my dear friends, for the apostolate that you accomplish! Therefore, I beg you not to stop doing such an apostolate. It is time to think about it in order to remain what we are, what we want to be, and what Our Lord Jesus Christ wants us to be, simply what the Church wants that we be.

All the catastrophes throughout the history of the Church came in general from the clergy. The clergy had abandoned the way of holiness, had abandoned the Way of the Cross; and it is in the measure that the clergy abandoned the Way of the Cross, in the same measure society was degraded. And there was need that the Good Lord raised founders of orders and founders of religious congregations to give back to the priests the way of holiness. We hope that the Society is precisely willed by God so that priestly holiness remains in the world. Let us hope that the Society shall be a light in the world, and also the other foundations which through the grace of God have understood with us the necessity of living the precepts of Our Lord Jesus Christ, the precepts of the Gospel, and who are here present. I don't want to name them but they also are searching for holiness, are searching for an example of prayer, of abnegation, of renouncement, of the Cross.

This is our *raison d'être* [reason for being], my dear friends; if we lose this, we lose our *raison d'être*. If we lose the way of holiness we lose the very reason of our existence.

Lastly, let us ask the Blessed Virgin Mary, she who was the Mother of the High Priest, who brought Our Lord to the temple, that she remain with us, my dear friends. She is certainly there; the Virgin Mary accompanies you and when you shall present yourself in a few moments with your cassocks to ask the bishop to bless them, Mary is with you. What she did with her Divine Son, she is doing for you now, hoping that you shall be "other Christs." In the Name of the Father, and of the Son, and of the Holy Ghost. Amen.